A Woman's World
"*A Woman's World* is not just a book for 'Everywoman'.... It's also a book for 'Everyman.' It shows how women travel through the world and how the world relates to them."
—*The New York Times*

"*A Woman's World* not only gives us a special sense of place and a glimpse into the women traveling through it, but also insight into ourselves. The book is packed with stories of courage and confidence, independence and introspection; if they don't inspire you to pack your bags and set out into the world, I can't imagine what would."
—*Self Magazine*

Gutsy Woman
"Packed with instructive and inspiring travel vignettes and tips."
—*Boston Globe*

"Essential reading for women travelers of any age."
—*Chicago Tribune*

A Woman's Passion for Travel
"Reading this book is dangerous. You'll quit your job. You'll cash in your savings—or take out a loan. At the very least, you'll ache to follow in the footsteps of these fine writers on their exciting travels."
—Lucy Jane Bledsoe, author of *Working Parts*

A Mother's World
"Heartwarming and heartbreaking, these stories remind us that motherhood is one of the great unifying forces in the world."
—John Flinn, *San Francisco Chronicle*

TRAVELERS' TALES BOOKS

TRAVELERS' TALES

A WOMAN'S EUROPE

TRUE STORIES

TRAVELERS' TALES

A WOMAN'S EUROPE

TRUE STORIES

Edited by

MARYBETH BOND

Series Editors
JAMES O'REILLY AND LARRY HABEGGER

TRAVELERS' TALES

SAN FRANCISCO

Travelers' Tales and *Travelers' Tales Guides* are trademarks of Travelers' Tales, Inc.

Credits and copyright notices for the individual articles in this collection are given starting on page 294.

We have made every effort to trace the ownership of all copyrighted material and to secure permission from copyright holders. In the event of any question arising as to the ownership of any material, we will be pleased to make the necessary correction in future printings. Contact Travelers' Tales, Inc., 330 Townsend Street, Suite 208, San Francisco, California 94107. www.travelerstales.com

Art Direction: Michelle Wetherbee and Stefan Gutermuth
Interior design: Kathryn Heflin and Susan Bailey
Cover photograph: © Mitsuru Yamaguchi/Photonica.
Page layout: Cynthia Lamb, using the font Bembo

Distributed by: Publishers Group West, 1700 Fourth Street, Berkeley, California 94710.

Library of Congress Cataloguing-in-Publication Data
A woman's Europe : true stories / edited by Marybeth Bond. — 1st ed.
    p. cm.
  Includes index.
  ISBN 1-932361-03-0
  1. Europe—Description and travel. 2. Women travelers—Europe. I. Bond, Marybeth.
  D907.W66 2004
  914.04'082'0973—dc22
             2004009448

First Edition
Printed in the United States
10 9 8 7 6 5 4 3 2

It is never too late to be what you might have been.

—GEORGE ELIOT (a.k.a. Mary Ann Evans, 1819–1880)

Table of Contents

A Woman's Europe: An Introduction

by Mary Morris

I went to Europe for the first time with my mother. I didn't want to go. I was a reluctant teenager who had just learned to drive. I preferred to cruise around northern Illinois with my friends. But it was not to be. My mother marched me down to the passport office and away we went.

It was the grand tour. London, Paris, Rome. Cities she had longed to see. I lost her in the Hall of Mirrors at Versailles. I wandered the streets of London in search of fresh fruit, and in the Borghese gardens I was followed by herds of boys, and a few overage men. We saw our bus driver kiss his wife good-bye in Rome as she handed him his lunch and kiss another woman hello in Florence as she gave him his clean laundry. In Genoa my laughing mother hurled her cultured pearls into the sea.

I returned ever altered and my own journeys began. Many of them. Over years and continents, but at least once a year I try to go back to Europe where it all began. When I think of women and travel, I go back to my mother—so filled with longing to go places—and that first trip abroad.

There is something about "going abroad" which for generations has had its allure. As if crossing borders (not to mention the sea) enabled one to cross boundaries as well. While Americans claim heritage from around the world, Europe has shaped us historically in ways no other culture has—for better or worse. And to Americans going abroad, it offers art, culture, and free expression in a way that few cultures can. For generations, Americans have gone to Europe to learn. And to break free.

It was true for Henry James and for "The Lost Generation" of Hemingway, Fitzgerald, a myriad of painters, and, of course, Gertrude Stein. It was always true for the English and Irish writers—Beckett and Joyce, E. M. Forster who understands the impact of an old cathedral in his beloved *A Room with a View*. It was true for men. And, of course, it was always true for women writers as well, though perhaps less clearly defined. Edith Wharton, for one, understood Europe's allure.

As I have long suspected, and as this impressive volume confirms, women do move through the world differently than men. Whether we like it or not, the dangers women face, the connections we make, are based on who we are and a part of who we are is female. Whether being chased down freezing Moscow streets by drunken men, as Stephanie Elizondo Griest is in her essay "After Midnight," or needing a hand to hoist our luggage into an overhead rack as Lollie Ragana does in "Restoration," women's experience is not the same as their male counterparts.

That is why I welcome this volume. As Henry Miller wrote in *The Colossus of Maroussi*, "Voyages are accomplished inwardly and the most difficult are made without leaving the spot." The real journey, as anyone who has gone anywhere knows, is an inner one—an existential one. And the women here don't resist this. They understand that travel is about change. Life is a journey after all, one of constant vicissitudes and surprises.

For Frances Mayes in "Yearning for the Sun," a house sought becomes a home. Andrea Carlisle in a hilarious essay, "The Full Brontë," goes to England in search of the Brontës' ancestral home and finds them on soap and place mats. There are journeys that seek out family and roots as in Janis Cooke

Newman's "The Road to Balbriggan" and Drina Iva Boban's touching meeting with her Croatian grandmother in "Cement Pole." And of course there is just the thrill of adventure as Robyn S. Shaw parachutes over Scotland in "Flying with the Gulls."

The adventures of women in this volume come in many forms—through sheer sport danger or the danger of walking down a street, through the emotional baggage we try to leave behind to the physical baggage we try to carry with us. Like it or not, women make connections—with others, with landscapes, with themselves. Perhaps there is a gender stereotype here. A volume of men on Europe would surely be different. But then again it would be rare to see four drunk women chasing a man down the street. And that man running for his life. I am happy to see women, embracing what they do best and who they are. It is a long time coming.

When my mother turned eighty, she walked the Great Wall of China. She still talks about meeting me for a weekend in Montreal, maybe even getting back to Paris. The truth is she can't. But I can, and her thirst for Europe shaped, and continues to shape, mine. I am glad to have this book. I've never been to Vienna. And perhaps it's time to return to Provence. Or rejoice on a flight delayed and dance all night in Greece.

Mary Morris is the author of twelve books, including five novels, three collections of short stories, and a trilogy of travel memoirs, including Angels & Aliens: A Journey West, Wall to Wall: From Beijing to Berlin by Rail, *and* Nothing to Declare: Memoirs of a Woman Traveling Alone. *She has also co-edited with her husband, Larry O'Connor,* Maiden Voyages, *an anthology of the travel literature of women. Her numerous short stories and essays have appeared in such places as* The Paris Review, The New York Times, Travel & Leisure, *and* Vogue. *The recipient of the Rome Prize in Literature from the American Academy of Arts & Letters, Morris teaches writing at Sarah Lawrence College and lives in Brooklyn with her husband and daughter.*

JUDY WADE

✦ ✦ ✦

The Working Class

Some of the best surprises of Paris
are just outside your window.

PARISIANS HAVE A UNIQUE SENSE OF THE APPROPRIATE. From the fellow in green coveralls giving the cobbled streets an early-morning wash to the nattily dressed chap popping into the Hotel de Ville, the city's town hall, they seem to possess a feeling for what's fitting. Just how fitting I was soon to learn.

The tiny Hotel Saint-Louis on the fabled Ile St-Louis occupies one of the island's former seventeenth-century townhouses. It nestles agreeably between other such structures, giving no hint that the island was once a bucolic pasture where devout King Louis IX, the island's namesake, strolled as he read his breviary.

I hauled my duffel up three flights to a little room that faced the island's single narrow main street. The Ile itself is just six blocks long and two wide, making it more of an isolated village than a part of bustling Paris. I pulled back the lacy white curtains and opened the wood shutters. In this centuries-old setting, the buildings across the street seemed almost within touching distance.

1

On the street below I watched a woman in a green sweater walking her sleek brown dachshund. In a city where there are more dogs than people, the little creature's "calling card" would not be remarked on. At eye level, I could see into a series of rooms across the street that obviously were being remodeled. The sounds of hammering and of a radio playing American rock drifted across the way. A young workman appeared at the window and surveyed the scene below as he lit a cigarette. He looked over at me, grinned, and saluted me with a cheery *bonjour*. I smiled, waved a reciprocal greeting, and turned to unpacking.

Late that afternoon after a trip to the Musée d'Orsay, I could see my workman friend, along with three others all in white overalls, lounging in a series of three windows. They obviously were enjoying a rest at the end of their day. I placed two of them in their twenties, one was plump and middle-aged, and a grandfatherish fourth wore a navy-blue beret over a grizzle of gray hair.

My appearance at the window was a cause for calls and gestures inviting me to share a glass of wine at the little corner bistro. Between my fledgling French and their sketchy English I managed a gentle refusal, blaming jet lag and fatigue. When I started out the next morning around eight, the shutters across the street were closed.

That evening the four workmen were once again eagerly at the window. This time I explained as best I could that there were four of them and just one of me, which really didn't equate for a comfortable cocktail date. They nodded contemplatively. I got the distinct impression they were thinking it over.

Although it wasn't a weekend, my new acquaintances didn't appear for the next two days. I thought perhaps they'd finished the job, which my hotel concierge/owner had explained was the renovation of an apartment for a business-man and his wife.

As I returned to the hotel the next evening and passed through the small lobby-cum-breakfast room, Madame the proprietress called my name. She handed me a tissue-wrapped package of four dewy long-stemmed roses…one red, one white, one yellow, one pink. "*Les ouvriers*," she explained and pointed across the street. The workmen.

I carried the roses up to my room and threw open the shutters. In the window were my overalled friends. The two younger ones each held a pink and a red rose, the middle-aged fellow waved a yellow one, and the grandfather had a white one tucked behind his ear.

"*Choisis! Choisis!*" they chorused.

Choose? Ahhh. I looked down at the four roses in my arms and back at the workmen. Their smiles were sunshine. Without hesitating I extracted the white rose from the bunch and placed it behind my ear.

Over the glass of wine I later shared with Philippe, for that was his name, I learned that he was indeed a grandfather, and a craftsman in renovation. He asked about my travels and my job as a journalist. Later, when he walked me to my hotel, he folded my hand in both of his and kissed it gently. My last glimpse of him was as he rounded the corner, the white rose still balanced beneath his beret.

Judy Wade is a freelance travel writer who prefers to write about outdoor activities, including "mellow strolls through interesting countryside." She has authored three books, has contributed to dozens of others, and lives in Phoenix with her husband, photographer Bill Baker.

FERNE ARFIN

* * *

Smoke, No Fire

*Local men in uniform offer a lesson
in hellos and goodbyes.*

THREE YOUNG MEN AT THE NEXT TABLE KEPT TRYING TO talk to me, but I, a woman traveling on my own in Greece, had been warned: *Don't make eye contact with strangers...especially in the Plaka; hold on to your handbag, stay in the well-lit areas at night.* For my first trip to Athens, more experienced friends had been generous with sensible advice.

The young men persisted. The blond—a real storybook Apollo—was their spokesman. He was the one who spoke English, anyway.

"You are English maybe? American? Yes?... We are so nice chaps...You talk English with us, please?"

He was so pretty, I was almost tempted. Instead, pretending not to notice them, I buried my nose in a guidebook.

Earlier, after dumping my bags in a modest hotel near Syntagma Square, I hit the tourist trail: the Acropolis and the Agora, a bit of shopping. This was a flying visit, one snatched day between the end of an island vacation and the 3 A.M. departure of a cheap charter flight. I planned to sightsee through lunch. But Athens blazes at midday in June. Everything closes until late afternoon. That was how I found myself lunching in a taverna on the edge of the Plaka, an enclave of nineteenth-century island architecture in the middle of Athens. Besides the young men, a pair of picturesque tourists in C&W gear—she in pink gingham and crinolines, he in a ten-gallon Stetson—sat nearby.

The young men were persistent. They laughed and waved to get my attention. Without acknowledging them directly, I discovered they were firemen. Much of Athens is a tinderbox in the dry summer. The small van parked at the curb was a fire truck in which the three young men patrolled, looking for small rubbish fires.

The tourist in the Stetson had been listening as the firemen flirted with me. "Me, too," he boomed. I peered over the top of my book. "You firemen," the Stetson man said, pointing forcefully at the three young men. "Me fireman, too." He beat his hand on his chest in classic "Me Tarzan" style.

I couldn't help myself; I laughed. The firemen laughed, too, and the ice was broken.

"You like music? Greek music? You like that?" said blond Apollo.

"Yes."

"*Bazoukie* music? You know? You like *bazoukie*?"

"Mmm, I guess so."

"You come with us later. We play...for food, you know. Where you stay? We take you. Eat. Listen to music. Don't say no. You come. Say yes. Say yes. You eat. You listen. We play."

There was no stopping them and no refusing them. To extricate myself, I agreed that if I was in at 10 P.M., when they finished work, and if I had nothing else to do, I might go with them. I never really thought I would.

★

Ten P.M. Foot-sore and bored, trapped in a grim hotel room, I had hours to kill before my flight. I considered three hours on a lumpy bed, staring at peeling, yellowed wallpaper, and hoped the firemen wouldn't show so I could be sensible. But they did show and by then my caution had been eroded by the dripping faucet.

Outside, Apollo took charge. In a flurry of commands a taxi was summoned, all my bags were loaded, and one of the three-some climbed in. Before I could follow, Apollo slammed the door. "You ride with me," he said, indicating the back of his motorcycle. The taxi bore all my possessions—handbag, pass-port, tickets, currency—off into the Athens traffic.

Motorcyles scare me. Now, as we left the bright heart of Athens, I had more to worry about. I had no identification and no money. I couldn't communicate in Greek—even to call for help. Where were they taking me? How could I have been so stupid? I had to keep my wits about me.

We rode into deep residential suburbs, down deserted streets, past closed shops and silent, shuttered houses. I pictured terrifying scenarios and mentally rehearsed self-defense strate-gies, discarding them one after another. There were two of them, only one of me. They would be faster. They would be stronger. They knew where the heck they were. They might even have accomplices lying in wait. Feverish imaginings added hours to the fifteen-minute journey.

At about the same time that I decided I was doomed, we arrived at a local party. A half dozen people ate and drank at candle-lit tables arranged on the pavement. There were no neon signs, no blazing windows, no menus or waiters to indi-cate that this was, in fact, our destination, a local taverna.

Inside, a motherly woman hugged my companions and ushered us to a table where the third fireman—with all my belongings—waited. A typical Greek meal, as served in a typical Greek neighborhood taverna, appeared on the table. Steak and french fries, in case you're wondering. Then two mandolins and a guitar were produced. For the next two hours, my new friends sang and played for our supper.

Other patrons joined in or sent us bottles of retsina and ouzo. In between songs, we four struggled to converse.

I could have danced all night, as they say. But my appointed hour at Athens airport approached. I asked Apollo to ring for a taxi.

"Oh, no," he said. "We take you. We sing for you. We go together, everybody. Yes?"

It was not a question.

Once again, my bags were loaded into a cab, this time accompanied by two mandolins and a guitar, and we left in convoy—the taxi and two motorcycles—for the airport.

The 3 A.M. flight to London was delayed; nobody knew for how long.

"Don't you worry," said Apollo. "We don't leave you to be alone."

My three firemen—by now I had become proprietary—settled comfortably on the floor to tune up.

"How old you are?" Apollo said.

"That's not a very polite question to ask a woman," I said. I guessed I was at least a decade older than any of them.

"I think you are same old as my Auntie," he laughed, "...but she is very young and pretty Auntie.... So now you tell me, what music you like?"

The only *bazoukie* tunes I could name were "Never on Sunday" and "Zorba the Greek." Both choices seemed inadequate.

So Apollo chose—one song after another.

Soon, we attracted an audience. In groups of twos and threes, the backpackers who throng Athens airport were drawn to the music until we were encircled.

Now and then, slim, tanned young girls approached my troubadours with requests. Each time, Apollo nodded at me. "We play for her," he would say. "You ask her."

So I was serenaded until my 6 A.M. boarding. And here is the best part. They never asked for anything; wouldn't accept a cup of coffee, never even told me their names. Perhaps, like me, they found sheer joy in a gallant gesture.

Ferne Arfin works part-time as a prison writer-in-residence, teaching creative writing to "murderers and fraudsters" twice a week. A London-based (homesick) American freelancer, she writes short stories and travel journals to finance an expensive habit: fiction writing.

✦ ✦ ✦

Yearning for the Sun

Home is where the heart opens.

MY HOUSE FACES SOUTHEAST, TOWARD A ROAD LINED with cypress trees, toward the foothills of the Apennines, and toward Lake Trasimeno, where Hannibal defeated the Romans in 217 B.C. I am amazed at how often Hannibal comes up in daily conversations around here; previously I had not heard him mentioned since World History in eighth grade. Now I know the weather conditions the morning of the battle (foggy), the route and the number of elephants Hannibal took over the Alps on the way to Rome, even what the Roman soldiers wore as they were driven into the misty lake and drowned.

Because I grew up in the American South, where hardly a day goes by that the War Between the States is not mentioned, I am used to the past intruding on the present. But the past in Tuscany goes back far beyond the reach of my most indefatigable Georgia aunts: I am driving with a friend and she points out the villa of someone she knows, saying, "That's where Luca Signorelli died when he stepped backward on

the scaffolding to get a better look at the fresco he was painting." She speaks as though recalling an unfortunate accident
last year, not the fate of the Signorelli, who died in 1523.

I wonder if this is why I came here, why I instantly felt so
at home in Tuscany when I have not a drop of Mediterranean
blood. In the South of my childhood, every house contained
a story; those who lived earlier seemed about to walk in the
door at any moment. It is the same here, only the people of
the Tuscan past stand against a mighty background of art, philosophy, history, and religion.

Since 1993 I have been a part-time resident of Cortona,
which remains an essentially medieval hill town with layers
and layers that peel back to pre-Etruscan times. Farmers still
plow up in their furrows small bronze horses that Etruscan ar-
tisans made in the sixth century B.C. At the same time, the
Tracy Chapman rock concert on a summer evening draws
thousands to the parking area in front of the church where the
incorruptible body of Saint Margaret of Cortona (folk rock
pulsating in her bones?) has lain since the thirteenth century.
The one-day photo service thrives in a dark twelfth-century
rabbit warren of a shop with a new glass front, and there I re-
ceive faxes from faraway California.

For me, buying a house in a foreign country was an audacious act. The end of my long marriage seemed to return me
to the adventurer I was in my youth. When the smoke from
the divorce cleared, I found myself with a full-time job, a
daughter in college, a stash of stocks and bonds, and a new life
to invent. I was in no hurry, but I had a clear desire to transform those static blue chips into something pleasurable—a
house with land. I could hear the echo of my grandfather's
voice, "Buy land, they aren't making it anymore."

In my (scary) freedom, I began to vacation in Italy. Since I
teach in a university, I have three months off. For five summers

I rented farmhouses all over Tuscany. I tried Cortona, then Montisi, Florence, Quercegrossa, Rignano sull'Arno, Volterra, Siena, Vicchio—two weeks here, a month there. Always I was drawn back to Cortona, to my first impressions of old houses tawny as loaves of bread and the bells of thirty-odd churches ringing over the fields. I thought that here I would begin to write poems, not in the usual way, on a legal pad or a laptop, but with a pen and real ink in one of those handmade, marbled-paperbound books, a big one, with thick, creamy pages.

That fifth summer I began to look seriously for a place to buy. I was no longer amused by the caprices of rented houses, however charming: sagging beds, no hot water, bats roosting in the fireplace, a caretaker who, uninvited, flies through the rooms shrieking and banging shutters whenever it rains. Because I was by then establishing a relationship that seemed permanent, the quest for a house was linked to whatever patterns Ed [my husband-to-be] and I would create in the future. He shares my passion for Italy and also the university boon of free summers.

My daughter, Ed, and friends who came to visit drove with the agent and me over back roads that turned into paths, participated in discussions about how cow mangers could be turned into banquettes, cooled my enthusiasm for one enchanting place that had no access road at all and a family of blacksnakes guarding the threshold. We found several houses I wanted, but Tuscans hate to part with property so owners often changed their minds. One ancient contessa cried to think of selling, doubled her price, and seemed cheered when we walked away.

By the time I saw my house, I had given up. I was leaving in two days, had thanked the local agent, and said good-bye. The next morning I ran into him in the piazza. "I just saw someone who might be interested in selling a house," he greeted me.

Outside town, he took the winding road that climbs around to the other side of the hill Cortona is built on. He turned onto a *strada bianca*, a road white with pebbles, and after a kilometer pulled into a sloping driveway. I caught a glimpse of a shrine with a ceramic saint and then looked up at a tall apricot-colored house with green shutters and tumbles of overgrown bushes and briars. I was silent as we drove up. There was a lovely wrought-iron fanlight over the door. The walls were as thick as my arm is long. Old glass in the windows wavered. I scuffed through silty dust and saw smooth terracotta floors in perfect condition. He showed me two bathrooms, rough but functioning bathrooms—after all the houses I had seen with no water, much less plumbing. No one had lived in the house for thirty years, and its five acres seemed like an enchanted garden rampant with roses and blackberries. Ivy twisted into trees and ran over fallen stone walls.

The agent shielded his eyes and surveyed the land. "*Molto lavoro*," he pronounced, much work.

"It's unbelievably romantic," I answered. I already envisioned myself snipping sun-warmed herbs into a basket, setting a long table with a checked cloth under the linden trees, Ed roasting boar in the big fireplace. I wanted to hang my summer clothes in an armoire and arrange my books under a window with a view of the winding row of cypresses beside the road, each one planted for a boy who died in World War I. After weeks of looking at ruins with collapsed roofs or at tasteless modernizations, after miles of dusty roads, this house seemed to have been waiting all along.

The Tuscan sunlight pouring into every room warmed me. There is something especially beneficent about the Italian sun; it seems to seep farther in, clarifying the mind. I felt renewed, excited, and calmly right, and I suppose this is part of what it feels like to be at home.

In America I have bought and sold a few houses—loading up the car with the blue-and-white Wedgwood, the cat, and the ficus for the drive across town or across the country to the next doorway where a new key would fit. Choices were always practical, bound to graduate schools or jobs. But this time the new door's iron key weighed half a pound and the doorway was 7,000 miles from home. The legal language and the baroque arrangements of buying baffled me. Currency rates were falling. My broker was selling my life savings and chiding me about *la dolce vita*. But years later I still feel stunned by my good luck, although I can also wake up thinking, *What on earth have you done and why, when you could have had a cottage right here on the California coast where you would buzz up for the weekend?*

One San Francisco August, I had looked for idyllic cottages and had even made an offer on a log house on the foggy Mendocino coast. I was instructed by how relieved I felt when the offer was turned down. I already knew what to expect from California, and from my home state of Georgia, which I also considered. I was running on instinct, and instinct said time for a new kind of home. Time for the unknown. Time to answer the question Dante faced in The Divine Comedy: What now to do in order to grow?

My little villa made of enormous stones perches on a terraced hillside covered with olive trees. Close to the house some intelligent soul planted fruit and nut trees—apricot, fig, plum, apple, hazelnut, almond, and many kinds of pears that bear in sequence. From summer through late fall I find pears to pick and a reason to stock the kitchen with the local Gorgonzola, the perfect accompaniment.

A neighbor said, "Your house is only a couple of hundred years old—mine is a thousand." He's right, the house is not old by local standards. It is not the classic stone farmhouse called *casa colonica,* nor is it a real villa. Although there are fourteen rooms, none have the ample proportions of a house of the nobility. It might have been the country place of some genial Cortona parvenu who brought his family here when July heat struck the stones of the town. The symmetrical house rises three stories with a fanciful iron balcony on the second floor above a double front door. From it I train hanging nasturtiums, but I can imagine someone, sometime stepping out to hear a lover sing "Ecco Maggio," or some equally corny popular song.

I bought the place from a doctor, who had recently bought it from five ancient sisters of Perugia. The doctor thought to make it a summer house, then changed his mind (turning a great profit, no doubt). I never think of him because he never lived here, but I often think of the five sisters. They must have been girls here; I can see them simultaneously pushing open the shutters of their five bedrooms and leaning out in their white nightgowns. This is the kind of fancy the house inspires. Why? Because it is a dream house. Not a dream house that has a perfect kitchen and ideal floor plan—I don't think dream houses have albino scorpions in the bidet—but it resembles a house from a dream, one where you discover a room you did not know existed and in it a dry plant bursts into full bloom. Oddly, everyone who visits comes downstairs to breakfast the first morning and says, "I had the strangest dream." Here I have a recurrent dream of swimming without effort in a clear green river, totally at home in the water, buoyantly carried downstream.

Reality is just as remarkable. I am dazzled by the remains of a Roman road at the edge of my property. I follow that stony path through the poppies into Cortona for espresso. I am dazzled by the cistern near the well. When I shine a flashlight into it, I see a brick archway underground. The caretaker at the Medici fortress on top of the hill claims that an underground escape route runs from the fortress all the way down to the lake. He shrugs. "Possibly your cistern was part of the passageway." How casual the Italians are about such things; that one is allowed to own something so ancient amazes me.

I am still learning to be casual about far more everyday experiences. Even the roof is extraordinary. I climb up the terraced hill and look down on the old tiles, formed over someone's knee and now alive with lacy gray moss. What else? The deeply satisfying tilt of the demijohn as I draw off some of my own olive oil for tonight's salad, oil from olives we picked and had pressed at a local mill. Also the thick, cool marble kitchen counters where the pizza dough never sticks, the small owl that lights on a windowsill and looks in, the straight stone stairs with a wrought-iron railing that kept some smith busy an entire winter.

Ed stripped and waxed each room's chestnut beams—some genius had slathered all of them with a sticky mud-colored varnish—and all the rooms are newly whitewashed. In one bedroom, a friend painted blue domes over the windows and filled them with Giotto-like gold stars. Walls are bare, except for a few of my daughter's paintings; tabletops are bare; casement windows are bare except for their sets of solid and louvered shutters. This house is now ready for long afternoons of reading or baking or putting up plum preserves—once we prune the olives and reset the stone terrace walls.

At least once a day I go out on the second-floor terrace and look up the hill. I can see a section of Etruscan wall that has the exact orientation of the house. If the wall had not securely kept vigil over this land for twenty-six centuries, I would be afraid it might tumble down on us: blocks of stone as big as the flat I rent, blocks on blocks. Etruscan walls form part of Cortona's town wall, and a couple of Etruscan gates and tombs remain scattered about.

From its position, historians think this wall is a remnant of a sun temple. The name of my house is Bramasole, from *bramare*, to yearn for, and *sole*, sun: something that yearns for the sun. I used to be surprised that everyone knew this house. "*Ah, Bramasole, si, una bella casa,*" they say. Delivery people, even from miles away, do not need a map. "*Si, si, la villa Bramasole,*" they say. They have picked cherries or nuts here during the thirty years of abandonment, or even earlier. They have gathered mistletoe from the almond trees at Christmas. Their grandmother picked figs every September.

One day in town, I spotted a postcard of the Etruscan wall said to be "in the locality of Bramasole." The owner of the shop, a lifelong resident and neighbor who lives just under the wall, explained that our whole section of the hillside was once known as Bramasole, not just my house, and long before my house existed. Perhaps the name goes back to the ancient purpose of this site, to the lost temple where people like me came when they were yearning for the sun.

Frances Mayes has written for The New York Times, House Beautiful, *and* Food and Wine. *She is also a widely published poet and food and travel writer. She divides her time between Cortona, Italy, and San Francisco, where she teaches creative writing at San Francisco State University. Her books include* Under the Tuscan Sun *and* Bella Tuscany.

LOLLIE RAGANA

✦ ✦ ✦

Restoration

Hard work on an old castle
is a salve for the spirit.

My first concern when I boarded the TGV, France's "fast train," was that the G-force would flatten my face. Having conquered the fear and boarded anyway, I am now feeling rather smug, as I shoot like a silver bullet on this earthbound Concorde, crammed among Friday afternoon commuters on their way home. Using my best French sprinkled with pantomime, I ask a manicured Frenchman unlucky enough to have an aisle seat if he will help me heft my suitcase to the overhead rack. *Un, deux, trois…*Oh, geez, do these things really stay up there? (And more importantly, am I liable if mine doesn't?) I whisper my thanks while squeezing through folks camped in the aisles. My breath is tight. I feel an anxiety attack coming on. I am suddenly certain the train is hermetically sealed and they've forgotten that human beings need air. I make a conscious attempt to breathe—in and out, in and out. O.K., I can do that. The train careens and I spill across a woman hoarding several bags (including one unfortunately placed wine bottle) that seem to spew from her like

17

serpents from Medusa's head and I tumble into my seat, letting
my eyes float to the window and my reflection. I am pleased
to find my face intact so I dare to peer beyond to a cobalt blue
sky. I don't have to be here, I remind myself. It was a choice. I
stare harder at the rolling hills sprinkled with stone houses and
downy fields of cheerful-looking wildflowers and wonder if
they're deliberately mocking me. But as Paris begins to fade in
the distance, I feel myself shedding layers of skin. My breathing becomes more rhythmic as my lungs respond to the endless horizon of friendly, green, oxygen-emitting plants. But the
thought still nags: Where am I going? Why am I here? Well, I
tell myself, a journey isn't really a journey if you already know
the path.

I wanted fun and adventure. I needed escape. I have been
caring for my father who is suffering from Alzheimer's,
steadily drifting away from the world and me—and the effects
from enduring physically and emotionally have been taking a
toll. Someone in the latter stages of Alzheimer's is a bit like a
ghost: one who needs to eat and sleep and has chronic ail-
ments that need tending, but without much to offer in the
way of thought or emotion. Over the past few years I've taken
him through endless rounds of specialists in the desperate
hope of curing him, which has now left me struggling with
the reality that it can't be done. Not long ago I used to tell
people that this man was really only a reasonable facsimile of
my father; today he's no longer even that. A friend who had
hiked Ireland with me a couple of years ago recommended a
little R & R working on the restoration of a medieval castle
in St. Victor la Coste, a village of 1,600 about fifteen miles
northwest of Avignon, and I thought, why not? Since I had
failed at restoring my father, maybe I could restore a castle instead. Promising that the work was invigorating but fun (lasting only until noon), the people friendly and interesting (from

all over the world), and the countryside a hiker's paradise, my friend painted an irresistible picture. Which is why I am now huddled on this tiny seat trying to nap as we dash from town to town, pausing for passengers to spill from the train, having no idea what to expect when I reach my own destination.

That "having no idea" part is scary. So is traveling alone. I have studied abroad and taught abroad. I have worked abroad as a documentary filmmaker. But I have always been with at least one other person and a plan. Never have I simply put myself at the mercy of someone else, which is an act that requires trust, always a challenge for me. As the train approaches Avignon I realize I am facing an existential moment. I decide I do not like existentialism, so I attempt to calm myself by painting a picture of what I would like to experience. Attempting to conjure "thrill" at the prospect of returning to France after a thirty-year hiatus, I reminisce on a summer I spent in Grenoble, a southern Alpine village. I rewind the mental tape and recall images from that summer that transformed me from gawky girl to (at least budding) woman. And I realize that I am at the point of another transformation in my life. Maybe I have unconsciously put myself here to encounter this existential moment? And, if so, what will I discover? My mind jumps to that dark place that reminds me that I may not want to know. I bolster myself and admit I need that summer again: like Alice in her Wonderland or Dorothy venturing through Oz, I am primed to escape into a new world. I pull out my journal and begin writing as that existential panic soars back, tearing through page after page, my pen hurrying to transform this menacing monster into an image of hope.

As I disembark, visions of Peter Mayles's Provence of artfully laden tables and robust peasants dance in my head. Instead, I am greeted by a van that any hippie would have been proud to own, say around 1968, and ride off with three other Americans to our new home away from home. We bounce along a highway cut between vineyards vibrant in the summer sun, then plod up a winding dirt road. Clambering out we follow our driver down a cobblestone path, up stone steps and through a beaded doorway (fly intervention), to enter the mansion built by the castle owners when castles were no longer necessary and they decided to move down the hill closer to the village. A high-ceilinged room with rustic antique furniture, tiled floors, and a large sink for hand-washing clothes makes me realize I am far from home. In a moment tinged with romanticism, but also brimmed with hope, I know I have stepped into not only a new world but also a new past that, maybe if I'm very lucky, will let me rewrite my future.

Surrounded by trees and ancient stone, I start to relax and laugh at the thought of my panic attack on the train. (Actually it is more of a high-pitched giggle, reminding me that the attack might still be lingering.) My new friends are also excited, so we toss bags and backpacks onto our cots and head out to explore the town, which consists of two small restaurants, a post office, a courthouse and a *tabac* (a shop selling cigarettes, newspapers, and knickknacks) where we stock up on postcards that come in three photographic choices: endless vineyards, endless rows of sunflowers, or endless fields of lavender. By standing next to the statue of Saint Victor in the middle of the square, I can see the entire "city center." I want to see more. We stroll past small houses built from the local limestone, with kids and dogs frolicking in the yards and lavender gardens enlivening the air with their sweet scent. I recall reading somewhere that lavender is used for tranquility in aromatherapy, so I stop at each garden and inhale deeply.

It takes about ten minutes to reach the outskirts and I am immediately charmed by this village of snugly-fitted houses nestled between rolling vineyards, dusty hills like trunkless elephants, and the Rhone River snaking its silvery path in the distance. Time moves slowly here, with none of the mindless, helter-skelter turmoil I'm used to. I even notice the sun setting in a friendly musky pink while a honey-colored full moon rises between two distant hills. Then the sun drops below the horizon and the night becomes black. And I mean black. There are no streetlights and I'm surprised to find no light glowing from houses either. Where is everybody? I think of Stephen King and what he could do with a story about a peopleless town. This place strikes me as downright creepy. Not only are there no lights, there's no noise from cooking or talking, TVs blaring, or traffic. In fact, there are no cars. Only silence. And scattered stones crunching under our feet. We're walking uphill and, as I look up to find my next step, my eye is drawn to a velvet sky cluttered with stars and I think about our ancient ancestors who had only stars to light up the night. I'm not used to a night sky so luminous and its effect is startling. I am suddenly insignificant as a puny human being among such vastness. The impersonal universe reminding me I am but an insect with a one-minute life span compared to the scope of the cosmos. It feels like the trapdoor just opened and I'm free-falling, all my foundations ripped away. I want to hug myself, to soothe the ripples of angst in the face of such reality. Overwhelmed, I sit in a patch of something soft and presumably green, then lie down and close my eyes to enjoy its coolness on my arms and legs. Something happens as I'm lying there. When I open my eyes my feelings of insignificance have been replaced with a sense of, oh…"specialness?" at actually being a part of something so primordial yet powerful.

Awed by this awareness, I stumble up to the house where I crawl into my cot tucked beneath low eaves and drift to sleep listening to the quiet.

And wake to a rooster crowing, a donkey's bray, and early morning sun soaring across my bed. I make my way to the stone patio where earlier risers are already ripping into over-sized baguettes, and I devour *café au lait*, yogurt, and bread which I lather with fresh peach preserves. Three more Americans, a Brit, and a young French couple have joined the group, and we resemble a scraggly army as we hike almost a mile up the hill. A rather daunting task at 8 A.M., but invigorating as it leaves me with precious little to worry about other than carrying a couple of buckets filled with shovels and hard-bristled brushes. When we reach the castle I feel like a kid, delighted by the massive stone towers and imagining the lives that were lived here.

I fear my restoration skills may be a bit rusty—castles being somewhat scarce back home—so to delay the inevitable I prattle on with questions and am told that the castle began as a chapel in the eleventh century, then became a full-fledged fortress soon after; by the seventeenth century the family had dismantled parts of it to build their estate down the hill (where I now eat and sleep). The castle is not going to be completely restored (thank goodness—I wasn't sure I was up to that), just simply made safe; 300 years of weather and neglect have left it unstable. O.K., so where are the bulldozers? Cranes? Electricity? I point out that these rather essential items seem to have made off in the night and Ginou, who orchestrates this process and reminds me a bit of Gepetto, informs me that we will be working in pretty much the same fashion as the original builders: with our hands. I spend the morning using a trowel and a brush to remove dirt and loose stones from one of the castle's interior walls. As I work I steal glimpses of the village with its miniature stone houses sprinkled between vineyards and discover the joy of digging my hands deep into the dirt, rousting frustration by ripping out dying plants while clearing stones that have been sitting for three centuries—the lazy buggers.

Work ends at noon. We trudge down the hill to a lunch prepared by the staff chef where we are treated to an authentic Peter Mayle moment. I gorge on vegetables baked in tantalizing sauces, lettuce so crisp the crunch echoes, the ubiquitous bread and a gentle rosé. After lunch one of our crew thinks a hike would be fun. I'm thinking nap and wonder why the French never adopted the endearing habit of siestas. Afraid that I'll miss out on the most spectacular moment of the whole trip—one that the others will be telling their grandchildren about someday while I sit silently—I decide to join them. Besides, I like a good hike.

But not heat and humidity. Unfortunately, we get an abundance of both as we start down a dusty trail that winds through vineyards etched in a chaotic checkerboard of young vines. *Cigalles*, French cicadas, roar so loudly we think they must be the size of hawks as we trek from sunny vineyards to a forest dense with cypress, oak, and pine in half an hour, then spend the next two hours struggling in said heat and humidity to clamber up mossy paths to the top of a hill famous for its view. But it's worth it. Like eagles soaring over the land, we can see our castle, endless miles of fluffy green, fields of sunflowers with their faces bent to the sun, and soft hills rolling like waves. I find a large rock to sit on and splash some water over a blister from the morning's work. My friends do the same, grumbling about bruises and sore ankles. Before heading back we snap group photos featuring our castle in the background for keepsakes. Then we start down, which I find easier than going up since I spend most of it sliding down steep, dank, leaf-strewn paths, almost sailing off a sharp cliff rather strategically placed if the plan is to doom hapless hikers.

Once safely back on the terra firma of the vineyards, I am reminded of Vincent van Gogh's vivid colors as I watch the hills turn purple in late afternoon sun against a sky the blue of polished sapphire. Mother Nature is apparently not only alive here, but thriving.

And our castle, too, continues to thrive as we reach the high point of our work: wall restoration, which is more complicated than it sounds. We spend a day collecting and sorting a load of stones according to size, shape, and beauty. The stones aren't cut but are used as is, so size and shape are important for stabilization of the wall and, of course, aesthetics: you want the beautiful ones to show. We mix mortar from sand dropped by buckets from a helicopter—which seems incongruous as I stand among medieval ruins with village and vineyards spreading at my feet, looking like they did centuries ago—then painstakingly create layers of stone until our wall begins to take shape. It's a great feeling to restore a life that will hopefully continue long into the future (and be forever known as "my" castle).

As the wall continues to grow, the time nears for my return to Los Angeles; I begin to have feelings of foreboding. Time is up to her old tricks: I feel I've just arrived, but it's actually been almost three weeks since I left home. One of the resident workers who has been coaching me in castle restoration (even heroically jumping over a short wall on a steep hillside to retrieve a bucket I inadvertently tossed) offers to take me to a Druid cave in the nearby village of Lirac (Druid caves seem rampant as several have been pointed out and I begin to think that all French caves are "Druid caves.") I am hungry for more time in the wilds and excited about the added bonus of exploring something ancient and sacred, so I cram my pack with fruits and water and meet my friend on the patio. We trek across boulder-strewn hillsides—I discover a blister that hasn't quite healed and wistfully imagine myself a goat—and through fields of wildflowers whose sweet perfume mixes with dust to create a musty scent until we finally arrive at the foot of the hill housing this mysterious site.

From here the cave is invisible, tucked within the rock face of a cliff. We begin up a switchback path and the limestone facade looms ever larger. Higher and higher we climb, pausing at each turn to gaze from ever-dizzying heights to the fields below. Vineyards shrink to dollhouse toys, trees look like parsley and the road a path etched by someone's finger.

When we reach the entrance, I pause and take a breath before stepping into the darkness. Inside it's cool and damp; limpid rays of sun seep through the opening. As soon as my eyes adjust, I find myself in a tunnel that hints at more passageways ahead. I follow my friend to emerge in a towering cavern and feel as if I've just made a mythological journey to the underworld. Shaped by Time and Mother Nature, the stone bulges and dips in its own chaotic pattern. Pillars brace themselves on the floor, supporting the ceiling which soars some forty feet up on broad shoulders like Atlas holding the world. My words echo, reminding me that we are alone in a dwelling older than I can imagine.

I climb steps carved against one wall, running my hand along the cold stone for guidance, and find myself in another chamber with an opening like a window revealing all the world's splendors. I stand like a goddess gazing down on her creation of gentle vineyards, a rainbow of flowers and a horizon iridescent in the sun. I wonder how many people before me have stood just here, enjoying this same view, for how many hundreds or perhaps thousands of years. No wonder this cave is sacred.

After soaking up as much of the verdant beauty as possible, I return to the main chamber. It's hard to imagine how much patience Time took in creating this womb so magnificent and so perfect and this thought reminds me of the stars I saw when I first arrived and the 12 billion years it took to create all that. What a trickster Time is. Sometimes a memory from my childhood seems so vivid I feel as if I could just step right back into it and live it again. As if I had simply blinked my eye and a couple of decades had passed. Maybe the universe blinks its eye and a couple of millennia pass. Maybe if I never blink again I can freeze time and stay here forever.

I sit where the lazy sun from the entrance can warm me and lean against the familiar white limestone bruised where lit tapers have singed it and dampness has mingled with dirt. I hear Druids chanting to ensure nature's endless cycle of life, death, and regeneration. Reluctant to break the spell, I think about time. How you can't freeze it and you can't relive the past. All you can do is move forward to an unknown future like a river creating its own shape as it moves across the earth. Eventually, I pull myself up, wriggle through the tunnel and step into the blazing sun. Like a sunflower awakened from sleep, I turn my face to soak up the warmth before beginning the journey home.

Having completed my contribution to an experience that restored me as much as it did the castle, I say good-bye, exchange addresses with my new friends, and retrace my ride on the TGV (no fear of flattened faces this time) to Paris.

After a trip over the Atlantic Ocean and the breadth of America, I am once again in Los Angeles, where my father is the same. I show him photos of my trip, but he just looks at me with wistful eyes. With a new respect for this primordial drama unfolding in my life, I stroke his face. I know the only gift I can give him now is love, but somehow that's enough.

Lollie Ragana wrote, directed and produced television for thirteen years, creating projects for PBS, KCET, numerous news/magazine programs and commercials, receiving two awards for a series of multicultural folktales. She is also an accomplished playwright and award-winning stage director: four of her plays have been produced by Los Angeles theaters. She is a regular speaker at Women's History Month events and Take Back the Night rallies. She has also been featured on KPFK radio discussing literature during Banned Books Month and the Celtic roots of Halloween. Her publishing credits include the Santa Monica Outlook, LA West, Trojan Family *(USC alumni magazine),* Mobius: A Journal for Social Change *and the* Los Angeles Times. *Lollie's father died ten months after this trip was taken.*

NANCY HILL

* * *

In a Soldier's Care

A guardian angel with a phrasebook
keeps watch over a traveler.

THE WISH TO HAVE MY LIFE ORCHESTRATED AS IF IT WERE a film was fulfilled in Verona, Italy, the summer I turned twenty-one.

I was part of a summer program for young musicians that was held in this city of golden light and arched bridges. We were housed in a magnificent old building with high ceilings and windows so large I could curl up on a windowsill for a nap.

The building's old stones kept the secrets of countless people who had lived in the rooms, but they could not keep out the awareness that for centuries, human dramas had been played out within the walls.

Dedicated to their art, the young musicians in the summer program were up before dawn perfecting their pieces and I awoke to the gentle melodies of Vivaldi, Bach, and Stravinsky.

While I dressed, Lalo played in the background and while eating breakfast, gypsy music urged me to hurry up, that there was much life to be lived.

28

But it was the melancholy music that best expressed my state of mind. Not a musician myself, I had been invited to the program to study photography and my teacher had never shown up. All the other students were musicians who studied and practiced all day and so most of my time was spent alone. I couldn't speak a word of Italian and wandered the streets with my camera longing for someone to share the discovery of hidden restaurants, unexpected frescos, the brooding statues in the cemeteries and the celestial art in the churches.

After a couple of weeks of wandering down winding streets and weaving in and out of alleys, I had the odd sensation that I was being followed. I'd walk faster, turn a corner and abruptly stop, looking back, hoping to catch someone. There was never anyone in sight. Yet the feeling persisted.

After a few days of this, I took a seat outside a small cafe on a dead end street and decided to sip lemon sodas until I was certain there was no one pursuing me. I passed two hours looking at pictures in an Italian newspaper, writing letters, and photographing children who played nearby. When I had just about given up the notion that I was being followed, a dark, handsome man in a military uniform quietly slipped into the seat beside me. He gestured to my camera. Assuming he wanted his picture taken, I picked it up. He put his hand over mine briefly, shook his head, and pulled an Italian/English dictionary out of his back pocket.

For over an hour, we took turns looking up words and pointing them out to each other, trying to communicate.

He was intrigued that I was an American and wanted to know why I was in Verona. He was a soldier serving his mandatory tour of duty. He took off his hat and showed me a series of lines he'd written under the brim to keep track of how many months he had been in the service. Altogether, he would have to serve fifteen months.

I asked if he had been following me. He leaned forward, took my hand, looked into my eyes. I melted. Would he kiss me? We were total strangers, couldn't even understand each other's language, but we had found each other. Ah, for a student nearby to fill the air with triumphant music.

But there was no kiss. He dropped my hand and went back to the dictionary. "Alone. Dangerous. Bad. Places. Hurt. Protect. Duty." How sweet. He was concerned about me and had decided to be my bodyguard.

I took the dictionary in turn. Pointed out "Thank you. No fear. Safe."

He shook his head, tipped his hat. "No safe," he said.

I pointed to my watch. He nodded. We both rose, and he walked me back to the building in which I was staying.

"Care," he said, and gestured to himself, then to me.

True to his word, he began looking out for me. When I left in the morning, he was outside waiting for me. Sometimes he would walk beside me, sometimes a block or so behind. Sometimes we would have a lemon soda together and he would insist I order them so he could laugh with the waiter over the odd way I pronounced the word "lemon." Sometimes I would think I was alone, but would turn around and find him there. Sometimes he was with another soldier or two, but usually he was alone.

We found out little things about each other. He had a large family, just like me. He wanted to go to college, to do something great with his life, but first he had to get out of the military. He would like to go to the U.S. where mail is delivered at the same time every day. We both loved ice cream and he thought eating pizza with hands was a good idea no matter what everyone else in his country thought.

He told me what was good and not so good to order in

restaurants, and took me to places he thought I would want to photograph.

I was no longer lonely and the melancholy music that used to define my life in Italy no longer fit. I begged the music students to play gypsy music and pieces fast and joyful.

The other students noticed that the soldier was often near me, and one of the students followed us to a park and took out his violin and played while my soldier and I ate fruit and freshly baked bread.

Time passed too quickly and there were but a few days left. I wondered if I was nothing more than someone to watch over or if my soldier was falling for me as I was for him. But I was too shy to ask and certainly would never make the first move.

He knew when I would leave, and on my last day asked what we should do that night. I took his dictionary and pointed out words. "Group. Students. Opera. Late."

His face lit up. Perhaps he did not understand. I pointed out more words. "Must go. Not alone. Home. Leave. Early." The word for tomorrow I knew, "*Domani.*"

He grinned, took my hand, held it for a minute and raised it to his lips. "Good-bye," he said in English. "For now."

That was it, then? He was content to say good-bye, leaving with the suggestions that we might meet again some day? I was devastated.

That night all the students and teachers went to the opera. Ah, how lovely it was, held in an amphitheater over 2,000 years old. The costumes were magnificent. The music almost too beautiful to bear. But I could not lose myself in it when I knew I would not see my soldier again. I tried not to cry, but a tear or two slipped down my cheek.

I felt a hand on my shoulder and looked up. My soldier!

He handed me a rose and motioned for me to follow him. I didn't hesitate. He led me to a higher seat where the breeze moved the music through the air. The opera came to life as we sat hand-in-hand, shoulder-to-shoulder. When the final curtain came down and the crowd rose to their feet, he leaned forward and kissed me to the sound of a full-house clapping. The applause, no doubt intended for the opera, was, in my heart, intended solely for my soldier and me.

He slipped a piece of paper into my hand, kissed me again, and walked me back home. He kissed me once more at the door. A long kiss, one that would linger for the rest of my life.

Later that night, when everyone slept, I climbed up on the windowsill and read the note he had given me by moonlight. "Always. Remember. *Domani*. Love."

I have never forgotten, and whenever I hear the sweet notes of a violin, I can feel my soldier following.

Nancy Hill is a writer and photographer living in Portland, Oregon, dreaming of adventure while living days of practicality. But change is always just around the corner.

CATHERINE WATSON

* * *

Pilgrim's Progress

*Camino de Santiago works its magic
on a non-believer.*

I HAVE ALWAYS BEEN DRAWN TO HOLY PLACES. NOT because I'm particularly religious—just the opposite, in fact. I was raised in the Presbyterian church because, as my father explained, "That will be the easiest one to drop out of later."

So it's not faith that draws me to the world's shrines, it's the faithful. They infuse a place with holiness, and I take comfort from being near them. I feel a sense of relief in being part of something they're sure of, even if I'm not. It's a lazy way of being spiritual—the religious equivalent of second-hand smoke.

As a pilgrimage groupie, then, I'd been tempted for years by the Camino de Santiago—the Way of St. James. In the Middle Ages, it was Europe's most important pilgrimage route, running west for nearly five hundred miles along the top of Spain to the foggy province of Galicia and the city of Santiago de Compostela.

But if you do it the old way—the right way, my vaguely Puritan conscience kept whispering—it takes four to six weeks to walk from the French border to Santiago. I'd never had that much free time.

Then I ran across a perfect compromise: a small tour company offering Camino samplers. We'd be part-time pilgrims, hiking eight to ten miles every day, but in the afternoons, we'd pile into a van and drive for an hour or so, cutting out the boring stretches and shortening the journey to a tidy twelve days. I signed up. The trip turned out to be a better fit than I dreamed—and one I would desperately need. All trips are pilgrimages, if your mind is in the right place. Mine wasn't. Two days before I left for Spain, my doctor announced that chronic pain in my arms and hands was caused by bone spurs, the result of too many years of lugging camera gear on travel assignments and hunching over a keyboard when I got back.

I was devastated. "What am I supposed to do now?" I asked her. "Don't pick up any suitcases," she said. She didn't see the irony. And I didn't see the gift: Fate in a white lab coat had just handed me one of the main reasons why hundreds of thousands of people—millions, perhaps—had walked the Santiago trail over the past 1,100 years.

They went because they were sick and wanted to get well. Or because they'd gotten well and wanted to give thanks. To have their sins forgiven or to shave their time in purgatory. Because they were curious or idle or bored or all three. To find love or to escape its clutches.

Some were criminals whom the court ordered to go, the way juveniles now are sometimes ordered to go to boot camp. And some went for the sheer adventure of going, like any modern tourist, like me. Europe's first guidebooks were written for Santiago-bound pilgrims.

Our group was to rendezvous in Pamplona. I got there a day early so I could explore the city that Ernest Hemingway put on America's literary map with *The Sun Also Rises*. The famous bulls had run two months before, so there was no fiesta spirit in the narrow streets—just long afternoon shadows between old buildings, people carrying supper home from the shops and young couples strolling in the warm September air.

A proud Basque taxi driver showed me around. I told him I'd come to walk the Camino. It's not that hard, he said. Just watch out for the wolves. What? The wolves. They eat pilgrims. But you'll be O.K. They ate a couple last week, so the coast is clear.

There were just six of us in the group: Dee, a vigorous widow in her 60s, and her daughter, Doree, both from Colorado. Juan Carlos and Joaquin, Spanish friends of the group leader, came along as helpers and guides. And the leader herself, Judy Colaneri, who spends her winters as a caterer in Aspen and her summers traveling. She had loved walking the full length of the Camino and wanted to share the experience.

There are many roads to Santiago, but the most-traveled starts at Roncesvalles, just inside the border with France—so close that the spot has a French name as well, Roncevaux. (It's believed to be where the army of Charlemagne was decimated by Saracens and where his nephew, the legendary hero of the "Chanson de Roland," was killed.)

The four main pilgrimage routes across France converged there, funneling medieval pilgrims through the Pyrenees and into Spain. We drove there from Pamplona, on our first morning.

Roncesvalles is a wooded hillside, with a church and a few stone buildings along a twisting road under old trees. In the Middle Ages, there had been a pilgrims' hospital here; perhaps five thousand of the patients died. Their bodies were put into a charnel house—popularly called "the silo of Charlemagne"— a consecrated pit grave next to the church. If you look inside, you can still see their bones.

It's said that the decomposing bodies gave off a strange light—*la luz de los muertos,* the light of the dead. The pilgrims' spirits rose up, guided by the light, and continued their journey in the sky. You see their trail whenever you look at the Milky Way.

Back on earth, painted yellow arrows on trees and buildings showed the way, but most of the time we didn't need them. Millions of passing feet had worn the way too clearly to miss.

From Roncesvalles, the Camino was a wide, flat path that ran like a green tunnel through sunny forest. We walked at different speeds, and I was quickly alone. There was plenty of time to think. Every day was like that.

In Spanish, the verb for what we were doing is *peregrinar,* "to go on a pilgrimage." But it has a deeper meaning. Like many Spanish words, it connects to another idea in a way that English usually leaves up to poets. *Peregrinar* also means "to exist in this mortal life."

To exist in this mortal life. To be a pilgrim even if you stay at home. I exist, therefore I am traveling. I travel, therefore I exist.

At Larrasoana, the next big town, we stopped at the mayor's office to get our pilgrimage *credenciales* stamped. A stiff card, the *credencial* is like a passport. You get stamps at key stops en route, and it proves you've made the journey. If you're a Catholic, it earns you a special certificate at the end; if you're not, it makes a great souvenir.

I chatted with five middle-aged Scots, also getting their cards stamped. They'd been gone only three days, but they were already blissed out. "When something happens on a trip," one of the women observed, "you think, 'Well, that's what happened.' When something happens on a pilgrimage, you think, 'That's a miracle...'"

I agreed. I was in the middle of one: As soon as we started walking, the ache in my neck and arms began to fall away, like a heavy cloak slipping off my shoulders. The pilgrimage had already walked me through the pain.

The Camino ran on ridge tops and in valleys, through pastures, woods and tiny villages, sometimes as an aisle between green fields and banks of blackberries, sometimes a leafy archway like a rabbit run, sometimes a farm lane where you could hear sheep bells tinkling, pigs snuffling, and placid, pinkish Basque cattle chewing their cud. It was that close-up ordinariness that I loved.

On the map, the distances we walked looked no longer than hyphens, but they seemed to hold all of Spain. As we passed, local people called to us from their doorways, leaned over garden walls to chat, offered drinks of water or sun-warmed apples from their orchards. It's always been good luck to help a pilgrim, but mostly I think they just wanted to see who we were. "I know America," one elderly woman told me. "Honduras and Argentina." Every encounter made me smile.

Because we went at our own speed, the pilgrimage was different for each person in the group. "This is all about what's in us already," I wrote in my notebook one afternoon, leaning against an old wall around a chapel garden, with the sun on my back and birds chirping in the shrubs. "The road gives you the chance to let it out. To hear your own small, quiet voice. To see how little we need. How little makes us happy." I felt at that moment as if I could walk forever.

The real pilgrimage puzzle, I thought, isn't why pilgrims did it, but why Santiago? The answer gives me a ghost-story tingle. About A.D. 850, local monks in Galicia noticed strange hovering stars—*estrellas* in Spanish. They investigated the field beneath—a *campo*—and discovered human bones, which promptly began to work miracles. Religious authorities concluded the bones belonged to a saint—and not just any saint. These were the bones of St. James, the apostle, whose body had come to Spain from the Holy Land in a miraculous boat.

Rumors spread, and people in need of miracles began coming to pray. Over the centuries, the monks built a chapel, then a beautifully austere Romanesque church, then a lavish rococo shell around that—today's cathedral of Santiago de Compostela, last resting place of the patron saint of Spain, Saint James of the Starry Field.

After the Reformation, the flood of religious pilgrims shrank to a trickle but never really stopped. During the past decade, they've been wildly outnumbered by thousands of hikers and bikers. El Camino has become, once again, the most popular trail in Europe: 61,400 people walked it in 2001.

This was Europe's hajj, and for the faithful, every inch was a walking prayer. My feet did their praying in beat-up Nikes. That's how gentle the track is—anybody can walk it. Dee's hiking boots hurt, so she switched to backless scuffs and did just fine.

You've always been able to tell a pilgrim by the clothes. You still can: fleece by Patagonia, boots by Mephisto, rain gear from Land's End. I favored a long-billed cap, with a sun-proof French Foreign Legion-style drape around the back of the neck. Early in the trip, I caught a glimpse of myself in a mirror and was struck by how much my headgear resembled a medieval wimple. Whattayaknow, I thought. Me and the Wife of Bath.

In the heyday of the pilgrimage, pilgrims wore a prescribed—and spartan—outfit: a long robe, a walking staff, a gourd for wine (water wasn't safe), a leather pouch for carrying food, and a big, wide-brimmed hat. Spanish images of St. James show him in a hat like that, with the brim pinned up on one side by a cockleshell.

The shell is still the emblem of the pilgrimage. It looks exactly like the logo of Shell Oil—a scallop, flat and pinkish, larger than a large man's palm. You see them everywhere—cast up on Spain's northern beaches, edging flower beds in Galicia, emblazoned on pilgrim's caps and T-shirts. And in fancy restaurants from Paris to California, wherever the menu lists coquilles St. Jacques, the scallops of St. James.

As more and more pilgrims took to the trail, priests and monks moved to protect them, building hospitals, bridges over dangerous streams, refuges for pilgrims to stay in, and churches like little fortresses, which made sense: The Moors had claimed the southern half of Iberia before the pilgrimage began. Up north, the pilgrims were doing what the military could not: nailing down this part of Spain for Christianity.

A thousand years ago, one of those monk-engineers was canonized and a church and a town named for him: Santo Domingo del Calzado, St. Dominick of the Walkway. I liked him. He's always depicted with a pair of white chickens, participants in his most famous miracle. A callous judge had had an innocent young pilgrim hanged for theft. The saint intervened while the judge was dining on roast chicken. The judge scoffed: "Why, you could no more bring that boy back to life than these dead chickens could stand up and crow!" Of course, the chickens revived, and so did the young man.

Inside the church, there's an ornate hencoop holding two live white chickens. Every so often during my visit, the white rooster would rear back and crow, and I would rear back and laugh out loud. It seemed sacrilegious, but I couldn't stop. Neither could the chicken.

A middle-aged woman with a sad face interrupted. "You are going to Santiago?" She'd mistaken me for a real pilgrim— must've been the hat. I felt embarrassed and started apologizing: "No, not really, I'm just..."

She didn't let me finish. She stepped closer, looked earnestly into my eyes and said softly, "When you get to Santiago, say a prayer for us. For Monique and Giles"—herself and her quiet husband—"and for my mother, who is very old."

Then she started to cry. I was overwhelmed. I reached out to give her a hug and burst into tears, too. We stood like that for a moment, total strangers crying in each others' arms in a church with a chicken crowing. Yes, I promised, yes, I'll say a prayer for you. Then we both turned and walked away. I never saw her again.

But from that moment, I was a pilgrim. It was Monique's faith, not mine, that had made me one. I never gave the "not really" speech again.

We started our days Spanish-style, with rolls and big cups of *cafe con leche*; we ate Judy's catered picnics in the afternoons and dug into hefty Spanish dinners at day's end. We slept in small hotels and, once, in a *refugio*, a dormitory like the ones the old pilgrims used.

Each day had its landmarks, sometimes a place, sometimes a person, sometimes both: The Cross of Iron, for example, a small thing on a tall pole with a huge mound of stones around its base. Pilgrims bring them from home and leave them there, hoping to leave old worries with them. I contributed a black pebble from my front yard and walked on.

Villafranca del Bierzo, where a chorus of local troubadours, wearing beribboned capes and strumming guitars, surrounded me and sang. The loveliest song was about their hometown—"*como te haces querer*," the refrain went, "how you make us love you."

And the young couple from Madrid who became fast friends because we walked together for two hours. People have always bonded like that on the Camino, the wife said, always: "It's like a family." When we parted in the next town, I missed them as deeply as if we'd walked together for months.

Sometimes the same conversation spilled across several towns and over different people. In Rabanal del Camino, a pretty, once-impoverished village that the modern pilgrimage is bringing back to life, I talked for a while with the manager of the *refugio*. "The point of a pilgrimage isn't to get somewhere," he told me, almost fiercely. "It's to come home changed!"

Farther west, at O'Cebreiro, the Celtic-looking mountain village that was my favorite spot—fog-bound, a Spanish brigadoon—an Englishwoman picked up the same thread. She knew what she was talking about: A convert to Catholicism, she had walked not only to Santiago before, but to Rome and to Jerusalem. "Once you get home," she warned, "everything in your daily life will conspire to keep you from living what you learned on the road."

In between encounters, my thoughts jumped around as if I were dreaming—from matters of faith to the gravel in my shoe, from ancient saints to how much I wanted a Coke. Even so, I felt more completely in the trip than any before or since. This was Travel, capital T, and I was living in the details. My journal again: "I fall in love with mossy tree trunks, remember individual stones. It takes so long to walk through a landscape. And it is so completely gone once you have: You don't waste steps second-guessing yourself. So is every step a commit-ment? It must be."

I'd made a vow about our last day: No riding. I intended to start on foot in the morning, stay on foot all day and enter Santiago on foot, no matter how long it took, because that's how the medieval pilgrims would have done it.

I started walking in a eucalyptus forest, pain-free and grate-ful. Thirteen miles later, hungry and shaky-tired, Santiago's suburbs were rising around me, and in the distance I could make out the spires of the cathedral through a haze of pollution above the city. This was the grail, but I was almost sorry to see it—I didn't want to let go of the Camino. I envied the old pilgrims who got to turn around and walk all the way home.

It was rush hour, and the traffic around me was fast and thick. Then the streets narrowed, and narrowed some more, until I was trudging in ancient alleys. I turned a final corner, and a huge paved space opened up—the plaza of the cathedral. Journey's end.

I went up the stone stairs and stepped through the outer doors. Inside was a second entrance, the Portico de la Gloria, the lovely, simple facade of the earlier church. Tradition demands that pilgrims kneel down before crossing its threshold.

A stream of pilgrims was flowing in—foot pilgrims, bike pilgrims, car pilgrims, bus pilgrims, pilgrims in high heels, pilgrims who'd never set foot on the Camino. But everybody knelt. When it was my turn, I knelt, too, reaching out to steady myself with a hand on a nearby pillar. Touching it gave me a burst of happiness. So many other hands had steadied pilgrims there that they'd worn a smooth, deep, undulating groove in the column. It fit my hand like a stone glove, comfortable, comforting.

Ahead, in the center of the distant altar at the back of the cathedral, I could see a small gleaming figure surrounded by a blaze of silver and gold: the saint himself. The actual reliquary holding his bones rests beneath the altar, but the pilgrim tide was flowing toward this statue, smaller than life-size, wearing a pilgrim's hat trimmed with a cockleshell.

We passed up a narrow flight of steps, into a tiny warm space behind the saint, and I did what pilgrims do: I gave him a hug. I put my arms around Santiago's silver shoulders and prayed, first for Monique and Giles and her mother, who was so very old, then for myself. Thank you, I said, thank you, thank you, thank you, thank you.

It took just seconds, and then I was going down the steps on the other side, through the portico, out onto the front steps again, then off to find my companions and drink a glass of Spanish red and talk about it all. The pilgrimage felt over then, but, strangely, it doesn't now. Maybe that's what the verb *peregrinar* really means: that the pilgrimage itself continues to exist in this mortal life.

Did I come home changed? A little. Did daily life conspire against me when I got back? Yes, but I was braced for it. Were there lessons? Some. I've been a more mindful traveler because of the Camino; I take more time along the way, listen for more stories, notice more details. Words and images gleaned in Rabanal and O'Cebreiro are still with me. And so is the lesson of my private miracle: When it hurts, hold your head up and keep on walking.

Catherine Watson is the award-winning travel editor of the Minneapolis Star Tribune *and the author of* Travel Basics.

✳ ✶ ✶

Naturally Baked

Yoga Provençal requires a good sense of humor.

WE WAKE EACH DAY TO THE SOUND OF A DIFFERENT hippie instrument. Day one was a Tibetan bell; on day two, Instructor Roger plays the piccolo; today, a man we call Guido because of his oiled hair and handsome gold neck chains, walks around strumming a guitar. My brother emerges furrily from another corner of the biodynamic farm, teeth unbrushed, ready to hike to the field for our yoga matinal.

Fifteen aspirant yogis wait in the field for Instructor Roger. All of them are French, deeply earnest, and committed to the principles of biodynamic agriculture. At dawn exactly, Instructor Roger arrives, smiling and bright. He and Instructor Claire are leading this week-long yoga and hiking retreat in the Alps of Haute Provence. Both are disciples of the Indian guru Patanjali and dedicated biodynamic vegetarians.

The sky, like the fragrant wildflowers, is a luminous purple-blue. The air smells of lavender and wild thyme; a palomino horse whinnies in the distance. The milk cows are returning from the fields, making low cow noises, the bells around their stout necks tinkling. Instructor Roger waves *bonjour* and produces a small teapot from his baggy trouser pocket. He murmurs something in Sanskrit, then cautions us in French to watch attentively. He begins pouring water into his right nostril. It drains directly out the left nostril and on to the dry ground. My brother and I are revolted and fascinated. "I'm sure it's very healthful and all," my brother whispers, "but I wouldn't do it on a first date."

I agree that it's definitely not a first-date thing.

Roger proceeds to blow his nose boisterously, spraying the wildflowers with lavish plumes, then attends to the opposite nostril. Properly purged, he launches into a lecture about the healthful effects of proper nasal hygiene. With Roger, everything becomes a lecture. The practice is called *neti*, he tells us, making the word sound more French than Sanskrit, and if practiced faithfully, will cleanse the body of impurities, physical and spiritual.

In the distance, we can see Mont Ventoux; the dawn is so clear that it is possible to see the white flag that flies from the peak. I am not sure what the flag symbolizes. Perhaps the French are surrendering again. The earth is tinder-dry, and a breeze rustles pleasantly through the grassy slopes and stirs a chorus of beating crickets, eddies of variegated butterflies.

Every morning begins with yogic nasal hygiene. We are not yet advanced enough for the teapot; instead we practice ritual noseblowing. Surrounded by golden rolled wheels of hay, we blow our noses with huge gulping snorts to Roger's cadence. Inspire! Expire! Inspire! Expire!

My brother leans over and whispers again: "If you do this right, you'll get high as a kite."

I blow and I blow. Nothing much happens.

Disappointingly, none of the other yogis are below the age of forty. My brother is inconsolable. "I thought this would be, you know, a hippie thing," he says to me. "With great-looking blond hippie girls, you know the kind with little anklets, the ones who just really like to pass the bong and stretch?"

"Maybe someone stretchy will show up tomorrow," I say.

He takes no comfort, and mutters to himself. "I can't believe it. I'm here with ten women old enough to be my mother, a fat guy with gold chains around his neck who wears a tiny leopard-print swimsuit, and my sister. This is not what I had in mind."

Josette and François, members of José Bové's Confederation Paysanne, run the biodynamic farm. They are not yogis themselves, but in the summer, the farm becomes a hostel of sorts for visiting groups of New Age *stagiaires*, students of yoga, astronomers, collectors of essential oils. The farm's sun-splashed dormitories sleep groups of four or five; there is an oak-paneled communal dining room with huge windows that open onto the mountains, and an activity room with walls made of local stone, cool and pleasant in the afternoon. The hostel is spotlessly clean and redolent of lavender oil. The dining room is filled with brochures denouncing the International Monetary Fund, leaflets decrying genetically modified organisms and battery farming, and Greenpeace literature. To round out the activist palette, a prominent stack of tracts calls for the interposition of an international police force in Occupied Palestine.

Josette is a tall woman of handsome peasant stock and an imposing sternness, with a thick wedge of chin-length iron hair, high color, and broad shoulders. Her arms are muscular from years of heavy labor. She instantly conveys that she is not to be defied and will brook no bourgeois nonsense, no nonsense of any kind. The word formidable comes to mind. My brother and I imagine her children, sitting on the psychoanalyst's couch. "My mother was a formidable woman," we imagine them saying. She is clearly running this show; François stays in the fields and wears a series of proletarian uniforms: gray overalls, green overalls, thigh-high rubber boots suitable for mucking stalls.

In the dining room, at lunch, we examine the leaflets about biodynamic agriculture. We learn that the principles of bio-dynamic agriculture were delineated by the Austrian mystic Rudolph Steiner, in 1916. The ideal farm should be self-contained, he argued, with just the right number and combi-nation of animals to provide the manure needed to revitalize the soil. These animals in turn should be fed from the same land. Biodynamic agriculture forbids the use of chemical fer-tilizers and pesticides, relying instead upon crop rotation and composting. Steiner, influenced by the Theosophists, posited subtle cosmic formative forces on plant growth, and claimed to be able to see back in time to ancient events imprinted on the cosmic ether. In his portrait, he is wearing a high starched collar and a heavy black overcoat; his eyes are wild, staring and mad.

As Steiner would have wished, the farm we are on strives for self-sufficiency, and the vegetables we eat—carrots, beets, lettuce, and fresh herbs—come from the garden behind the stable. François raises his own wheat, from which the daily bread is made. The bread is just awful, like lead.

The life of the farm appears to be organized around the daily rhythms of the twenty milk cows. They come in for milking, they go out to pasture, they come in for milking again. Each cow's name is hand-lettered above her stall. Jacinthe, Marguerite, Koala, and their companions are milked twice daily, herded to the fields by means of affectionate slaps on their marbled rumps, and allowed to graze freely. They ap-pear to be in glorious bovine health. A calf is born the first morning we are there, white and brown with a pirate-patch of sorrel over one of his enormous eyes. He is hopelessly touching, following his mother around on unsturdy splayed legs. Behind the stable a family of black pigs and piglets scarf down slop, as Steiner would have wished: They are eating the acidic waste produced during cheesemaking so that it does not contaminate the soil. The pigs grunt happily. "Doesn't get much better than being a biodynamic pig on a vegetarian farm," my brother says, wandering over to scratch a pig behind the ears.

Later, we are dismayed to find a leaflet promoting the farm's own pâté. The farmers are vegetarians, evidently, but some of the customers are not. "This is disturbing," my brother whispers to me, showing me the leaflet. "Very disturbing."

While we do yoga, the farmhands work. They pitch hay, or whatever it is one does with hay. They sweep the stables. There is incessant labor involved in collecting the milk, making the cheese, and keeping these beasts warm, dry, and happy. The farmhands are always doing something disagreeable; someone is always brandishing a pitchfork, driving a tractor, industriously hauling something heavy from a truck.

The farm does not belong to Josette and François, but to a fraternal, nonprofit organization called the Earth and Sky Society. According to its charter, the organization exists to foster cultural exchanges and "make the world a better place for human life while finding a good relationship with the earth that nourishes us, a forum of life where respect for humans and nature forges a positive attitude toward humanity and its future on this planet." Major decisions about the farm are made by committee, and loans to the farm come from a fraternal bank. The farm is staffed by volunteers, many of them conscientious objectors from Germany.

The food is just abominable, but everyone keeps raving about it, because it's biodynamic. Every day Josette puts exactly the same thing on the long wooden picnic tables beneath the linden trees: dark bread with the weight and density of plutonium, a bowl of undressed lettuce garnished with edible marigolds, lentils, grated carrots, and stone-hard peaches. There is never quite enough, and even though it is a dairy farm, milk and yogurt are rationed sharply. After each meal the yogis lunge ungraciously for the scraps, bargaining savagely with each other for the last few lettuce leaves. The meals are dreary and monotonous. But no one admits it. "*C'est délicieux!*" the yogis declare, smacking their lips. "How much better it tastes when it is prepared naturally!" By the third day, my brother and I are desperate. At lunch, my brother looks down the table and whispers, softly, to no one in particular, "*coq au vin*."

Half the table looks scandalized, as if he had revealed a fetish. But a dreamy look passes across the face of a plump woman named Anne. "*Ah oui*," she sighs, "*avec des frites*." Her husband looks at her indulgently, tenderly, but the rest of the table glares. "Of course this too is very good," she says quickly, applying herself to her naked lettuce leaves.

That evening I spot Jonas. Jonas is at least six-and-a-half feet tall, not yet twenty-one, strapping, handsome, well-muscled, blond. He speaks excellent English, although very slowly, with a thick German accent that makes him sound exactly like Arnold Schwarzenegger. He looks as if he was born to invade Poland, but in fact he volunteered to work at the farm to avoid German military service. At first he thought he was clever, Jonas did, getting out of forced marches and night patrols to spend a year in Provence, but after a year of shoveling manure and slopping hogs—ten hours a day, six days a week—those night patrols are sounding better and better. He loathes the farm, loathes everything about it, is dying of boredom and hatred. He yearns to be in Berlin, listening to the music of Kraftwerk and taking Ecstasy at the fashionable clubs. He regards the yogis with pure contempt. He has lived for a year now on Josette's flavorless biodynamic cooking, and when we ask him one morning whether he will share his pot of real coffee with us—the yogis drink only decaffeinated chicory brew—he clutches the pot to his chest and growls like a cornered beast. "Not enough!" he snarls. "Find your own!"

We leave him and his coffee alone.

This is no life for a young man of his sensibilities. There is no one his age on the farm except for Josette's and François's daughter. She is plump and pretty, but Jonas suspects that François is the kind of man who knows how to use his hunting rifle. Jonas receives room and vegetarian board. They pay him a little bit every month in pocket money, not even enough to pay for gas to drive to the nearest city.

"Well," I say, "it's got to be better than the military. At least no one's shooting at you."

"Yes," he replies. "But maybe if I see another cow I shoot myself." As if to punctuate his comment, a cow moos stupidly in the distance.

How does it work, I ask him, doing public service instead of joining the military? Can you work anywhere you like?

"They like it if you work for one of Germany's enemies. You know, Ukraine, Russia, France, Israel. I think it is stupid. I wasn't responsible for that war. I wasn't even born."

Young Germans always want to tell me that they weren't responsible for the war. They say it as early in the conversation as they can.

He asks me what I do in Paris. I tell him I write novels.

"I want to write a novel, too," he says. "Like Bret Easton Ellis. He is my favorite writer."

"What do you want to write about?" I ask.

"This place," he nods toward the cows.

"What about it?" I ask.

"The story of how I sell my soul."

"You sold your soul?"

"I sell my soul to work on a biodynamic farm. I do it for my future, but I sell my soul."

"I see," I say. I am not sure what he means.

"I would write about these people. You know, François is a communist. A real one." He flings his cigarette into the flowerbed with a flick of his wrist.

"Which one is he, exactly?" I ask, trying to place him. Josette is a commanding presence, but François is just a specter.

"He is the one with all the hairs growing from his ears." Hay-uhs gro-ving frum his ee-yahs.

"You don't get along with them?" I ask.

He shrugs. "They don't like me because they think I am bourgeois. They hate all people who don't want to work with their hands. All intellectuals, they hate them."

I nod.

"Once," says Jonas in his Arnold Schwarzenegger accent, "I complain about the food. I say that it is always the same." All-vays duh same. "But Josette, she freak out." He shakes his head to indicate that something awesome and terrible occurred. "I never say that again." I neh-vuh say dat a-gain.

As he contemplates his lot, the Tibetan chime sounds, summoning us to afternoon yoga practice.

My brother and I remark that Instructor Roger is a dead ringer for Marshall Applewhite, the leader of the Heaven's Gate cult who prompted his disciples to ingest poison mixed with applesauce in the hope of quitting their earthly vessels to ride the comet Hale-Bopp. This resemblance is especially pronounced when Roger dons his long white yoga robes. But Roger is jolly and good-natured, with a kind of softness to all his body parts. He prefers lecturing about the theory of yoga to practicing it. He lectures for hours at a stretch, winding his way slowly through each of the eight steps on the path to enlightenment. He begins each discourse with a rhetorical question: *Qu'est-ce que c'est le Pranayama? Qu'est-ce que c'est les Asanas?* He pauses for effect, scanning the class with his eyes. *Eh bien.* Then he reaches for the original Sanskrit authorities, a voluminous set of notes, photographs of a pretzeled Indian guru, and the illustrated Larousse, and begins methodically to answer his own question, saying nothing at great length.

Alors, j'explique.

My brother and I came to practice yoga, not to listen to lectures on yoga theory, and we are maddened with impatience. But we are amazed to see that the other students appear to love these lectures, and pronounce Roger's endless disquisitions to be *très, très bien.* They encourage him. They raise their hands and ask long, complicated, completely incoherent theoretical questions. We are not sure whether this is because they are French, or because they are old. We suspect, though, that it is because they are French. After a two-hour lecture on the theory of yoga postures, as we become progressively more cramped and stiff from sitting motionless on the floor, my brother turns to me and asks, "How on earth do these people make love?"

Instructor Claire is deathly thin. She is nothing but bone and veins covered in translucent skin, like a jellyfish. Her spine can be viewed from the front as well as the back. My brother and I worry about her. When we go hiking, I ask what we would do if she suddenly dropped dead.

"No problem, just sling her over your shoulder and skip down the trail," my brother says.

"Could probably fit her in your backpack," I agree.

We can't figure out why she is so thin. She seems to be filling her plate with biodynamic food at every meal. Later at lunch, my brother leans over to me and whispers: "She's a chewer."

"Huh?"

"Watch how many times she chews each bite."

I watch. She is chewing every bite for a minute or more. I ask my brother what this means. He thinks that maybe she belongs to an Indian chewing sect, one in which devotees are obliged to chew each bite thirty times. The effect is nutritionally devastating, he says: The salivary enzymes decompose the proteins so thoroughly that the body can no longer use them. There is a lecture on nutrition for yogis on the schedule, but my brother declares that we will boycott it. We are not taking any nutritional advice from Instructor Claire, he says. No way.

In the afternoons, when yoga theory crawls to a close, the gentle stretching begins, although Instructor Roger interrupts us after every pose to correct us and then offer the lengthy theoretical justification for his correction. To my side sits a plump gray-haired woman who bears so striking a resemblance to my brother's second-grade teacher that we rename her Mrs. Loeb, and cannot thereafter think of her by any other name. She is unable to do any of the yoga postures, but greatly enjoys the nose-blowing. For the entire week, she is a one-woman nose orchestra. Especially when we try to meditate. Instructor Roger's voice urges deeper and deeper relaxation, a gentle breeze stirs the dry afternoon air and rustles the grass, we focus on our breath, inhale, exhale, and—Snort! Blast!—there goes Mrs. Loeb's nose.

No, they are not young and lithe, these yogis. This is not the place to come to meet hippie chicks. There is Mrs. Loeb, of course, with her orchestral nose, and Christine, a drooping creature with large hips and very pale skin and sad eyes, and

Marie-Thérèse, another painfully thin woman, in her sixties with dyed red hair and a pinched prune of a mouth. She complains of constipation. But we have to admit that these yogis are the gentlest, kindest group of earnest middle-aged people we have ever met. Mrs. Loeb spends hours trying to teach us the genders of French nouns. The classification of the American states is a source of puzzlement and vexation to my brother; Mrs. Loeb goes through every state in the Union with us: It is *la Californie*, but *le Kansas*, and *oui, le français*, it is not always *logique*. They are solicitous, concerned: We have arrived unprepared, without water bottles for our hikes, without raincoats. They offer their own. "But it's not raining," my brother protests. No matter; he is the youngest. They bundle him up in an enormous raincoat; his bare legs stick out underneath and he looks like a human mushroom swaying on its stalk.

At night, the yogis sit in a circle in the stone-walled activity room and sing French songs from their childhood. Together, their voices are sweet and lovely, almost childish. They sing of picking daisies, gathering wildflowers, first love. They all know all the words to the songs. Anne-Marie becomes nostalgic when they sing a song about the train that whistles. It reminds her of her first love. "How I cried," she says. I try to imagine her as a young woman.

The farm reminds them of their childhoods; they all agree. "The cows, they look like the cows when I was growing up," says Marie-Thérèse. Everyone nods vigorously. "Cows don't look like that any more," someone says. The cows do look happy, as these things go. They are outside all day; their stalls are spacious and clean; their hay is fresh. The mother and her calf are inseparable. The food tastes awful, it is true, but in the end we are glad that meat is never served. "Imagine waking up in the morning and finding just an empty stall and a cowbell where Koala used to be," my brother says.

Once, we are attempting to meditate in the activity room, when a cow walks past the window and moos loudly, making the most absurd bovine sound, a sound of pure comic stupidity. It sounds just like Mrs. Loeb blowing her nose. My brother and I begin to giggle and can't stop. The more we try, the worse it gets. We are doubled over on our yoga mats, trying to stop laughing, dying of embarrassment. The moment one of us gets a hold of ourselves, the other one starts again, and we lose control. We ruin everyone's concentration.

On Thursday evening, we are shown a videotape about biodynamic agriculture. The video shows a woman casting astrological charts, a man spraying his crops with some kind of crystal, cows being cured of hoof-and-mouth disease with homeopathic tinctures. Then Josette gives a lecture. We sit in a circle, legs crossed lotus-style. She begins by asking us each to introduce ourselves and explain what we do in the "*marche de la vie.*" I'm puzzled by the phrase, and as we go around the room, it is obvious that everyone else is puzzled too. The other yogis stammer and babble, talking about how they do yoga to relax. Josette is looking at them as if they are fools, she didn't ask about yoga and she couldn't give a damn what they do to relax. Finally, it is my turn, and since I have an excuse, I ask, what does this French expression mean, *marche de vie*? Josette stares at me, her expression stern under her iron hair. "It means," she says in French, marching her two forefingers briskly in the air, "what do you do in the walk in life?" I am no closer to understanding, but somehow I know intuitively that she is asking what sort of meaningful physical labor I do, and that no truthful answer I give will be remotely satisfactory.

I write, I say.

Her gaze is withering. Finally, she says, "What do you write?"

Feebly, I answer: "Maybe a book denouncing factory farming?"

Her face softens, slightly. "*Ça va, alors.*"

I have joined Jonas in the club of sold souls.

Wide-bottomed Yogini Christine has been flirting with Yogi Serge all week; she slaps his bottom coyly as we hike up Mount Chamouse. She seems to be flirting with Yogi Guido, too, cuddling up to him as he plays his guitar. Watching this with puzzlement, my brother asks whether I've noticed that these middle-aged French women give off an air of hideous sexual desperation. "Insane crazed lust," he says. "Like if they got their hands on you they'd tear you to shreds."

Suddenly, we both have the same idea.

"Jonas," we say in unison, and look at each other. My brother imagines Marie-Thérèse emerging from the stable, hastily rearranging herself and shaking her short dyed hair. *Oh la la! J'ai tiré un bon coup, moi!*

We know we have a moneymaker on our hands.

Later, we pitch the idea to him. "Look, Jonas, this is a strictly commercial proposal. We arrange everything and we take 10 percent. One night of work, you could make enough to spend next weekend in Biarritz."

He looks at us, the muscles in his jaw twitching. He's not sure if we're serious.

"I already sell my soul. I don't want to sell my body." Boh-dee.

"Aw, c'mon Jonas," I coax. "You wanted to write a novel, right? Let me tell you, no one's interested in a novel about shoveling cow shit. But a novel called I Was a Biodynamic Gigolo—straight to the top of the bestseller list, man, I'm telling you."

He stares at us some more. "Really?" he says at last.

"Really," I assure him.

He is thinking about it, and his head is getting warm from the effort. In the distance, we hear the cowbells and the low

cow sounds. The crickets stir and croak. The children are playing *petanque* outside the stable and their voices are a gentle
gabble. Jonas thinks. Christine returns from the field with an
armful of fresh lavender and Spanish broom, which she will
arrange in a bouquet for the dinner table. Jonas follows her
wide hips with his eyes. The Tibetan chime sounds; it is time
for the afternoon yoga. We leave Jonas, pitchfork in hand,
golden hair gleaming in the sun, staring into the distance, con-
templating the state of his soul.

Yogi Serge insists that it is possible to feel the trees' energy.
On one hike, we summit a hill and find the yogis on the other
side, holding hands in a ring around an ancient oak, eyes
closed, expressions rapt, attempting to pass energy from hand
to hand in a circle. When they are finished, each of the yogis
hugs the tree in turn. My brother and I look at each other; he
raises an eyebrow. We go over to the tree to try to feel the energy, too. I close my eyes and stretch out my hands just like
Serge. I don't feel much of anything, but of course I say that I
do; I tell Serge that the energy is *très très forte*. "Did you feel
anything?" I whisper to my brother afterwards.

"I felt a sort of rumbling," he says.

"Rumbling?"

"It's all those lentils, I think. All this biodynamic food is
making me really turbo-charged, if you know what I mean."

I know exactly what he means.

I have almost given up on feeling the energy, writing it off
as a bad job, but on the last day, Instructor Roger leads us in
special yogic breathing exercises in a shady copse in the
woods. The temperature of the air is exquisite, like dry champagne. We place our mats on the ground and sit with our legs
crossed and our spines erect; we inhale, holding our breath, re-
laxing our muscles, then exhale, then inhale again. The wind

rustles in the grass and the leaves of the trees. The air is so soft, the breeze so gentle, the sky so blue, the lavender so fragrant, the light so golden, that after two hours of this gentle breathing I am transported. We breathe energy into our fingers and toes, breathe energy into our scalps and our jaws and our ankles and our fingertips. We inhale and hold, we exhale and hold, my body feels as if it is lifting off the ground. My hands and my feet feel tingly and light, as if they are humming. I think I can feel the energy, yes, definitely I can feel the energy. I am willing to believe that the trees are speaking to me personally, telling me their sad tree stories, I can really feel it, I can, for a brief moment I can really feel it—

Then Mrs. Loeb blows her nose—Snort! Blast!—

My brother begins to snicker—

And the moment passes.

Claire Berlinski is a writer, freelance journalist, and the author of the novel, Loose Lips. *Since receiving her doctorate in international relations in 1995, she has worked in print media, taught at the university level, and worked for the United Nations, living in England, Thailand, Laos, San Francisco, and Washington, D.C. She is now living in Paris.*

MARYBETH BOND

⋆ ⋆ ⋆

Pedaling Through the Emerald Isle

A cyclist discovers that Ireland has a song
in its heart, and chivalry at its core.

IF LIFE SEEMS RICHER, GREENER, AND MORE MELODIC IN Ireland, that's because there is simply more clear air, clean water, verdant countryside, and heart-lifting music in everyday life.

For ten entrancing days, I cycled the quiet back roads of the Ring of Kerry and the Dingle Peninsula in southwest Ireland. By day, I wheeled down corkscrew lanes aflame with red fuchsia and yellow gorse, through frog-green hills crisscrossed with ancient stone walls, dotted with medieval ruins, and grazed by baaing sheep. By night, I basked in the musical revelry of a local pub or the warmth of farmhouse hospitality.

I quickly discovered that, for a relatively small island (the size of Maine), Ireland offers an extraordinary variety of scenery and a network of intertwining trails and bike-perfect country lanes. Indeed, Ireland is a hiker's and cyclist's paradise.

Spinning through pastures of myriad shades of green, past high hedges, and rushing rivers, I felt the earth roll under my pedals, smelled the peat bricks burning, and tasted the salty air of the coast, where the ocean foamed onto rocky shores.

Along the Dingle Peninsula I stopped often to rest on a towering cliff above the treacherous coastline and watch 3,000 miles of Atlantic surge towards the beach.

This was my first trip to Ireland and I traveled alone. Although I would have enjoyed biking with a buddy or significant other, no one had the same vacation time, so I took off solo—to a country reputed to be safe and hospitable. The glossy photos in the tour brochures I consulted showed smiling guests at sumptuous feasts, experienced guides, a support vehicle for cyclists, and luxurious accommodations in castles and manor houses. But an organized bike trip didn't fit my slim budget, so I spent my nights in cozy cottages, farmhouses, and small B & Bs, where the matron of the house would tuck a hot water bottle in the toe of my bed while I went out for dinner.

And while bicycle tour companies provide their guests with twenty-one-speed hybrid touring models, my rented vehicle was a one-speed, heavy black bike with a wire basket in front, resembling the bicycle Dorothy's wicked neighbor rode in *The Wizard of Oz*. I squeezed my backpack into the basket and headed for the open road.

For me, the allure of exploring rural Ireland by bicycle was the slow pace and the up-close contact with the land and the people. I could pedal along the most scenic routes, stop often, breathe the fragrant air, gaze out upon the verdant landscape, and remember every heart-pounding hill that passed under my wheels. My feelings of exhilaration came in a smug, distinctly self-satisfied way, in the burn I felt just before I hauled myself by pedal power to the top of yet another hill. Or after a long day in the saddle, knowing my muscles were harder. Or in the slight tingle in my calf muscles that reminded me I just had the most inspiring day's ride ever.

Starting in popular Killarney, I rode around the Ring of Kerry, along the perimeter of the Iveragh Peninsula, and then along the Dingle Peninsula, following many off-the-beaten-path roads to avoid the tourist traffic.

Killarney is a busy tourist center, packed with tour buses, shops, discos, and cabarets. Yet the stunning beauty of the surrounding area—a combination of heather-clad mountains, deep-blue lakes and lush vegetation—remains unspoiled. Killarney National Park, famous for its lake and mountain scenery, occupies a large part of the valley.

Light rain is typical in southwest Ireland, but it seldom lasts long. The clouds billow over the lakes or hills, showers follow, and within minutes, brilliant sunshine and rainbows emerge. During the month of April, when I biked in Ireland, there can be more rain and cooler weather than May to September. The temperature ranged from 50 to 60 degrees Fahrenheit.

In good weather, the trip to the Gap of Donloe is an idyllic bike and hike excursion from Killarney. The gap is a four-mile trail that winds along the ridge above steep gorges and five deep glacial lakes.

Leaving the Ring of Kerry, I pedaled toward the Dingle Peninsula where the movies *Ryan's Daughter* (with Sara Miles and Christopher Jones) and *Far and Away* (with Nicole Kidman and Tom Cruise) were filmed.

The Dingle Peninsula is a meeting place of sorts, where wave-carved cliffs and rolling hills fend off a moody, restless Atlantic, and the memories of sea battles merge with the scent of wildflowers. The natural stage of the Dingle itself, often veiled in mist, enlivened by the pounding surf, is a draw for travelers in search of solitude, renewal, and natural beauty.

Many evenings, after a hard day's ride, I visited the local pub to share lively conversation and music over a pint of nut-brown Guinness. I would take a seat, call for a drink, and listen as the tune was handed on from fiddle to flute, from strings to pipe. Toe tapping began and I could feel the rhythm deepen as it went around, strengthening and gaining in confidence. I often found myself happily lost in the intricate melodies.

A green-eyed, bearded young fiddler assured me, "There isn't a corner of the country where music isn't central to the gathering. You see," he continued, "it doesn't have to be organized, and the group of musicians may change as the evening wears away." When it was late and the fingers were flying, my heart would soar.

One memorable day, after six hours of pedaling over the hills through the soft Irish mist, I heard a hiss from my front tire and knew I had a problem. It had been hours since I'd seen the sun, my leg muscles screamed, and my back end burned. My only companions, black and white cows plodding across the road, were indifferent.

Enviously, I thought about the pampered guests on the organized tours. Had I booked my trip with a bicycle company, a support vehicle and guide would have come to my rescue to repair my tire, while I joked and commiserated with my fellow cycling companions. But alone, with a leaking tire, a wet body, and a soggy spirit, I wondered if Ireland's terrain defied the laws of physics and the entire country was uphill. It was time to break for hot coffee and a warm scone—or perhaps, a reviving Guinness.

In the distance, at the crest of the next hill, I could see white cottages with gray slate roofs. Through the thin clouds one chimney rose above the others, pouring out a fragrant plume of peat smoke from a turf fire. "Ah," I thought, "that must be the village pub." After an hour of low-tire pumping, I was there.

I tramped into the pub's inviting warmth, drenched and disheveled, feeling conspicuous, but the man behind the worn wooden bar put me at ease. As he served my Guinness, he grinned and asked, "Can you sing?"

Now where else in the world would a bartender ask this question of a young lady who stood dripping water on the floor?

"Yes, I think I can sing," I answered. Lord Guinness worked his magic and loosened my tongue, and out flowed, "When Irish Eyes Are Smiling," which my half-Irish mother used to sing to me when she tucked me into bed. An elderly man in tattered tweed coat and wool cap stepped up to the bar, squared his shoulders, took a deep breath, and then belted out, "Mine eyes have seen the glory of the coming of the Lord."

Other customers left their darts and conversations to gather around us. "Sing another one, Yankee," they urged and then joined in. They knew two or three verses to each song. It's hard to stop a song session from taking shape when everyone loves to sing and it's warm inside and spitting Irish dew outside.

An hour and a dozen tunes later, when I was ready to leave, the impromptu choir members insisted on paying for my brews and then escorted me to the door. As I stepped outside—miracle of miracles—the sun was shining again.

The men stood in the door and watched me start to wrestle with my little bicycle pump, ineptly trying to fix my flat tire. With loud and teasing guffaws, they poured out of the pub and organized a work party; the baritone fetched a repair kit from his barn. As they worked, we sang another song and I passed around the last of my Cadbury chocolate bars. It didn't take them long to patch the leak, and as I pedaled off, I turned and waved. They waved back, smiles a mile wide.

Biking through a land of more rainbows than I'd ever seen in my life, over hills and through mist, pushed me physically, but my real discovery was the people. I learned that the sun in the Irish soul is expressed through song, and the smile in Irish eyes is contagious.

Marybeth Bond (www.marybethbond.com) is the editor of this book, as well as A Woman's World, A Mother's World, A Woman's Passion for Travel, *and the author of* Gutsy Women *and* Gutsy Mamas. *She is also the adventure editor for* travelgirl *magazine.*

LUCY McCAULEY

★ ★ ★

Expatriate, with Olives

Sometimes understanding comes by getting
your fingernails dirty.

I AM IN SOUTHERN SPAIN, WALKING TOWARD AN OLIVE grove. It is Catherine's, bought last year when she first came to live in the village. The grove has about fifty trees, said Manuel, who knows all of those trees better than Catherine does, from years of picking there.

The dog, the small curly-haired one who doesn't look as fierce as he is, barks to announce my arrival. Catherine is there, and Bernhard, the young German, and Manuel. Manuel is seventy-three. Lines carve out his jaw and mouth and deep-set eyes, filmy with cataracts. His clippers are going full speed, a great claw squeaking as the dull blades clutch a branch and pull, strip it of olives, the fruit falling green-purple-black in soft drumbeats on the net below.

Since he was eight years old he's been picking olives. He tells me: "I was even born under an olive tree."

"Is that true, Manuel?" comes Catherine's voice from behind a leafy branch.

"Well, no," he replies, and we laugh. "But almost—in a farmhouse *near* an olive grove."

Catherine is a Pennsylvanian who is tall and stands perfectly straight, long auburn hair flowing down her back. I have seen her walk for miles uphill and even then her back remains straight. On one of those walks she showed me the rosemary that grows wild near the side of the road in this part of Spain. "She who passes by rosemary and doesn't pick it," she said, reciting a village proverb, "neither has love nor dreams of it." I watched her pick some, bring the pungent leaves to her nose, and drop them in her pocket.

Catherine divorced her husband and came to live in the village near this grove a year ago, after having visited every summer for twenty years. She is a poet; she came to the village, she says, because it is where she feels most at home in the world. She has had her disappointments. When she first came here she fell in love with a man from a neighboring village. Like many Spanish bachelors, he had lived at home with his mother all his life, but even after she died he could not bring himself to stay with Catherine, a woman of whom his mother disapproved because of her divorce and her foreignness.

But Catherine has her home in the village, her walls and tables draped in richly woven textiles, colorful clay pots and plates in the cupboards. She has her friendship with Manuel and other villagers who have come to love her.

And she has her olives.

This is Catherine's first time collecting the olives of her trees. Harvesting comes once a year, late fall, and lasts a little over a month. Today at twilight she will take the sacks we have filled to the *molina* in town that you can hear grinding away when the winds blow a certain direction, even from up here in the hills, making oil from the villagers' olives.

Clip, slide, *snap, whoosh*—we skin olives from branches and they tumble to the ground like rain. The sun gets hot and bright in southern Spain, even now in late fall. But the breezes from the Mediterranean dry the sweat beading on my forehead before it can trickle down my face. Bernhard and Manuel use the two pairs of clippers, so Catherine and I use our hands, better for feeling the round bubbles of meat, smooth and taut, as we gently clasp the branches and pull through silvery-green leaves.

Before I came to this village, I'd never seen an olive tree up close—only from a distance, driving past groves of them on Spanish highways. An olive branch really does look like a symbol of peace. Graceful, with small feathery leaves that finger outward optimistically from a bumpy little spine, the larger branches bending and twisting together in one direction—toward sun or away from wind or downhill with gravity.

I like standing among the olive branches, enjoy the communal feel of encircling this tree with my companions, each with our own group of branches to clear but still working in tandem, accompanying each other with fragments of conversation and the *whoosh-whoosh* of falling olives. Bernhard tells me he is an artist. He came from Germany five years ago to live in the countryside and to paint, and to collect olives by day for cash. His Spanish is fluid with a German lilt, flattening vowels long at the ends of words rather than spitting them out as a Spaniard would. He paints landscapes, uses fat swirling strokes to form clouds and olive groves.

The conversation lags for a moment, and I think how grateful I am that Catherine has invited me here to pick with her, Bernhard, and Manuel. She has befriended me, taken me out of the isolation of static days at my writing desk in the small house I'm renting in the village. We have stayed up together late into the night, drinking wine and reading poetry, listening to Miles Davis in a cavelike den she's made in her home for the express purpose of listening to music and reading. Its door is a pair of heavy drapes; its floor the terracotta from an old goat shed that once stood there. She lights little fires in the hearth, and burns incense.

On nights like that sometimes she tells me of the pain of losing the man she fell in love with when she arrived in Spain. How he often still passes through the village on the way to his own; he'll walk by her on the road without so much as a hello.

Catherine has given me a glimpse of what it might be like to leave home and family behind, to transform oneself, make a new start in a place that is a home for the heart. But she has also shown me how life is life anywhere you go: you cannot run from heartbreak, or from the daily routines that inevitably set in.

And just as there is everywhere, there is work to be done here. So now I stand in Catherine's olive grove with the sun in my eyes, light glinting from the shiny fruit as we harvest it ripe from the bough.

First, you must place the nets on the ground—it takes two nets, side by side, overlapping slightly—wrap the tree trunk close with them, then spread the nets across the dirt so the olives from every branch have a place to fall. These are Manuel's directions, which he projects with an edge of impatience to us novice harvesters. Catherine has known Manuel since she began visiting the village two decades ago, knows the gentle heart beneath his bark, and she laughs at his gruffness. Still, she defers to him in her olive grove, cocking her head when Manuel gives a command, grateful to have this expert midwife for her harvest.

"The strings of the nets *abajo*—down," Manuel says emphatically. The strings tie the downhill part of the nets up, on the branches of a neighboring tree, so that when the olives tumble downhill, they run up the end of the nets like a soccer ball would, caught in a net-gutter.

After standing in one place for so long, stripping branches of olives, I like bringing the nets to the next tree like an offering, spreading them out to form a perfect chalice. The branches offer themselves, boughs leaning low. We begin taking the olives again, reverently, as if counting prayer beads, thumbs and forefingers moving along branches and over the round pebbles of fruit, pulling through the leaves, olives raining down. Reach, pull, bend, lift; these movements feel imprinted on my brain like an archetype, a ritual known to humans since the first tree appeared in the first garden.

I watch Bernhard's dark bristled hair bob through the high branches where he sits, trying to reach reluctant olives. The tree is picked when only the leaves are left shimmering in the sun, no circles of olives spotting the branches dark. Manuel and Catherine lift the net from the upside of the hill to let the straggling fruit roll down, roaring quietly like ocean in a conch shell. At the downhill part of the net, Bernhard unties the strings. He directs me to hold up one corner, the net heavy with olives, and I feel the weight of my obligation to keep our work for the last half hour from streaming downhill in one great river.

By now, almost halfway through a day of picking together, all this is done like a dance, each of us knowing what needs to happen next, the same sequence for each tree. Sometimes we switch roles, but no matter; someone does a job and the others do what's left: get the *cubo,* the bucket used to scoop fruit shining in the sun then shadow where someone else leans over, plucking the large branches out.

I hold open an enormous burlap sack as Manuel pours in olives from the *cubo* we have filled. The bag grows fuller with each scoop until olives threaten to spill from the top. Bernhard shakes the sack to settle the olives, then ties the corners together. His face is already shining with sweat before he hoists the sack to his shoulders in one graceful motion and walks uphill, his broad back one with the sack and the incline.

We lunch under a tree near the edge of the grove, away from our work. I unpack the garlicky green olives I have brought, and everyone groans. But we each take one anyway and nibble in communion. Manuel passes me a *granada,* a pomegranate lusciously pink, seeds spilling like forbidden fruit—"*Tómelo, tómelo!*" he commands—passes a chunk of bread to Bernhard who has none, only a can of tuna he opens in a zig-zag with his knife. But Bernhard has brought oranges, picked from the trees behind his house, and he passes them around. They smell sweet as we rip them, the scent mingling with the dirt and olive oil on our palms and under our nails, and the juice is thirst-quenching in the hot Spanish sun.

Catherine has wine that she pours in a mug to share among us. I watch her pour, and I wonder if she gets lonely here in the village, even among so many friends. I wonder if her nights are long, and how long she will continue to feel the sting of losing her love.

When we are full, our bodies growing languid in the heat of the day, Manuel announces it's time to pick the next tree. It feels good to be standing again, moving my arms like pistons, the branches like udders of a cow that I milk, the olives pelting my tennis shoes and rolling down the net. Manuel bends to find his walking stick and whacks the tree for straggling olives. Bernhard reaches into the high branches. I untie the corners of the net; Catherine lifts the edge and watches her harvest cascade around her feet.

She looks at me and her eyes shimmer, pleased at the olives

that we have picked from her tree and will load into bags to take to the *molina*.

And whether her love returns or not, at Christmastime Catherine will make presents to friends of her olive oil, drop into the bottles long stems of rosemary that she has picked on one of her long walks. And throughout the year, until the next harvest, the smell of her oil and the rosemary will waft from her kitchen and wind through the streets of this village that she now calls home.

Lucy McCauley is the editor of Travelers' Tales Spain, A Woman's Path, *and* Women in the Wild. *Her writing has appeared in such publications as* The Atlantic Monthly, Los Angeles Times, Harvard Review, Fast Company, *and several Travelers' Tales books. She lives in Dallas, Texas.*

✦ ✦ ✦

In the Bosom of Switzerland

Certain times and places are filled with magic.

IN THE SWISS CANTON OF VALAIS THERE PERCHES AN Alpine village so pretty that the postcard of it looks shamelessly contrived, as if the village were assembled in some movie studio.

This village is a collection of old, green-shuttered wood chalets, each one decked with lacy white window boxes overflowing with red geraniums. The chalets are set into a steep hillside, and are gathered up and around a gray stone church. There is no main street, for there is no street in this tiny vertical hamlet, merely a square where all cars must be parked, and which holds an incongruously tall flagpole and an inn that sports some large medieval emblem. A minuscule general store, a shed with a coin-operated washing machine and dryer, and a small grammar school are the only other public buildings. The name of this village is Troistorrents, for it is here that three tributaries of the Rhone are combined. Troistorrents hugs the slope above the rich, green Val d'Illiez—between the Alps to the south and their foothills to the north. It faces Les

Dents du Midi, that jagged ridge of teethlike peaks that bite the sky. And though Troistorrents is so unimportant it doesn't even appear on many Swiss maps, it is for me a significant place.

I held a romantic vision of Switzerland from my obsessive childhood reading of *Heidi*, so when my husband and I traveled there as newlyweds in our VW van, I found Switzerland the only country more beautiful than any photograph of it. I loved it so much that Stephen got a job as a French-speaking liaison for a new laser company in Monthey, a contract for one whole year. My joy knew no bounds.

The other Americans working for this company rented apartments in the industrial town of Monthey, but *Heidi* haunted me so that I *had* to live in a real chalet in a real Swiss village. Within just a week, we managed to rent a house in a mountainside village for only twenty-five dollars a week. That's how, in spring, we came to Troistorrents, and to our new home: an old fir-tree wood chalet with all the trimmings. Hearts carved into the shutters. Window boxes. Wood veranda. Knotty pine walls, kitchen garden, flower garden, and antique furniture. And, of course, it was aglow with cleanliness.

When in my mind now I see this chalet below the green meadows and behind the stone church, framing sublime views of the Alps from every leaded-glass window, I remember the man who once said he thought the Swiss greedy for wanting to go to heaven *after* death, too.

The first day in this chalet I think I just walked around looking at everything again and again with the greatest tenderness. The bedroom held a big sleigh bed piled with the whitest, warmest, and fluffiest down comforter—not at all like those comforters we use that lie flat as hospital blankets. No,

I'm talking about a *comforting* comforter—an eiderdown that is so feather-filled that it fluffs up over you like a cumulus cloud. Next to the bed, against one wall stood a carved pine armoire with an oval beveled mirror, and in the corner was a washstand with an antique pitcher and bowl. The bedroom window looked directly onto the church steeple and beyond to the wide cow-dotted valleys and up to the soaring crest of Les Dents du Midi. One could have lain in bed in that room and photographed a travelogue.

The back guest bedroom held a small bed, and arranged about it was antique marble and mahogany furniture. Its window looked upon the road swooping down to Monthey and the dozens of chalets that were scattered about the hillside like children's toys.

And the kitchen! The only word for it is perfect. What other word could describe this small refurbished kitchen that contained color-coded European faucets, the most modern of electric stoves and appliances, *and* an antique wood-burning stove? The new pine cupboards made the whole room smell of an Alpine forest, and when I opened them, I saw they were lined with scalloped white paper, and held every conceivable food preparing and serving device—all brand new: an orange enamel fondue pot with eight forks, each in a different color; a large crepe pan; a small, heart-shaped crepe pan; a cast iron skillet, wide as a manhole cover; and a blue enamel ragout pot. Opening one drawer, I found tablecloths—snowy white, flowered and checkered, laundered, starched, and ironed with matching serviettes. Opening another, I discovered a line-up of tiny dentist-type implements for digging nuts or snails out of shells, or for writing words on a cake or etching designs into butter. Then I opened the deep drawer and voila! *Faience* platters from France, egg cups in the shape of chickens and chefs, ramekin dishes, pâté pans, and madeleine molds. Also, a set of *pots de crème*, a ravioli roller, and a crowd of various-shaped wooden spoons for beating the most fractious food into submission. On the very top shelf: a *chocolatière*, a *cafétière*, a *théière*, each encircled by their own family of cups. And in the glass cupboard? Snail servers and a porcelain asparagus dish with a *trompe l'oeil* picture of cooked asparagus painted on the bottom. Also miniature copper pots, no bigger than your fist, for the béchamel, for the velouté, for the hollandaise. Whiskey glasses, brandy snifters, wine and champagne glasses. And to top it off, six tiny liqueur glasses decorated with daisies on their own daisy-dotted tray.

The only problem was that I couldn't cook. My greatest accomplishment in this kitchen would be to pour mueseli into a bowl without spilling it. I had no idea what you did with veal, fish, chicken, or beef. When in doubt, I threw everything in a pan and fried it. As for vegetables, I boiled them all to a kind of porridge. I had never tasted a fondue, and had no knowledge of tortes, tarts, or terrines. And at the age of twenty-two, the very thought of serving liqueur seemed too curious to consider.

I was standing in this kitchen in the early evening after our arrival when I heard a knock at the front door, then the soft, musical voice of an old woman. My husband led our landlady, Madame Carroux, into the kitchen. She had come expressly to welcome me, she said, and to bring some additional things she thought would come in handy: a bundt pan, a small tin bucket with a lid which I thought was for ice cubes, and an additional set of liqueur glasses. This set, old and of a lovely golden color, was even smaller than the first one, as if brought down from the attic of a doll house.

"In case, Madame, you should have many guests," she explained, handing me the tray of thimble-tumblers.

We thanked her, and she seated herself at the kitchen table.

Madame Carroux was in her late sixties, a plain looking woman with gray hair parted in the middle and knotted into a small bun at the nape of her neck. She wore gray sweaters, wool skirts, and floral aprons. Her feet were always encased in boot-like black shoes. She wore neither makeup nor jewelry. Madame Carroux was a refined farm wife who had grown up in Troistorrents and had never, ever left it. She lived in the large chalet, the next one up the path from ours. Her husband, Remy Carroux, was a dairy farmer, but now it was her son who did the most strenuous pasturing and milking work. All this she told us in her polite, modulated French.

As my husband had found this rental and had negotiated for it without me, I sensed that she had come now in great part to check me out. The Swiss are a cautious people, and it was daring enough for her to rent to foreigners in this isolated village. Now she was going to see whether I was a good gamble. Madame Carroux watched me all the while she talked, and after a few moments I felt I should at least look domestic. So, as if I were preparing dinner, in my nervousness I peeled an onion, placed it on a board and with an immense meat-carving knife began to chop it. I thought myself very clever for I used the professional-looking method of a Chinese chef I'd seen on TV who held a large knife in two hands horizontally over the onion and brought it down like a guillotine blade again and again over it.

As I chopped with affected concentration and my eyes welled with tears, Madame Carroux informed us of many things. We could have all the vegetables in the garden and all the flowers, too. She'd do our laundry for us at no extra charge, and by the way, there was no need for me to buy milk, as she would give me fresh milk if I came to her each morning with the tin bucket. At last she stood up to leave, and in the overly-polite and sing-song way of the Swiss, we bade

each other good-bye in what sounds like mountain echoes—
merci Madame, merci Madame, au revoir Madame, au revoir Madame, merci encore, merci, au revoir! au revoir!

Stephen escorted her out. I heard some murmuring and then the closing of the door. When he re-entered the kitchen, he told me that upon leaving, Madame Carroux had whispered significantly in his ear, "*La jeune madame sait bien couper les oignons.*"

I was accepted and became to her *la jeune madame.* I don't remember my landlady ever calling me anything else, but I didn't mind, for in the months that followed I came to understand that these words contained all her respectful affection for me.

Our liking for each other grew quickly. I soon found I very much enjoyed carrying the little tin pail up the path each morning to Madame Carroux's house. A knock on the door and she would bid me enter into the main room of her chalet, which was a large kitchen. Unlike my kitchen, hers had no modern appliances, merely a small gas stove, a large wood-burning stove, a giant cabinet filled with crockery, a sink, and a rough wood table. The only other room on this ground floor was the dining room, nearly completely taken up by its great table, twelve or so dining chairs, a low couch with lace doilies, and a big color television which balanced atop a china cabinet. The door to this room was always closed, however, so the kitchen would retain the heat from the wood stove.

When I arrived each morning Madame Carroux would call her son, and he, a dark-haired man in his early thirties, would come good-naturedly and take my pail. While he was milking in the pasture for me, my landlady would, without fail, ask me to take coffee with her. I never refused. She had an elaborate way of making coffee. She ground the beans in an old coffee-grinder by hand, then she put the grounds into what looked like a scrap from a mummy's shroud and spread it over an aluminum pot. She boiled the water on the gas stove and poured it over the ancient muslin. The result was rich and delicious coffee which she topped for me with hot fresh cream. Then while she churned butter, we talked.

At first I only wanted to stay and take coffee with her so I could practice my French and watch her work the butter churn, which seemed to me the quaintest thing on earth, but after the first visit I knew that I was staying because I liked her. I liked her old country ways, her simplicity, her hospitality. But especially I liked her politeness. Her manner was courteous and very genteel, in a way perhaps few Americans have known. Madame Carroux never pried into my life. She never commented negatively on anything I said, and she never allowed herself to become overly familiar. She was not sly, but rather subtle in the most charming way. She never, for instance, insisted I take another cookie or a bit of cheese, or a slice of sausage, but only pushed by the tiniest centimeter-fractions the plate closer to me as I talked.

I have no idea what she thought of our exuberant tourism—our jaunts to Geneva and Lausanne, our frenzied drives with friends to Zurich, and, one night, just for a lark, to Rome. And why we would go once a month to the Thursday market of Thonon in France was beyond her understanding. No matter that there were more than three hundred cheeses for sale there, she made her own cheese, she said, and anyway could get whatever she wanted from the market in Monthey. Besides, why travel so far as France to shop! She herself had never been to France in her life for, as she explained, it was not only different, but far—twenty-six kilometers away.

Her life seemed to me narrow and isolating, yet she talked to me of the most interesting things. She told me about her older son who was a blessed man, for he was a priest doing missionary work in India. She told me about food and its preparation. She informed me on a host of things that were perhaps more charming because of their uselessness to me: butter-churning, meat-smoking, sausage-making, and mushroom-gathering. She told me her philosophy on eating fish, a practice of which she greatly disapproved. Well, it was all right for other people to eat fish, but not people in the Val d'Illiez! It was Madame Carroux's belief that people must eat only what lives naturally in their region. As there are no fish in that valley's rivers, it was unwise for the people to eat fish at all. *Contre nature!*

I loved living in Troistorrents. In spring I began studying French in Monthey, and became adept at buying from the farmers at the Wednesday market. We went to films and concerts in Monthey, and on weekends visited the other villages in Valais: the ski resort of Champery, the medieval, gray-stoned Sion, and the colorful Martigny, where we could eat delicious cabbage sausages and watch parades. There was the steep ascent up to the barren, windswept peaks of Rochers de Naye, jaunts across the border to the elegant café-town of Evians les Bains, and of course there was, again and again, graceful, romantic Montreux with its beautiful hotel-cafés, lake steamers and poetic castle. But always when we drove up the road or took the tiny cog-wheel train that chugged up the steep mountainside from Monthey to Troistorrents, I felt the bliss of coming home.

In summer, I'd climb the hill above my chalet and write letters under the fir trees. From my perch I could hear the hourly grinding of the little train, the incessant chiming of cowbells, and the periodic pealing from the church steeple. Troistorrents had become my timepiece.

By summer's end Madame Carroux's generosity seemed to me boundless. She now made regular visits to my chalet to bring me, among other things: a brand new bedspread, several bouquets of dahlias, sacks of tomatoes, her own smoked meat, a bottle of homemade wine, a new steam iron, a bag of beets, a bunch of grapes, and a *tarte aux pommes*. With each offering came the added gift of her visit, for our times together now had become cozily peaceful.

But one autumn day when I knocked on the door of the Carroux chalet, I found her household in an uproar. It seemed that Madame Carroux's cow had a sore leg, and the vet had to be called. But this stocky, gray-haired doctor was now running about the kitchen being chased by Madame Carroux's son! The two men ran around and around like wild schoolboys playing tag, simultaneously laughing and shouting at each other. The schoolboy impression was heightened by the fact that the aged doctor wore knee-length breeches and knee-high green socks and was crying, "*NON! NON! NON!*" Strangest of all, Madame Carroux seemed neither agitated nor surprised by their behavior; she looked upon the odd scene with only an air of amused patience. At last the chase ended when the veterinarian shouted, "*D'accord! D'accord!*" and Madame Carroux's son triumphantly stuffed a wad of francs into the man's jacket pocket. Then I understood it. The veterinarian had finally agreed to accept payment from them, and as an added admission of his defeat, took a parting gift of a large cabbage.

As funny as the whole scene was, I thought the veterinarian's prescription for the cow even funnier: a month-long stay in the house, and four aspirin every day in a bowl of *café au lait*.

The cow was brought into an alcove of the kitchen that could be closed with a sliding door. Now it was here that the cow was milked, and Madame Carroux's son invited me to watch him milk her. As he sat milking on his stool, he'd comment to the cow on the amount of her milk. "*Bravo!*" he'd crow, giving her a congratulatory slap, "*dix-huit litres!*" Once he asked me if I'd like to try milking. I did, finding it more difficult than it looked, but the squirting noise seemed to me very funny, and I laughed too much to get it right.

By October, the air grew cold and was spiced with chimney smoke. The mountain peaks turned white, and all the paths in Troistorrents were carpeted with yellow leaves. Then down these paths came the long, slow procession of cattle from the high meadows. Their heads waggling from side to side, their large bells making a jangled Balinese harmony, the cows solemnly paraded past our homes to their winter barns.

And then, late one November night, arriving like a mute guest, snow came. As we slept, it fell silently on Troistorrents— all its chalets, all its pine, elm and fir trees, all its roads and paths, coating everything in starlit whiteness, turning our high Alpine village into a Christmas card.

It was in November, too, after I had been in Troistorrents more than eight months, that I discovered that indeed I had not only been watched by the other villagers, but I had also been discussed. I learned this one evening from my husband, who informed me that the postwoman, who in the snow was forced to deliver the mail on foot rather than on her *motorcyclette*, asked him whether he was married to the American, the one the villagers called, "the woman who goes very slowly downhill."

This label was a complete mortification to me because I had been privately embarrassed by the fact that I did not know how to walk down a snowy path, such as the steep one that led from our house to the village square. I had no clue at all! I had only been in snow twice in my whole life, but now, living in Troistorrents, I was forced to contend every day with icy steps and slushy roads. I thought that the only way to manage on the slippery white stuff without breaking bones was to go very slowly. So I'd make my way extremely slowly each day down to the village. I went along as if I had bound feet and sometimes sideways like a crab. It's embarrassing now to even think how peculiar I must have looked, especially since along the way I often reached out to clutch a branch, a fence post, or even a low cauliflower stalk when I felt the sudden terror of falling and skidding all the way down to the village on my rear end like a kid on a slide.

The words of the postwoman made me see that I had become an object of not only curiosity in the village but amusement. I didn't have time to let it bother me, though, for the next week, two weeks before Christmas, we were abruptly forced to leave Switzerland.

Stephen's work permit was refused by the Swiss government. The reason: 5 million Swiss and already 1 million foreigners in the country. The refusal was part of a nationwide crackdown on foreign workers. We appealed, but without luck; so with heavy hearts we planned our hasty departure. As we wanted to see Asia, we decided to drive there in our heaterless VW van. And it was just at this time, when our thoughts turned from the Alps to the Himalayas, that Madame Carroux's son—the priest, Père Carroux, arrived from India. A few nights after his arrival, he came to visit us and tell us about that strange land. He was a tall, handsome man in his forties. His manner was kind and dignified, like his mother's. He spoke about his work in India, about growing up in Troistorrents and, between and around the Taj Mahal and his Alpine childhood, to our painful surprise, he made an allusion to his mother's battle with a small but stubborn tumor. As he spoke, at chance moments his French and English swapped places, so that he'd unexpectedly end a French sentence with an English word or an English sentence with a French one.

The night before we left, Madame Carroux gave us a little farewell party. For the first time we were ushered into the dining room, and there, around the enormous table, we sat with Madame and Monsieur Carroux, their farmer son, and their priest son. As we chatted, we picked at Madame Carroux's homemade cabbage sausage and apple tart, and drank her homemade non-alcoholic cherry wine. We spoke bravely of our route east and all the marvels we, too, would see in India. Yet it was a subdued gathering, for we didn't want to make the trip now. Not in winter.

The next morning, the snow fell steadily. Our bags packed, we were having a last breakfast in our chalet when there came a knocking at our door. We opened it to see Père Carroux. "I have come to tell you our whole family urges you not to leave today. The weather is very bad. Wait, please, until this storm passes. To go today over the Alps over the Saint Bernard…it's too *dangereuse!*"

So much real concern was expressed in his face that right then we agreed we would wait. In two more days, though, the storm passed and we left, stopping at the Carroux's to return the key. There was a lot of wishing us well, though I can't remember what was said exactly. What I do remember is how, before we went out the door, Madame Carroux suddenly covered her face with her hands like a child playing peek-a-boo, and wept. I wept then, too, and I remember it well, for it was the only time in my life I ever left anything and cried for it.

We drove over the St. Bernard Pass in a bitter blizzard. We drove from Switzerland all the way to Pakistan. Months passed. Our lives took on adventures. Years passed. Our lives took on responsibilities. Troistorrents became a dear memory, unsullied by correspondence. Then a few years ago, more than sixteen years after I'd lived in Troistorrents, I returned.

I was traveling with a friend through Switzerland. We had driven to Montreux from France, and the weather was cloudy, raining on and off. After re-visiting the Chateau de Chillon, we decided that, yes, we would go see this village I had talked about so much. Of course, it was a foolhardy idea. Not only because it was already late afternoon and we had no place to stay that night, but because going back to a place you once loved is so hazardous to the memory of it. As we passed Monthey, which had expanded grossly, and as we ascended the road that curved up to Troistorrents, my thoughts became gloomy. Troistorrents must have grown, too, I thought, and suddenly I remembered the cancer. When we arrived in the village, I asked in the shop whether Madame Carroux still lived here.

Without even looking at me, the shopkeeper asked, "Carroux? Which one! Almost everyone here is a Carroux!"

"Madame Remy Carroux," I answered.

At that moment a young man standing behind me in line beckoned for us to follow him. We did, and he motioned for us to get inside his little VW bug, which we also did. Then he drove up the road beside the chalets, and stopped in front of the very chalet I had once lived in. I knocked on the door and—Brigadoon! Time simply had not happened. Madame Carroux opened the door looking exactly as before. She was now living in this smaller chalet with her husband, who now seemed, if anything, as if he'd grown younger.

Madame Carroux acted not in the least surprised that I had returned to see her. She bade us enter and led us to the back bedroom, which she had converted into a cozy, cluttered sitting-room. Then while she poured and re-poured glasses of her homemade wine, "*sans alcool, Madame,*" we all chatted for an hour. When the shadows stretched long on the mountain peaks, we said good-bye, and I took a picture of the couple in the doorway. Then my friend and I walked about the village. She marveled at its extraordinary, picturesque beauty, and I marveled that Troistorrents was exactly as I remembered it.

It's now about six years since my second visit there. The other day Stephen said something about going on a walking tour of Switzerland where you stay in hikers' huts along the way.

If we went, I mused for a moment, I could re-visit Troistorrents. The moment passed quickly, for deep inside I know I don't want to go back. Ever. Memories are fragile as glass, and cherished most when tinged with longing. I fear one day I might find something diminished or melancholy in Troistorrents that would forever revise my original remembrance of it. That's why I won't go back. It's too *dangereuse*.

Maxine Rose Schur, a former actress, is now a speaker, guest lecturer, and writing teacher. Her award-winning travel essays have appeared in numerous publications, including the San Francisco Examiner, The Christian Science Monitor, Los Angeles Times, Escape, *as well as Travelers' Tales anthologies and* Wanderlust: Real-life Tales of Adventure and Romance. *Twice a Lowell Thomas Award winner, she is also the author of ten books and gift journals.*

Aisle K

Many years ago, a young woman joined
the strange pantheon of regulars
at the British Museum.

"THE READING ROOM WAS HIS TRUE HOME; ITS WARMTH enwrapped him kindly; the peculiar odor of its atmosphere—at first a cause of headache—grew dear and delightful to him."

When I found this passage in George Gissing's *New Grub Street*, I felt a pleasant shock of recognition, the more so as I happened to be sitting in the Reading Room at that very moment. Both Gissing and I are referring, of course, to the Reading Room in the British Museum, in London. For a moment, I felt such kinship with the author that, though he has long been dead, I looked around half expecting to find him sitting at one of the desks in my aisle—K. I always sit in Aisle K unless it's full when I arrive. It is no use asking me why I prefer it. I don't know, because there is absolutely no difference between Aisles J and K, and any other; they all radiate like spokes from the hub, a circular counter in the center of the great circular room, surmounted by a dome inset with grimy glass. Aisle K is where I sat on my first day in the

Reading Room, long ago, and I make tracks for it every morning that I go in. I went there to begin with because I had been hired to look up local color for an overworked American writer of historical romances, and, once there, immediately became, and have remained, a regular reader. We are a peculiar lot, but—with some few exceptions, such as Karl Marx—we are harmless. Though I am not sure which aisle Marx preferred, I do know that he, too, kept going to the same chair.

We are unobservant, too. Though I've been frequenting the Reading Room for thirty years, off and on, I recognize very few of the others, and few of them recognize me. We are too busy with our own books and thoughts to waste time frivolously summing up our neighbors. Only when a man has an *outré* beard or wears really odd clothing do I mark him in my mind and know him when I see him again. I mean, of course, when I see him in the Reading Room. Other contingencies do not arise. Though I do occasionally encounter in the Reading Room somebody from the world outside—my husband, or a friend from an out-of-town university—I have never met genuine, dyed-in-the-wool readers in shops or at theatres or restaurants, or anywhere at all but at the Museum, where they belong. Once, I bumped into a Museum guard in an Underground station—the man who usually stands at the Reading Room door in a little sentry box. In the station, he was in mufti, and though he tipped his hat politely, I didn't recognize him at first without his blue coat and peaked cap. This was disconcerting. After all, *he* knows *me*, no matter what I'm wearing, and what's more, he always lets me go in without asking to see my ticket, which I appreciate, life being enhanced by such small triumphs. Therefore, I was ashamed of myself for having even seemed to snub him, but that's the way we readers are—absent-minded.

There is only one regular reader whom I would recognize anywhere, even at Harrods or the Zoo—not that she would ever be in either place. For a long time, I didn't speculate about her. A less regular reader—that is to say, a less self-centered person—might sometime have wasted a few minutes wondering where she goes when the Reading Room closes for the night, what aerie furnishes her shelter. But I never had. It took me twenty years to learn that her name is Stuart, and I learned that only because one day I happened to hear an attendant address her.

Yet I saw Miss Stuart the first time I ever went to the Museum. I had stopped at the outer gate to ask where to go to apply for a reader's ticket. As I paused there, she rode past me on a bicycle, through the opening in the great iron railings, and on across the courtyard toward the steps that stretch imposingly across the building's face. Idly, I watched her set up her bicycle in a rack at one side of them. She had a jaunty manner—a sort of certainty that impressed me, because I was brand-new in England and very timid—but there was more than a manner to be noticed about Miss Stuart. On a cold, raw, dark day in January, in an era when women never wore bifurcated clothing for anything but the most drastic activities, she was attired in very short running shorts, a cotton sweater without sleeves, and socks. I gawked as I went after her, but by the time I had followed her to the top of the steps and into the building she had vanished. I went into the office I had been directed to, and forgot all about her in the perplexity of filling in the required form. I learned that before I could get a ticket I must be vouched for by three individuals—a property owner, a bank manager, and a clergyman. It seemed too difficult to contemplate. I was near giving up the whole idea of England and retiring to New York in disgrace. It wasn't as if I had ever passionately wanted to be there, I reminded myself. Where I wanted to be was the Belgian Congo. Naturally, I had welcomed the chance of getting out of Depression America and having my first venture abroad, but now I regretted being so impulsive. I am a chilly type, whose hands and feet remain cold even in the tropics, and I was already half stupefied with the London wintertime damp, the cold, and the dark. It was impossible to feel the emotions I knew I should be experiencing. I saw no magic in London and possessed no mysterious conviction that I had been there before. The streets did not make me think of Dickens; they were just streets. The traffic reminded me more of Brooklyn than of anywhere else. People in dirty raincoats stumped along pavements that were apparently coated with machine oil, and I could not blame them for looking as bad-tempered as they did. Henry James, I decided, must have been out of his mind.

But a trouble that went deeper than chilblains or sniffles was that I was an American and thus an object of curiosity. It may sound strange nowadays, but the fact is that at that time a lot of Londoners had never seen an American or heard American speech until they saw and heard me. Though they didn't seem particularly pleased with the experience now that it was theirs, they were curious in a dour way, and whenever I spoke in a public place, on no matter how banal a subject—asking my way, buying a newspaper—people within hearing distance would fall silent and stare at me. They were familiar with other accents, such as German or French or Scandinavian, but American was something new, and they didn't hold with it. It was weak of me to mind, but I couldn't help it. I wasn't used to being abroad and I minded awfully. So it was actually an effort to leave my lodging house in the morning and face the city.

I felt better, though, after I had cleared the hurdle of the application form and become a reader. I did so with the help of

my landlady; a property owner herself, she was good enough
to supply her own bank manager and clergyman. After that, I
was eager to get out of the house and into the Museum, for
there, in the Reading Room, I had found peace. There all was
for the most part silent, for, after all, it *was* a library. But even
when circumstances did compel me to speak, nobody so
much as raised an eyebrow. They were sophisticated at the
British Museum. Almost every American professor or student
who came to London—and there were such, even in those
dark ages—went to the Reading Room. There, alone, my accent was nothing new. I suppose this relief marked the beginning of my lifelong fixation. I was the panting fox I have read
about who takes refuge from the hounds in a badger's set and
gets so emotionally attached to the place that he stays on,
moving in on the badger for good. In the Reading Room, I
found my set. I *belonged*.

Life had a regular pattern. The lodging house, in Torrington
Square, was near the back of the Museum. Every morning, I
dressed as fast as I could, because the room was cold, and ate
breakfast from a tray, huddling close to the shilling-meter gas
fire. Then I went out. I always walked fast in the morning, and
the sidewalks were always wet. By the time I had rounded the
Museum's flanks and reached the pillared portico, the backs of
my legs were so splashed with black that they looked like a
Dalmatian's. Breathlessly, I crossed the enormous entrance hall.
(Everything about the Museum is outsized, as if the official
wanted always to be prepared for giants who might happen to
drop in for tea.) Towered over by the roof, dwarfed and intimidated by huge stone gods, I was glad to reach the other
side and the door to the Reading Room.

I felt that the Reading Room was cozy, though in general
effect it is not unlike the old main hall of the Pennsylvania
Station. Inside there was no further need to rush, for I was

safe. The peace that descended on me, and still descends, had an even more magical effect. It convinced me that I was warm. This was an illusion. In the old days, everyone but Miss Stuart kept his coat on, and sometimes I was reduced to writing my notes wearing gloves. In those days, my feet were heavy, insentient lumps until I got home in the late afternoon and went to bed. Nevertheless, I felt warm in the Reading Room and was reluctant to go out to lunch, and as lunchtime came I envied the self-confident Miss Stuart, because she had perfected her own method of saving the trouble of going out. She always brought a bottle of milk with her in the morning, and at noon she emptied it through a straw in the Ladies' Room. It was forbidden to eat or drink in the Ladies' Room, or anywhere else in the Museum, but Miss Stuart ignored the rule. She knew the attendant, and would chatter away with her customary air of owning the place and drink her milk unquestioned.

Fixation or no fixation, illusion of warmth or not, I never went so far as to sit tight when a loud bell told us, at the end of the afternoon, to turn in our books and get out. I was always ready to go by that time. I was tired and had stored up enough reassurance to carry me through until morning. On the way back to Torrington Square, I didn't rush. The world was dark—had been dark since before tea time—and I plodded by instinct through the badly lit streets, between enormous walls and billboards. I might have been that small, featureless figure sketched in an architect's plans to show the scale of the drawing.

One evening, I was surprised to realize that my road back was not as dim as usual. There could be no doubt about it—the sun had been late in setting. Until then, I had not grasped the fact that the seasons in England bring noticeable changes, but now that I was alerted I began to check up. Sure enough, in the morning the world was lighter when I set out on my hasty journey. After that, things improved rapidly. The weather remained wet most of the time and my stockings got as spattered as ever, but the added light made a great difference to my spirits. Besides, I knew people; somehow I had gathered acquaintances. Sometimes I went out to dinner. Sometimes I would invite a friend up to have a drink in my room, though I learned that this was not always a good thing, because people didn't seem to admire the lodging house. "You ought to live in a better place than this," said one man sharply, and I was puzzled. What did he mean better? The room was all right, I told myself. It had a row of hooks on the wall, and a chair and a bed and a little table in the corner where I kept a bottle of Black and White and a bottle of seltzer. Who needed more than that? He laughed at my bottle of Black and White, too, and said, "You Americans!" When I demanded an explanation, he said that English girls didn't drink whisky, or gin, either. Sherry was what they drank, he said. "And other wine as well," he added. "Wine's absolutely all right. Why don't you stick to that?"

Spring crept in. The grass in parks and squares, which had bothered me from the beginning by being green in a manner unseasonable, now grew greener and longer. The sunlight, though still watery and uncertain, was enough to plant a hint of restlessness in my winter heart. Suddenly I found my self-imposed hours in the Reading Room too long. I never became abandoned enough to stay away from the Museum in the morning, but sometimes I turned my books in early and went out into the sweet, thawing air. There was no errand to run, no meaning to it; it was only the fox putting his nose out, sniffing the wind, growing cocky.

Outside, I just mooned around looking in bookshop windows most of the time, but about once a week I took a bus and went to my new friend Julia's photography studio, getting there in time for tea. At that hour, as I had learned, there were always several people at the studio, who came in every day and brought things to help out when they happened to have the money—biscuits, or sugar, or tea itself. I liked to go there because being an American was not a bad thing at Julia's. If anything, it was good. She and her friends had such a dread of being insular that they would have made me welcome even if they had disliked me personally. They didn't dislike me—they teased me, but they didn't dislike me. And so I had another place to relax in, as well as the Reading Room. I seldom missed a week at Julia's, and sometimes we indulged in little extra sprees that were inexpensive—a bus trip to see the gardens at Hampton Court when the tulips were in bloom, or a meal in Soho. I didn't really enjoy long jaunts, though. I felt guilty about neglecting the Reading Room.

When summer was an accomplished fact, a blow fell on me. I finished my job. It seemed unbelievable that this could have happened so quickly, and again and again I checked the list of what I was to have read and looked at the notebooks I had filled. But there was no doubt—I had read everything I was supposed to read, and some extra books as well. Logically, I should have been glad, for there was nothing now to keep me in England; I could pack and go and leave behind the things that had so distressed me—the black-smeared pavements, the foggy air, the unfriendly faces of strangers. Yet the more I thought about it, the less I liked the idea. It had been weeks since I'd noticed the pavements, and somehow people did not seem unfriendly anymore. I had evolved a life that included Miss Stuart and her milk bottle, Julia's tea hour, even the black chimney pots outside my window, and it suited me. I simply could not face leaving the Reading Room. For the first time, I felt sympathy for those permanent undergraduates who are to be found in American universities, taking degrees in one subject after another, frantically looking for new courses until they are tottering around the campus. Indeed, I resolved to behave like them, and look for a subject that would keep me busy a while longer at the British Museum, at least until I came to the end of my money. After considering various possibilities, I selected the Royal Society of London for Promoting Natural Knowledge, an august body that, since it had received its charter from Charles II soon after the Restoration, was sure to have plenty of history. I would have a lot of fun reading about the Royal Society, I told myself, and nobody need know—nobody would care—if I was doing it for a practical purpose or not. I started on it at once.

There it is. That's my life, or, at any rate, a large part of it. I can't claim to be the British Museum's most constant reader. I've gone away from time to time, and on occasion have remained absent for protracted periods, but I have always gone back. I decided, after a bit, that absences don't matter a lot in a place like that; the years make little or no difference. When I got back the first time, after two years in the Congo, I felt as if I'd never been away. The familiar benison fell gently on my head as I went into the Reading Room and took my old place in Aisle K. At lunchtime, there was Miss Stuart in the Ladies' Room, dressed in her shorts as always, and I reflected comfortably that the Museum had borrowed timelessness from its own Elgin marbles or from the Egyptian mummies upstairs.

But I had come to this conclusion too soon. A time arrived when I overdid things, and strained the patience of even as permanent a spirit as the Reading Room's, by staying away a full decade. It was 1946 when I returned that time, and I felt a nasty little shock as soon as I set foot in the entrance room. The Museum *had* changed. Dust was everywhere—underfoot and on the cases and in the air. Wooden supports held up the ceiling, and here and there were rough screens barring the public from certain rooms. The Museum had suffered a nearly direct hit from at least one bomb, I learned, and gossip had it that consultant architects were not quite happy about the state of the Reading Room's dome. Repairs and investigations accounted for the dust, but I felt that it had really been stirred up when the bomb fell and had not yet settled, though two years had elapsed.

Not unnaturally, I assumed that after such a long absence I would have to begin the routine all over again, from the ground up. Surely my permission to use the Reading Room would have lapsed, I thought, if only because the records had been scattered, so I went to the old office and asked for an application form. The attendant, when I explained the situation, was hurt and surprised. "But Madam," he said, "if you already hold a card, all you need do is hand it in and we'll issue you a new one."

I said, "Alas, I've lost it. I know it was careless of me, but I was in China, you see, and what with the war and one thing and another—"

"Oh, I quite understand," he said. His pleasantness did not relax one tittle. "In the circumstances, we'll give you a new card even though you can't turn in the old one. Now, let's see—what was the name?"

He picked up an ancient ledger, blew off some dust, and opened it at the right letter. There my name was, just where I'd written it years before. And as I took my card I forgot the thing that had disturbed me—the dust and the bomb and the sensation of being disjointed. I was back in the Reading Room, and all was well.

There I stayed until the warning bell rang. I was going out, sunk in the old familiar stupor, when a man addressed me by name just outside the door. He was a gray man—his suit was gray, and so was his hair, and his spectacled eyes must have been gray, too, but I could scarcely see them. His glasses seemed dusty, like his hair and shoulders. He said, "We used to read next to each other in Aisle K. I remember you."

I said, I am afraid untruly, that I remembered him as well, and we shook hands. "And what are you doing now?" I asked.

There was a surprised reproach in his tone as he answered, "Why, still studying for my degree, of course."

I realize now that though the Reading Room didn't really change during the years I spent away from it, changes have come while I've been right there. It occurred to me with another shock, a couple of years ago, that Miss Stuart, of all people, has altered. I noticed, God knows how belatedly, that it is impossible to tell whether or not she is still wearing shorts, because, it has slowly dawned on me, nowadays her costume is covered, winter and summer, by a frayed mackintosh. Winter or summer, rain or shine, Miss Stuart keeps that raincoat tightly belted and buckled around her, and she now wears a hat as well—a thing like a basket pulled down over her straying, pepper-and-salt hair.

I noticed this the year we readers all had to move for a couple of months into the North Library, customarily reserved for rare editions and pornography, so that the building authorities would be free to shore up the Reading Room dome. Otherwise, it was said, everything might well come crashing down on our heads. In the North library, an oblong room, we had to work side by side at long refectory-type tables instead of our customary sheltered, high-fronted desks, and for many this interruption of habit constituted a trauma. That was how I came to notice Miss Stuart standing in line to pick up her reserved books; I had been jolted, and was looking around as a result. Even without the new outfit, she would have seemed unfamiliar against that strange background. On her face was a fierce scowl. I suppose readers in general behaved even more peculiarly than usual during the Diaspora. One afternoon in the North Library, I was chatting sotto-voce with the Superintendent. I had turned in my chair so that I could see him, standing behind me. All seemed quiet when suddenly he looked over my head and across the room, his face showing an expression that, for him—he was a controlled man—signified extreme horror. He said, aloud and sharply, "No, no, Mr. Schmidt!" I followed his gaze. Two attendants were already hurrying toward a stocky man with bristling cropped hair who was standing at his chair, books piled on the table in front of him, arms outstretched. One hand held an unlit cigarette, in the other was burning lighter. He was not trying to apply the lighter's flame to the cigarette, but when he was sure he had got the room's attention he said loudly, "I wish to protest. Why are we not allowed to use the Reading Room? I—" At that moment, the attendants got hold of him, one arm each, and, after extinguishing the lighter, hustled him with kindly efficiency toward the door. All the way, Mr. Schmidt kept repeating, "I protest! I protest!" until he had been ejected and the door was closed behind him. The Superintendent, taking up our conversation exactly where it had dropped, carried it on as if nothing had happened. But he was again interrupted, by one of the attendants who had taken Mr. Schmidt away. Somewhat breathless, but in a calm manner, this man asked what was to be done about Mr. Schmidt's books, and the Superintendent lifted his eyebrows, indicating that it was a question that should not have been asked.

"Are they still there at his place?" he inquired coldly.

"Yes, sir."

The Superintendent gave an impatient flick of the fingers. "Well, put them on reserve, put them on reserve for Mr. Schmidt."

Marginal notes, especially when I come upon them in a library book, are apt to startle me. One day, after we were back in the Reading Room, I found a marginal note in a Reading Room copy of Otway. In the preface, the author had spoken of Queen Elizabeth, referring to her as "the Virgin Queen," and the marginal commentator evidently had taken this amiss. Purple ink double-underlined the world "Virgin." In the margin, in the same ink, were written the words "Ha! Ha! Of such is history!"

No doubt I am foolish, but the thing haunted me. Who had done it? It must have been some other regular reader, I reflected. I reminded myself that we are a peculiar lot, and wondered how long it would be before I, too, became certifiable. I turned in the Otway without reporting my discovery—why borrow trouble?—but I went on thinking about it, and talking about it, too. I talked about it to a girl I was introduced to in a nearby lunchroom—a girl who was just starting out on her career in the Museum. She said eagerly, "Oh, I know exactly what you mean. It's quite frightening. I've been sitting in Aisle G, next to that crazy old woman in the mackintosh— you know the one? Well, yesterday I saw that she had a big book and she was spitting on it."

"Spitting?"

"Yes, that's what I said. She would spit on a page, then turn it over and spit on the next. She was very careful not to miss a single page. Well, I wondered—"

"Wait a minute," I said. "What sort of book was it?" I was aware that I have never yet tried to find out what subject Miss Stuart had been working on all those years.

The girl said, "It was some Victorian tome—*Lives of the Popes*. I didn't quite know what to do. One hates to be a tat-tle-tale, doesn't one? Besides, it's borrowing trouble. But in the end my social conscience prevailed and I knew I had to report it. To keep her from realizing what I was doing, I made the most devious trip to the desk, consulting *Who's Who* in that case over by the main entrance and then looking up something in the O.E.D. Finally, I got to the desk and told my story to one of the men. I must say, he took it very calmly, and he was awfully nice when I asked him not to give me away. He told me not to worry. I did so, and he waited a full five minutes before he did anything—*ever* so nice he was. When he got there, she was still spitting away, and he said, 'Now, Miss Stuart, you know you aren't to do that. You've been told before.' He took the book away from her and carried it off—I suppose to be fumigated. The woman just sat there without moving for a minute, and I kept my eyes on my work. Then she leaned sideways toward me and hissed, under her breath, *'Papist spy!'*" The girl paused, pondering unhappily. "Tomorrow, perhaps I'd better move to Aisle F," she said at last, and sighed.

Emily Hahn (1905-1997) was the author of fifty-two books, as well as hundreds of articles and short stories she produced for The New Yorker *from 1929 to 1996. Born in St. Louis, Missouri, she became the first woman to earn a degree in mining engineering at the University of Wisconsin. She did graduate work at both Columbia*

*and Oxford before leaving for Shanghai. Her wartime affair with
Charles Boxer, Britain's chief spy in pre-World War II Hong Kong,
evolved into a loving and unconventional marriage that lasted fifty-
two years and produced two daughters. This story was excerpted from
her memoir,* No Hurry to Get Home.

LINDA WATANABE McFERRIN

✶ ✶ ✶

On Pleasures Oral

The meal most longed for
is the meal not yet eaten.

LAWRENCE AND I HAD SAMPLED ONLY A SMALL PART OF
Venice when Monica arrived. Disembarking at the Piazza San
Marco, we crossed it, noting the Duomo's landmark rotunda,
the rows of apostles draped in scaffold and net. We checked
into our hotel, the Panada, at five o'clock and had dinner at
ten o'clock—a very light supper at the Pescatore Conte.

The next morning dawn awakened us, weaseling its way in
through the casements, creeping down draperies, columning
them in substance. The scent of baking bread followed the
light, then sound—the clatter of pots and pans, of children's
voices rising from the street below.

When Monica disembarked, we were seated at a sidewalk
café on the perimeter of the Piazza San Marco. Across the
wide, noon-bright circle of the piazza, she progressed, a scin-
tillating clove-brown figure, an exotic and imperious
Cleopatra clad in a saffron blouse and billowing peasant skirt,
preceded by a porter carting her enormous black suitcase and
a few smaller bags. Her head was uncovered, scarved only in

the straight black fall of her hair. She seemed made for the heat. Her Italian movie-star carriage had the usual grand and eye-stopping effect. Pigeons scattered. Heads turned. Men's hands reached involuntarily out toward her as she passed, thumbs and forefingers kissing in empty pinches that would never be consummated.

At that moment, I realized that I loved Monica in the same way that I loved my Barbie dolls as a child, with the passionate attachment one feels toward an ideal shimmering on the distant never-to-be-attained horizon. Men also had this feeling for her.

Lawrence and I pushed back our chairs, threw our napkins down next to our plates and advanced toward her with the well-choreographed precision of two chorus line extras supporting the principal dancer.

She rewarded us with a white flash of smile.

"*Ciao*," she sang out to us. "When did you get here?"

"Last night," we answered in unison.

"Don't you love it?" Monica crooned, echoing the pigeons that cooed, pecked, and preened around our ankles and feet, their plump, feathered bodies pressing carelessly up against us.

"More so now, because you are here," we responded.

"Well, I have to get rid of this luggage," she confided with well-practiced urgency. "Then, I will show you my Venice."

I've always felt very small next to Monica, small and child-like, like a pawn. My adoration only increases when I see the impact she has on everyone else. On her ample bosom, Lawrence's head had found a place to come, metaphorically, to rest. At least, I hoped it was metaphorical. I watched the two walk, arm-in-arm, ahead of me while I dawdled on bridges, and the chipped, gap-toothed buildings leaned toward us, leering like doddering courtiers drunk with the sunlight.

"Where did you eat last night?" Monica asked as we walked past a series of portside cafes on the Canale Della Giudecca.

"At the Pescatore Conte," Lawrence replied.

"Hmmm," she said thoughtfully as if trying it out in her mind. "I've never eaten there." She paused for a moment considering this. "Well, tonight," she said with a long, slow smile, "we will dine at the Bai Barbacani. It is better than that one, Au Pied de Cochon, in Paris, remember? You will love it. I'll introduce you to Aldo, the owner. I wonder if he will remember me?"

There was no doubt in my mind about this.

We expected other friends to join us in the afternoon, but they arrived exhausted and ill. Dinner for them was out of the question.

Night had pitched its black tent over the city. Monica, in her sunflower-yellow dress gleamed like a beacon beneath the lanterns that lined the narrow alleyways near the canal. On the marled stone walls that rose from the shadows on the opposite bank, small windows opened like the tiny doors in an advent calendar, torch-lit, adventures seeming to smolder within their confines. The entrance to the Bai Barbacani was behind one of these windows.

We crossed a narrow bridge to Calle del Paradiso, on the other side of the canal. At the portals of the Bai Barbacani we were greeted by a slender, tuxedoed waiter who escorted us into the cavelike interior to a round white-clothed table where the candlelight danced, sylphlike, over crystal, china, and silver.

Light flooded over Monica's shoulders pooling gracefully at the juncture of her breasts. Her eyelashes cast shadows on the rise of her cheeks. Lawrence's hair glinted fiery.

Our waiter seemed adequate, but Monica was still restless,

her eyes on a tall broad-shouldered man impeccably dressed in a double-breasted blue jacket cut to enhance a narrow waist.

He was making his way across the room, stopping at each of the tables and chatting with guests. His progress was arrested at the table next to ours for he seemed to have found among these diners several dear friends.

"Aldo?" I asked.

"No," said Monica. "Aldo is not here," she added with just a soupçon of petulance. I noticed that the slightest of pouts had settled upon her carnation-red lips. The restaurant seemed to have changed, to have been rearranged. Gone were the dusty bottles of homemade *fragolino* that Monica had raved about. The broad-shouldered man was laughing, leaning into the table right next to us, ignoring our table completely. He summoned a waiter who disappeared into the back of the restaurant and returned with what must have been a very special bottle of wine. It was uncorked with great ritual. The diner who sampled it nodded his head furiously. The broad-shouldered man squeezed his arm and moved on to us. His dark hair was thin and cut very short. He had eagle-like features. "Welcome to the Bai Barbacani," he said, in musically accented English.

"Where's Aldo?" Monica demanded in response.

"He is gone," said our host.

Monica let him know that Aldo was missed.

"I was here before Aldo," the man replied simply. "I went away and now I am back. Aldo is gone."

He said this with the finality of a man who is used to fitting his confreres with shoes of cement.

"I don't believe you," Monica whispered tauntingly. "I think you have Aldo locked up in the basement."

"So," the man said looking down at Monica, noticing appreciatively the way the darkness gathered at the top of her breasts like a pendant of jet and, sliding between them, disappeared into the soft yellow fabric of her bodice.

He lifted his eyes to us and smiled.

Monica told the man that Aldo had promised her certain secrets—"secret recipes"—when she returned and she wasn't pleased to find him no longer there. Our new host was given to understand that she liked him less.

He asked her, "You don't like me as much?"

Monica shrugged and smiled. "I miss Aldo," she said.

It was a challenge, a gauntlet thrown down. Then it began—the wooing. Perhaps it was the candlelight that bathed everything in a kind of fairy-tale beauty, perhaps it was the desire to best the chivalrous Aldo or maybe it was the Circean net that Monica carried for occasions like this one. Whatever the cause, though the waiter returned and was very solicitous, the man could not seem to stay away from our table.

"Come, come back to the kitchen with me. I can show you how to stir the risotto," he said archly.

We had visions of Monica being abducted into the back, into the restaurant's nether regions, into the basement where Aldo was most certainly buried.

Monica laughed. "Maybe," she said. "Maybe later."

For an appetizer Monica ordered a bowl full of mussels, and our host nearly swallowed his tongue. Piled high on their perfect white china bowl, each glistening shell held the tiny mollusk that has been compared to that most delicate part of a woman's anatomy. Pry open the shell, shut as tight as virgin's thighs, and you feast on the sweet mound of flesh in its own fragrant liquor. Dress them with wine or eat them undressed—either way, to consume them is heaven.

Paulo (by this time we knew his name) leaned over Monica's shoulder and asked, not so innocently, if she'd like him to put a little lemon on them. Monica said "yes," so he called over the waiter who arrived with the proper tools—a silver plate holding a gauze-wrapped half-lemon and a small silver spoon. Paulo expertly disrobed the lemon and took firm hold of the spoon. He very aggressively screwed his small spoon into the lemon, dribbling its juices all over Monica's mussels. Monica watched him. He continued to screw away, eyes upon hers, really building up a sweat in the process. It seemed to go on forever. I was amazed. I'm sure none of us thought there could be that much juice in a single lemon. But Paulo was determined to lemon-up the mussels to Monica's satisfaction or knock himself out trying. It was pathetic.

"Monica," I wanted to plead, "make him stop."

As if reading our minds, Monica finally purred demurely, "That's enough. Thank you." Imaginary handkerchiefs went to three foreheads—Lawrence's, Paulo's, and mine.

I had ordered sweet and sour sardines for an appetizer. I do not want to speculate upon their metaphorical value. Lawrence had ordered mussels as well, but all he got were a few cursory twists of lemon from the waiter.

Monica consumed her mussels with incredible gusto and even offered a few to me, though she knows that I'm allergic to shellfish. It's an allergy I developed recently and one that I never manage to recollect without a puritanical pang.

The appetizers had nearly exhausted us. I wasn't sure we were ready to deal with our entrees. To calm my nerves, I ordered risotto—a sweet pearly mixture, perfectly flavored, designed to comfort the taker. Lawrence had scampi—meaty pink prawns that he separated from their wafer-thin jackets of exoskeleton with fingers perfumed in lemon water.

Monica ordered gnocchi, a regional favorite. Satiny black pillows colored with cuttlefish ink and bathed in a fragrant salmon-red sauce—before us the simple potato dumplings lay, transformed into something incredibly sexy.

Round two, I thought. Victoria's Secret. Frederick's of Hollywood.

Paulo appeared, again, along with the entrees.

"This is the perfect choice for you," he said to Monica, his hand, braceleted at the wrist, gesturing toward her plate.

"I love those colors," giggled Monica.

"Come to the kitchen with me," Paulo challenged with a canine grin. "I will show you how it is done."

Monica laughed, "I'll bet," she said, and bit into one of the little black pillows. Her sharp teeth cut a tiny half-moon out of one side. I'd swear Paulo was salivating.

"Do you know," he asked, warming to the subject of food as he watched Monica eat, "do you know how I like to eat spaghetti?"

"No, how?" asked Monica.

"I float a wooden bowl of spaghetti in my swimming pool." His large hands placed an imaginary bowl upon the cobalt-blue waters shimmering in front of him.

"Then I float up to it."

We could now picture him in swim trunks approaching the spaghetti that bobbed in its big wooden bowl on the water's flickering surface.

"Then, I suck the spaghetti slowly out of the bowl," he said, looking down at Monica. He was grinning from ear to ear.

"Oh, that sounds wonderful," Monica responded, placing her napkin beside her plate and gazing up into his dark brown eyes.

"You could try it," he said, raising an eyebrow.

"Do you know what my favorite food is?" Monica countered. "It is *mascarpone* cheese. Do you know how to make *mascarpone*?"

"Yes," said Paulo. "This cheese takes a long time."

"It does," agreed Monica. "I make fabulous *mascarpone*. I can teach you to make it my way."

"I would love to make *mascarpone* with you," said Paulo formally. I half-expected him to salute.

"*La vie est belle*," Monica laughed.

"*Toujours l'amour*," Paulo chimed back.

The clichés began flying back and forth like shuttlecocks. Paulo would not leave our table. He catered to us to the point of neglect of the rest of his clientele. Diners ordered desserts and after dinner drinks. He ignored them. Regulars paid bills and left the restaurant. He ignored them.

We struggled through apple strudels and tortes and polished things off with homemade *fragolino*, a strawberry liqueur more fragrant, Monica declared, than Aldo's.

"This is my *fragolino*," Paulo said with great pride.

It was like perfume, really, a dark beautiful perfume. We chuckled and whispered that he probably had Aldo locked up in the basement making the stuff. Hours had passed. Candles had burned down to mere stumps. All of the other diners were gone.

"Will you come again, tomorrow night?" Paulo asked Monica, leaning over her chair, his mouth close to her ear.

"No," Monica said, turning her face to his, her nose nearly touching the sharp beak that was his. "No, but I'm here every year."

"Well," he said, as she rose from the table, "you must come again, next year."

He took Monica's arm and escorted her gallantly back to the restaurant's threshold. "I will give you the secret then, to the *fragolino*," Paulo said solemnly, exchanging cards with Monica, promising her the recipe "next year," if she came, just as Aldo once had.

Lawrence and I knew better, of course. We had seen this happen before. We knew that the meal most longed for is the meal not yet eaten. We knew that Paulo's appetite had been aroused. And we knew, for certain, that sometime—long before the promised next year—there'd be a knock on Monica's door, and there he would be—the man with a hunger for *mascarpone.*

Linda Watanabe McFerrin has been traveling since she was two and writing about it since she was six. She is a poet, travel writer, and novelist, who has contributed to numerous publications including the San Francisco Chronicle Magazine, The Washington Post, Modern Bride, Travelers' Tales, *and Salon.com. She is the author of the novel* Namako: Sea Cucumber, *and the short story collection,* The Hand of Buddha. *She is a winner of the Katherine Anne Porter Prize for Fiction, and lives in Oakland, California.*

LAURIE GOUGH

✱ ✱ ✱

Naxos Nights

A traveler from the cold north
discovers the heat of her soul.

NO SINGLE INCIDENT IN MY LIFE HAS BEEN SO STRANGE, so hard to grasp, so totally lacking in feasible explanation. It's the weirdest thing that's ever happened to me and it happened on a Greek island. I came to Naxos by mistake, but maybe there are no mistakes. Maybe sometimes we're meant to be led here and there, to certain places at certain times for reasons beyond our understanding, beyond our will or the spell of the moon or the arrangement of the stars in the sky. Maybe all the dark and eternal nameless things lurking around us have their own purpose and vision for us. Who knows?

When I was twenty-three, I was traveling alone through Europe. I'd been in the rain for two months in Britain and discovered I didn't like being wet. I wanted to dry out and perhaps I wanted more than that—an inner light, a deeper understanding of life's complexities, a friend. With all those rainy days traveling alone, a fire had been extinguished within me and I needed rekindling. One morning I woke up soggy. I was on a beach in Scotland at the time so soggy was to be expected, but I was also shivering and miserable. I decided to escape to Greece as fast as possible.

Three days later I was on a midnight flight to Athens. At six in the morning, dragging my sleepless, jet-lagged body around the port of Piraeus, I came to a clapboard sign of a ferry schedule for various Greek islands. I was still dripping wet psychologically and dead tired, but I wanted things: a beach, the sun, a warm dry place to sleep, a Greek salad. I bought a ticket for the island of Paros because the ferry was leaving in ten minutes. Arbitrary, yes, but I was young and still arranged my life that way. Six hours later we pulled into the Paros harbor. From the wooden bench on the boat where I'd been napping, I looked up to see a jammed crowd of passengers swarming the exit doors. Since I was groggy and exhausted, I decided to stay on the bench a few more minutes and let the crowd disappear. When I looked up again, in what seemed just a few minutes, I was appalled to see the boat pulling away from the harbor, the passengers all gone, and me left alone on the boat. For the next two hours I worried we were sailing back to Athens, and I was too embarrassed to ask the men who worked on the ferry about it.

Fortunately, in two hours we arrived at another island. I got off the boat on the island of Naxos and walked with my backpack along the dock where I was immediately swarmed by a sea of short, round, middle-aged women in polyester black dresses and black socks who wanted me to stay at their guest houses and sleep on their roofs. Assuming the roles of foreign eccentric aunts, they took my arms and patted my hands, trying to pull me into their lives, their doughy bodies.

I didn't go to the houses of any of those women. In the recesses of my drowsy mind I remembered I needed a beach, and sleep. Leaving the busy little port town behind, I headed south along the beach, walking for a long time through scatterings of

bodies lying on the white sand, topless French women playing frisbee, nut-brown boys throwing balls, incoming waves
and *tavernas* off to the side. A pure Aegean light fell on my
head like a bleached curtain draping from the sky. It was a lean
and haunting landscape, savagely dry, yet the light was uncannily clear with a blue sky big enough to crack open the world,
had the world been a giant egg. The crowds thinned as I
walked farther along the beach and music from the *tavernas*
faded in the distance. Finally, I spotted something under the
shade of an olive grove—a small bamboo wind shelter that
someone must have constructed and recently abandoned.
Perfect. I'd found the place to drop down and sleep. And, although I didn't know it at the time, I'd found the place that
would become my home for over a month.

I slept the rest of that day in the bamboo wind shelter
under the olive grove and when I woke up it was dark and all
the people were gone. A night wind danced across my face
and shooting stars crashed across the sky. I ran along the beach,
delirious, exalted, and finally dry.

My days on the beach took on their own rhythm. In the
morning, rose rays of sunrise from behind a dark mountain
would wake me, and if they didn't, the island's omnipresent
roosters would. The sea would be calm at dawn and I'd go for
a swim before the day's beach crowd arrived. Walking back to
my bamboo shelter I'd say hello and chat with the smiling
waiter, Nikos, at the nearby *taverna* as he set out his chairs for
the day's customers. Nikos was handsome in the way many
Greek men are handsome, which has more to do with the way
they look at you than how they themselves look. Nikos was
good at looking rather than good-looking, which was almost
the same thing in the end. When the sun got too high I'd escape its burning rays and read books in the shade of my olive
grove. I'm a redhead—an absolute curse in a desert like

Greece. The waves would gather momentum as the day passed and at some point every afternoon they would be at their fullest. That's when the old men would appear. From seemingly out of nowhere, a gathering of weathered, mahogany Greek men with sunken chests and black bathing shorts would converge to stand on the shore and survey the sea. The Aegean in dark-blue spasms would be reaching its zenith there in the afternoon light and, from my olive grove, I'd watch it also. The old men would enter the sea together, simultaneously turn to face the shore, and hunch over with their knees slightly bent, skinny arms outstretched, waiting. They'd look over their shoulders at the ocean beyond, ready to jump up and join it at precisely the right moment. They always knew when that was. I would join them and always laughed when riding the waves, but I never saw those men crack a smile. I decided that when I was eighty I would take the waves that seriously also. After that many years of life on earth, what could be more important than playing in the waves?

Sometimes I'd walk into town to explore, buy fruit and bottled water, and watch old men argue politics over their Turkish coffee served in tiny cups. The coffee was sweet and strong and one-third full of gooey sediment. At sunset the men would turn their chairs to face the sun as it melted the day into the sea. They'd sigh and drink their ouzo or citron or *kitro*—a specialty of Naxos, lemon liqueur—and stop talking until the sky drained of color. Parish priests with stovepipe hats, long robes, and beards would stroll the narrow alleys with their hands behind their backs looking exactly like movie extras. Old women in black would watch me as I passed, ask me about snow occasionally. I'd wander through the maze of whitewashed houses, the stark lines of white and blue, and stumble back home over the rocky land of dry absolutes in a heady daze. Nothing is murky in Greece, nor hazy, nor humid,

nor dewy. Lush doesn't live there. Greece is a rock garden of
shrubs and laurel, juniper and cypress, thyme and oregano.
Wildflowers spin colors that surge out of a pure clarity and
in this clarity the forms of things are finer. Greece shimmers
from afar, is hardy in the distance, and chill beneath your
bones. In the dry heat of this arid place, donkeys sound-off
at all hours, as if agitated. They'd wake me even in the dead
of night.

One evening at sunset a man on a moped zipped by as I was
walking along the beach. He came to a stop in the sand ahead
and turned to ask my name. I'd seen him before at the taverna,
throwing his head back to laugh when Nikos the waiter told
jokes. The man on the moped offered me a ride down the
beach and I took it. Naxos has one entire uninterrupted beach
and in twenty minutes or so we came to his village, a cluster
of houses and an outdoor restaurant overlooking the sea. The
man let me off, smiled without speaking and disappeared. I
went to the restaurant for dinner and chatted with some
tourists. We didn't say anything significant. Mostly we watched
the sky, which by then was blood red, cracked apart with silver shots of whisky. Shortly after I found a bus that took me
back to the town of Naxos.

By the time I finally arrived at the olive grove it was dark
except for the light of the moon heaving itself full over the
mountain. I came to my bamboo wind shelter and found it
creaking in the wind, desolate, as it was the day I arrived, abandoned by its inhabitant. My backpack and the little home I'd
made with my sleeping bag and pillows were gone, taken. For
approximately three seconds I felt a panic spread through me,
which didn't seem healthy, so I looked at the moon and seeing that dependable milky rock hovering up there like the
planet's eccentric uncle made me smile, and I remembered
that in the great scheme of the universe, this kind of thing

didn't matter. I had my money, travelers' checks, and passport with me and could buy the few things I needed. My backpack had been too heavy anyway, and traveling light would be a relief, a new challenge, something to write home about in postcards. Sitting on the sand I thought of the stolen things I would miss: my journal, my camera, some foreign change, a pair of Levis, my toothbrush, my shoes. My shoes!

I fell asleep surprisingly quickly under the full moon that night. Luckily the thieves hadn't stolen the floor of the wind shelter—the bamboo mats—and I was comfortable and warm, but an hour or so later a group of hysterical German women came and woke me. They'd been staying at a campground down the beach and they too had been victims of an annoying petty crime. Standing with them was a quiet, tall Dutch man with a blond beard and thick glasses. His belongings had been stolen also, even an expensive camera was gone, but I noticed that, unlike the women, he wasn't the least perturbed by it. In fact he was calm, even amused, and I felt an instant affinity for this unusual man. In the midst of the German panic, three Scottish backpackers came along and asked if this was a safe place to camp. I laughed, which seemed to irritate the German women, while Martin, the Dutch man, said it was safe except for the occasional theft in the area, but really quite peaceful during the day. The German women went off to search for clues down the beach. Martin and I lay back on the sand and watched the stars swirl over the wine-dark sea as we discussed the lapses and betrayals of the modern world. We should have been helping in the search, but what was the point? Our possessions gone, we felt free in a funny way. We didn't care. We were two whimsical souls colliding in the land of Homer. Half an hour later, the German women came running back, exhilarated and out of breath. "We found everything! Our things! Come!" It was true. Over a sand dune not far away, most of our belongings, including my backpack, were piled together like a happy heap of children hiding in the dark. My backpack had been slashed with a knife and anything of value, like my camera, was gone, but my journal was there and so were most of my clothes, even my toothbrush. It felt like Christmas. I found my sleeping bag and tent in another sand dune and since I hadn't used the tent since Britain anyway, I gave it to Martin because his had been taken. Somehow losing everything and so unexpectedly finding it again had given us a new perspective on what we valued. One of the German women gave me a book. A festive night! The best part of the thievery was that in the semi-crisis of getting our stuff ripped off, I'd met the strange, fair-haired Dutch man and he made me laugh.

Martin and I spent the next two days together talking continuously. Just being with him filled me with an excitement and a calm, deep knowledge. There are people with whom you feel mute and around them you forget you have a head and a heart full of ideas and wonder, poetry and longing, and there are those who can reach straight into your chest and pull songs and stars out of your heart. Martin wasn't quite like that—I didn't sing around him—but he was close, and he was the best friend I'd made in months of traveling. Traveling is so temporary, so peculiar to the nature of the human psyche, that you forget you need friends. When you find one, you remember the miracle of another person and you remember yourself. Talking to Martin made me feel I was availing myself to whatever was extraordinary in the world. He had a special interest in the spirit world, also in plants and modern history. He was a storyteller, too, with stories of his long journey through India and Tibet, stories of love, betrayal, auto accidents. I told stories also, most of mine involving medical mishaps in Third World countries.

On the third day Martin left to catch a plane. I walked him to the ferry. He limped because he'd stepped on a sea urchin. He was sunburned. I waved good-bye from the dock to the Dutch man with gawky glasses and violet eyes underneath, and I wondered if I'd ever see him again.

As the days passed, I found it increasingly difficult to leave my wind shelter. I had the moon, sun, stars, my books, the old men in the waves. Why would I leave? I'd seen enough of the world and I liked where I was. Perhaps the more you stay in a place, the more it grows on you, the way some people do. I'd wake at dawn thinking today should be the day to go to another island, go back to the mainland or to another country. But then I'd go for a swim and read a little, take a walk, jump through the waves. The sun would sneak across the sky making its way towards its great dip into the sea and I'd still be there like a lotus eater, lazy some would say, if they didn't know better. One day I decided to take an excursion away from my beach, maybe try to leave it for good. I wasn't prepared to leave Naxos yet. I'd just see more of it. I took a bus to the other side of the island and was gone for four days. It felt like forever.

The bus driver could have gotten us killed several times as he rampaged around hairpin curves into the mountains. From the window, I watched the dramatic patchwork of Naxos, its gardens, vineyards, citrus orchards, villages, and Venetian watchtowers. Farmers plowed with donkeys in the fields. Children played barefoot along the roads. The people of the island may have had only a scruffy flock of goats or a small grape orchard, a rowboat to search the night waters for fish or a *taverna* with three tables, but they weren't poor. Life brought them regular random encounters with friends and relatives each day, not just occasional carefully selected lunches with them. Their lives were rich, plentiful, and cheerful.

I stayed at a fishing village called Apollon on the roof of a house of one of the women in black. In Greece, a woman puts on a black dress when a loved one dies and she wears a black dress the rest of her life. That's devotion. That also cuts down on clothing expenses. Some women also rent out rooms to tourists and, if the rooms are full, they rent the roof. That's a good head for business. By that time I was so accustomed to sleeping outside, I chose the roof over an inside room. The woman in black gave me a fine example of a *tsk tsk*—something people the world over do with their teeth and tongue when they disapprove of you—and she said something in Greek, which was Greek to me, and gave me an extra blanket. For hours I watched the stars and thought of our dark ancestral past far away, the stars where we originated in some distant long forgotten explosion. Under the weight of the stars I could hardly bear the full force of the universe, the randomness, the chaos, the chance of it all. What is one to do with a life when eternity surrounds us?

One could return to a wind shelter under an olive grove. That was one option.

So I returned. And that's when the strange thing happened, the one for which there is no logical explanation. On the first night back from my excursion I had fallen into a deep sleep in my wind shelter when I had the distinct and uncomfortable feeling that something was moving towards me along the beach and I should wake up to chase it away. I tried with all my might to wake up but my eyes felt glued shut and I couldn't open them. The thing was approaching fast, faster every second it seemed, and it was determined, perhaps running, and I knew it was looking for me. Although I couldn't fathom what it was, it felt horribly dangerous and I knew it was imperative I wake up to protect myself. Yet waking was impossible. My body and eyes were paralyzed. Like a great black shadow the thing was coming across the sand and still my body was comatose. Then I could feel it close by and, I knew suddenly, this dark and unknown thing was with me in the olive grove. My heart seemed to bang out of my chest, loud enough to hear. I forced myself to climb up through layers and layers of a deep sleep, the sleep of centuries it felt like, and at last I broke out of it and woke, or so I thought. Pulling myself up on my elbows, I saw what the thing was: a tiny woman in black, no more than four feet tall, and very old. She lay down beside me, curled her body against mine, and shivered. Whatever she was, she was very cold and wanted inside. I knew instinctively she didn't mean inside my sleeping bag. She wanted inside me. No, I said, you can't come in. I live here. She pulled herself closer and her long, damp silver hair fell like sorrow, like misery, like an ancient sad longing. She needed a home, a warm body to live in, a place with a fire. Her face was that of a crone and I could feel her wrinkled icy skin on my cheek. Even her breath was the frigid night air of winter. Her eyes seemed bottomless at first, empty, like black holes, but buried deep inside were two brilliant stars for eyes, blazing stars light years away. Again and again I told her No, which seemed to make her unbearably sad. Please let me in, she pleaded. No, you can't. This is my body, this is me! For a moment an uncanny intimacy hung there between us as we stared at each other across the distance of two worlds. Her eyes shone so brightly they burned my own, burned straight through to my inner core. No, I told her again firmly. No. With that, she was gone. She raised herself up and drifted off down the beach, still shivering and still wanting a home. She left as she had come, with the night breeze.

The incident itself I could easily have dismissed as a weird dream, and did in fact do so the next morning when I woke to the call of the roosters, shaking my head at the previous night's dark madness. Although the dream had been unusually vivid, perceptible and oddly lucid, it had to be a dream nonetheless. A four-foot-tall woman in black trying to pry her way into my body? How rude. Crazy. What happened later that day, however, made me wonder how far dreams travel into the waking world.

That afternoon, the *taverna* near my wind shelter where I always ate lunch was closed, the tables, chairs, and the owner, Nikos, nowhere in sight. Strange, I thought, since I had never seen it closed in all the weeks I'd been there. Perhaps Nikos was taking a holiday. I decided to walk down the beach to the campground restaurant instead. By chance, my table happened to be next to some backpackers who were discussing where they would travel after Greece. As I ate my fruit salad I listened to their conversation, which fortunately was in English since they were of several nationalities. The conversation took a twist when a German woman began to tell the others about a strange dream she'd had the night before.

"It was horrible, a nightmare. I dreamt a little woman came floating along the beach. She was kind of like the women here in Greece, the ones who wear the black, but she was tiny. She was cold. It was terrible, terrible. Such a clear dream."

My spoon fell from my hand and I felt a sudden constriction around my heart. Had I heard her right? Was this too a dream? "Excuse me," I said to the German woman, "I couldn't help overhearing you. What did the woman want?" The German woman looked over at me, startled, almost familiar. Her face was pale.

"To get inside me."

In a land where myth and reality swirl around each other in a luminous haze, lessons clear and absolute can be found after all. I said nothing is murky in Greece but I was wrong. A woman came to me on the mist. She crossed over from the other side and sent me a gift. In all my life I have never known such a moment as when those haunting eyes from eternity stared into mine. Although she may not have intended to, she gave me a message: a human life is an extraordinary treasure. She wanted to feel life, maybe feel it again as she once had, and she wanted it desperately. I was alive, breathing, warm, strong, with a fire and light inside me she ached for. When I pushed her away, proclaiming my life as my own, never had I felt the life inside me so intensely.

I left on the ferry the next day. I didn't need to stay in Naxos anymore. I needed to see the rest of the world. To stay in my wind shelter and live amidst the lure and myth of Greece would be to believe in magic and fate, superstition and dark mysteries. I had this world to explore first, the one with cities and rivers, foreign faces and Woody Allen movies. From the boat I watched the island shrink on the horizon, getting smaller and smaller like a puddle evaporating in the sun.

Yet I knew then as I still know now, that from the shore where the sand dunes begin, the olive grove grows old, and from the bed where we sleep, the shadows of secret things lurk, forbidden, timeless, and forever calling our name.

Laurie Gough is the author of Kite Strings of the Southern Cross, *which won a silver medal for Foreword Magazine's Best Travel Book of the Year, and was short-listed for the Thomas Cook/Daily Telegraph Travel Book of the Year award in the U.K. She has also written for Salon.com,* Outpost, *and the* Toronto Globe and Mail. *Her work appears in several travel anthologies, including* Travelers' Tales: A Woman's World, The Adventure of Food, Greece, Her Fork in the Road, *and* Wanderlust: Real-Life Tales of Adventure and Romance. *She lives in Ontario, Canada.*

CAROL PEREHUDOFF

✦ ✦ ✦

Pilgrimage to Glastonbury

*An uncertain goddess searches
among the myths.*

"THERE A GODDESS CONFERENCE ON," SAID THE CLERK AT the third hotel I called. "No rooms available."

Well, I'm Nemesis, Goddess of Vengeance and Fate, I wanted to say. Any chance you can squeeze me in?

Nowhere else but Glastonbury would I be competing with over three hundred goddesses for a room. This mystical Isle of Avalon is a point of pilgrimage for Christians and Pagans alike. It's the site of the first Christian church in England, the hiding place of the Holy Grail, and the burial place of Arthur and Guinevere.

Maybe.

Myths abound in this tiny Somerset town and it's impossible to weed out the facts. But for many, drawn by ley-lines, legends, or even the huge annual music festival, it's a magical place. I'm just curious to see if this spirituality will affect me, or if, as I suspect, I'm mystically thick as a plank.

I finally find a room at The George & Pilgrims. A fifteenth-century hotel with a carved stone façade, it's been housing pilgrims for centuries. A tunnel underneath, now blocked off, previously connected it to the once mighty Glastonbury Abbey down the street.

A miniature statue of Henry VIII stares out at me defiantly from the wall of my Henry VIII room. Too much patriarchal energy for the goddesses? Maybe that's why it's available. I'm surprised pilgrims would want it either, as it was Henry who caused the destruction of the Abbey after his break from the Roman Church. A word with Oddvar, the Norwegian desk clerk who has made Glastonbury his home, assures me that Henry didn't actually stay in the room. If he did stay at the George, and that is debatable, it would have been in what is now the lounge on the main floor.

From my 500-year-old window, I look out over flocks of goddesses walking the street in colorful flowing skirts. Here to celebrate womanhood, no doubt. I'm a bit lonely with nothing but the statue of Henry for company so I decide to join them. I'm female, what more credentials do I need? I head to the town hall and leaf through a program. Labyrinth Ceremonies, Goddess Alphabet Dance Meditation, Weaving the Goddess E-Web.... I don't understand a thing, but decide to sign up. Until I learn the price. Forty-five pounds for one day. Reluctantly, I forgo goddess kinship for the solitary role of a pilgrim. It may be lonely, but it's free.

I head instead to the Tor, the strange grassy hill which rises like a cone behind town. I follow the posted arrows, but instead of the paved footpath, end up on a rambling dirt trail which winds around the back of the hill. The morning light slants across the path, the brush is rich with the smell of damp greenery and smoky traces of campfire...and it's not without danger either—a grunting pig behind a hedgerow scares me half out of my wits.

Finally I reach the base and start climbing the stone steps.

Some say the Tor is hollow, a dwelling place of the fairies. Others think it's the entrance to the underworld. It's certainly an unusual trek, much like hiking a wizard's hat. Panting when I reach the top, I flop on the grass and look out over the Vale of Avalon. Pale green fields stretch like waves, merging into a hazy blue sky. In the shade of the fifteenth-century tower behind me, the only remains of a much older chapel, a man softly strums the guitar.

It should be tranquil but it isn't. Either I'm adversely affected by the ley-lines which intersect here, I'm sensing the lingering spirit of Richard Whiting, the elderly abbot who was dragged up here and hanged in 1539 during Henry's Dissolution of the Monasteries, or I'm just feeling left out because I can't be a goddess.

On my way down I meet the minstrel guitarist, Murray, and his girlfriend, Wendy. Together we decide to go to the Chalice Well. Wendy tells me that just before she met Murray, she was doing her fairy cards, and turned up the pixie, which signifies unconditional love. So here I am off to an ancient well with a fairy and a pixie. My spirits perk up.

In the Eden-like Chalice Well Garden, I dip my feet into the healing Pilgrims' Bath, then drink three cold glasses filled from a lion's head spout. Wendy and Murray decide to stay for a spot of meditation, so I stroll to the back of the garden, where surrounded by the fragrance of roses is the well head, the source of the spring. Joseph of Arimathea, the Virgin Mary's uncle, hid the Holy Grail here. Either that or in the hills behind. We don't know for sure as it's never been found.

The next morning I slog through a downpour over to the town hall for the goddess procession up to the Tor. Not only is it open to the public, it's free. The crowd huddled in the doorway doesn't look as if it's going to be marching anytime soon, so after waiting around for twenty minutes I head around the corner to the Abbey instead.

It's a different world inside the Abbey grounds, silent and serene. Under the protection of my umbrella I walk through the vast crumbling ruins, walls half-standing like decaying trees in a forest of moss. The rain stops as I'm standing in the roofless Lady Chapel and I feel a tremendous sense of peace.

The chapel rests on a potent spot, my audio tape confirms it. Joseph built England's first Christian church here in A.D. 63—a mud-and-wattle hut dedicated to Mary.

Outside, on a smooth stretch of grass, a plaque marks the original tomb of Arthur and Guinevere. A leaden cross buried with them (which vanished in the seventeenth century) certified that, *Here lies the illustrious King Arthur buried in the Isle of Avalon.*

In reality here lies controversy—perhaps the oldest tourist trap in existence. The monks found the grave in 1191, conveniently when money was needed to rebuild after a devastating fire. What better way to attract pilgrim coffers?

Hungry from myth hunting, I head out to the High Street for a meal at the Spiral Café. Over chickpea stew, I chat with the British couple beside me. With his lavender shirt and pressed beige pants, I'd pegged Mike for a tourist, but he's well acquainted with Glastonbury, and has accompanied his wife, Liz, to the Goddess Conference. Mike's beliefs are hard to define, but universalist with neopagan and gnostic tendencies comes close, while Liz prefers a female divinity.

"It's a feminine energy, here," she says. "The hills form the shape of a reclining woman."

That explains the goddesses. And here the woman at tourist information had told me it was because the Tor was in the shape of a breast. But Liz informs me that Glastonbury is an age-old center of goddess worship. Avalon is Morgan la Fay's kingdom, and though she's usually seen as Arthur's enemy, she was also a healer; it was here she brought him to tend his mortal wounds.

"Morgan got a bum rap," Liz says.

With a surge of satisfaction, I recall that it was the Lady's Chapel in the Abbey that affected me the most deeply, the one place I truly felt at peace. Maybe it's not necessary to be part of the goddess group in order to find the feminine magic of Glastonbury. Without realizing it I find I've been celebrating the female spirit, too.

The restaurant fills up and two German women sit down at my table.

"Here for the conference?" they ask.

"No," I say cheerfully, moving over to make room. I may not be a goddess, or even close, but it's still nice to be mistaken for one.

Carol Perehudoff has been globe trotting ever since she could afford a round-the-world ticket. She spent two years in England, eight months in Spain and seven years in Korea. Now a travel writer based in Toronto, her travel column in the Toronto Star *"Going Solo" leads her on a never-ending quest to find a place she fits in.*

KATHLEEN COMSTOCK

Just Chicken

*A small place in Paris provided
more than exquisite meals.*

ON A RECENT TRIP TO PARIS, A PEEK AT MY DINING GUIDE
confirmed the Restaurant du Midi was still there. As I read
on, however, my heart sank, realizing my friend was gone.

> With the departure of Claude Menard, new talent
> arrives from Southwest France to re-adorn this
> adorable bistro, its copper moldings intact and still
> weathered by time, with the panache that it never
> would have lost had it not changed hands. The menu
> is more expensive with duck in luscious berry sauces
> and a solid, debonair wine list. But if there's a dish
> that really must be ordered in this tiny corner of a
> largely forgotten part of the 15th *arrondissement*, it's
> the chicken, miraculously endowed with simplicity
> and justice.

In spite of the review, I knew that without Monsieur
Menard, the place could never be the same. Instead of going
out for dinner, I settled back in my chair.

The man arose in my memory, his rosy face and snowy hair, those rugged arms, his pot belly smartly tucked—as the French will—under his t-shirt, and roving, twinkling, mischievous eyes ready for me each time I entered his establishment.

We met over fifteen years ago, when I was moving to the city and temporarily set up at the Holiday Inn in the 15th *arrondissement*. Near train stations and exits to major highways, the quarter idled between the dingy outskirts and the intimacy and glamour commonly appreciated as Paris. Dog shit stuck longer to sidewalks, migrants with wooden teeth and unsavory regards passed on the street, and at night cats furiously mated while drunks shouted. To awaken to the sounds of someone throwing up outside my window wasn't unusual in the wee hours of a Saturday morning. On occasion from above low-lying fog and largely decrepit buildings, the Eiffel Tower's pointy top helped me remember what city I lived in.

Starving one night after a day-long meeting without breaks, I alighted from the Métro and swore to myself I'd find a decent place to eat rather than submit to unexciting hotel cuisine. Wandering without regard, I followed a boulevard that turned into an alley which swung around to a cul de sac. Sore feet from walking on three-inch heels stopped me at an unassuming green façade with oversized windows and neatly tucked-aside interior lace curtains. The voice of an old friend whispered, "It's the little out-of-the-way places you will fall for. Do not overlook them."

By the time I swung open the door, briefcase weighing me down, hair flattened and sticking out in all the wrong ways, clothes smelling of the day's energies, and eyes maniacal from hunger, the man behind his bar had checked me out. With an abrupt, obnoxiously Gallic shrug, he turned his back on me.

"Damn French," I thought, tending to my feet by lifting one set of toes and then the other. At 7 P.M.—too early for "real dining" according to the haughtier side of the culture—his wordless message was clear: I was way out of line. He continued washing glasses but, each time his head rose to the smoked mirror in front of him, his eyes darted my way.

I couldn't help but stall over the tables for two and four, each decorated with white cloth, candle, and fresh pink rose. Empty green bottles lined two walls, labels from fine Bordeaux and Burgundy vintages organized alongside lesser-known Côte du Rhônes. The garlic and butter smells so seduced my appetite in the cheery place, that I decided to hold out on this French man. His rude shrug, I learned from previous similar encounters, was best served by ignoring. Two could play his game.

"We do not serve until 7:30."

"I can wait," I said, my gaze roving his walls rather than him.

"Suit yourself." He returned to his glasses. As he rubbed them dry, they squeaked happily. Afterward, he gently placed them on shelving behind the bar while humming a more throaty version of "*Je ne regrette rien*" ("No Regrets"), a song made famous by France's wartime crooner, Edith Piaf.

After a minute or two, he looked up. "Well, have a seat anyway, *rousse* (redhead)."

This reference to my hair drew a smile from me and from him a glance of curiosity. I nodded to a table that would place me dead center, able to study his bar walls containing the magnificent labels, selections that, if they remain at all today, lie carefully guarded in the *caves* of the wealthy and aficionados. From here I could also attract his wandering attentions once the place filled, which I knew it would, for it bore all the signs of a local hangout—no menus, no chalkboards, little in the way of luxury with its hardwood chairs and everyday silverware. I suspected, however, that anything required to dine well would appear at one's fingertips. He nodded back and I settled.

"Apéritif?"

"*Un petit Ambassadeur* (a sweet-sour drink), *s'il vous plaît*," I said.

"Ah, then you need nuts, too," he said, his voice scratchy yet more melodic than when we started out.

The nuts arrived in a tiny dish. I waited until he disappeared behind curtains to check out the bottom. Limoges. Simple and white, but Limoges china nonetheless. I began to relax, and the Ambassadeur sank to my empty stomach and then heated my sore toes, a massage without hands.

He waited until I finished my drink before returning to the table. "You are going to start with something."

"What do you have?" I asked with as much nonchalance as I could muster. I would have downed a napkin flavored with salt and pepper.

"Pumpkin soup."

"Anything else?"

"Take the soup. It's fresh."

"O.K."

"Tonight. Chicken for the main course," he said, scratching the back of his head. Free of any notepad to take orders, his other hand clutched the back of my chair for support. He studied a passing car, as though its driver might be someone he knew. His fingernails were clean, the only soil was on his apron.

"Just chicken?" I asked.

"Where are you from? The accent is lightly Swiss. Geneva?"

"Boston. That's in the United States."

From behind white eyelashes that made him look sleepy, his huge black eyes penetrated mine. He was either going to make love to me or kill me. I held my gaze and he let one bushy brow lower, then lower still.

"Red hair like that is Irish," he said.

"I'll take the chicken. And a half carafe of your house wine." I continued to gaze at him. From the back room, music began to play. More Edith.

He made a sweeping gesture with his arm, then wound around my table. Before again disappearing, he called to whoever was in the back that "we have a pumpkin and a chicken."

Served in a simple white bowl, the gourd this dish started out as was transformed to thick buttery swirls with a dollop of heavy cream in the middle. With smooth consistency touched with pepper and sea salt, its exact warm temperature invited immediate consumption. The owner did a double-take when he noted how rapidly it disappeared.

"You starve. Eat more in life," he said. "You won't be so frazzled like when you walked in here." He removed my bowl and poured me wine from a small handmade ceramic pitcher.

He allowed no time for a response because a foursome arrived, with whom he continued a debate likely started the day before about the status of mushrooms for the upcoming season. In short order, the place filled with elderly couples, families of three and four, lovers, a nun. Everyone knew the owner, who wound around tables just as he had my own, barely missing chairs and patrons, all the while removing coats, offering seating, and advising them of the soup and the chicken. Over the murmur of diners debating additional selections—yesterday's beef bourguignon, duck confit—he joked about the latest foibles at the Elysée Palace and the additional fast trains to support the upcoming Alpine winter holiday exodus. With a trailing, sweet ring, his words threaded every table's conversation. When not chatting, he hummed along with Edith. At times, voices lowered as did his massive body, to discuss the redhead in the center of the room. At one point I heard the word "American" and the couple to whom he spoke darted glances that I caught, which I think threw them off as they never looked again my way.

Chicken is chicken is chicken, they say. In my family, we were discouraged from ordering something as banal as chicken when dining out. So when he brought the meal, my expectations were set and I was unprepared for the deciding moment that it would become.

Indeed, chicken lay on the plate, a leg and small breast sitting contentedly in its own shining pale yellow juices, speckles of pepper on top, a sprig of parsley to the side. To look at, simple, fresh, inviting.

To eat, a journey through all that has made the French known for their cooking, yet more subtle and sublime than the world-renowned "book three months in advance" restaurants most tourists tend to seek out. Bites of perfectly roasted bird accompanied by the peppery, black currant flavors of the wine proved opera to my senses, and filled me aptly, in spite of the conservative portion. He had to bring me extra bread so I could sop up the sauce.

I finished the wine and bypassed dessert, wishing instead to appreciate the meal's lingering pleasures, even as fatigue started warning me. I had to walk home before hitting the sack. I paid and went to the counter.

A Parisian restaurant owner, however highbrow, wants dearly to know one thing before you walk out, and this owner was no different.

"So, *rousse*, did you enjoy?" he asked predictably.

I leaned into his bar, waiting for him to stop rubbing a glass. When he looked up, I got close enough so he could smell the garlic and wine on my breath.

"That was the best chicken I have ever, ever had in my entire life."

His eyes, clearly twinkling with my response, as well as the contents of what had been a full wine glass within his reach all evening, devoured me along with his now gregarious smile. An aura as effervescent as his chicken took over. "Well, when you come back, ask for the chicken. I will have it for you."

"What is your name?" I asked.

"Menard," he said, reaching his hand to shake mine with a clutch that was fixed and whole.

"Kathleen," I said.

"*Rousse* is better."

During my years in Paris, I returned time and again, with friends, with executives from my company, most often alone. The word got out at my place of work, all the way across the Atlantic. "Go with Kathy to the chicken man." The marketing vice president I worked for, a wealthy, flamboyant traveler who only ate at the name places in Paris, became the biggest advertiser of the Restaurant du Midi. So enamored was he of the chicken place, he told everyone, describing over and over with delight his first encounter with Menard in this unassuming part of the city. "He kept calling me BEEEG BOSS!"

When I dined by myself I always showed up at seven and so had time to linger afterwards while Menard served meals. I would sit at the bar and there we learned of one another. He told me of Simone de Beauvoir who, before she died several years prior, took a table in the corner most Thursday nights. I talked of how the mauve dunes of Cape Cod spill into the Atlantic, of Boston with its skyscrapers you can ride to the top of and, unlike in Paris, the fewer lines or waiting at most of our places of business.

He served meals to German military during the war.

"Didn't that just kill you to have to do that?" I asked. That night I had stayed for another glass of wine and leaned over his bar, comfortable in our ever-reversing roles of listener and storyteller. (He never charged for the wine those nights.)

For a moment, he stopped stroking the bar with his towel and gave me a sleepy, mirthful look. "There are ways of getting even, *rousse*. The soup is made with multiple ingredients."

We laughed, joked, and I always ordered chicken. Prior to my return to the States after a stay of three years, I went to say good-bye.

"You won't return," he said, wrapping up a bottle of Burgundy as gift for me, a 1985 and one of his choicest.

"I will. You wait."

"You will marry a rich American who wears a cowboy hat. You will have babies, a house with a pool in Hollywood or New York. Three times divorced, you will end up in Florida, white-haired and plump. You Americans are all alike."

Thus we concluded with our routine banter, he about the stereotyped Americans and me about the irascible French.

"Three-quarters of you French will not go to Heaven when you die. You will go to the Other Place, subjected for eternity to the tutelage of Miss Manners! You will sink in your own sewage because you do not make plumbing a priority in this country. You will fart to death from eating rich food. You will miss me when I'm gone!"

That night, I walked home, as I had so many nights, satiated by food and the richly succulent, ruefully attractive Monsieur Menard. Who I never did see again.

Kathleen Comstock lived in Paris for two years where she developed her love for fine dining and travel. She is the author of the novel, Orchid House, *and she now divides her time between a home in Central Massachusetts and one on Cape Cod with her family and two dogs.*

ISABELLA TREE

* ⋆ *

On Spétses

*A lifetime of summers in Greece
casts a spell that never fades.*

TODAY IS LIKE YESTERDAY AND TOMORROW. THERE IS nothing to ruffle the waters of the mind, no cloud on the horizon. The cicadas have made a nest deep inside my temporal lobe, and they rasp there incessantly, soothingly, an entomological lullaby shutting off all forms of conscious thought. The air is alive and warm and suffused with the intoxicating smell of pine needles. Nothing stirs. Only the breeze and the ripples of water sucking idly at pebbles on the beach.

We are moored in a bay on the eastern side of the Aegean island of Spétses. Our boat is a traditional caïque built of pinewood by local craftsmen who have worked it by eye, without plans, with the blueprint in their genes. It bobs on the sea like a cradle.

Beneath me the water is gin clear, and light twinkles through it as if the sun is rising from its depths. Diving in—which I will do in a minute or two, when I can stir some action into my limbs—is like bursting a bubble.

135

I will swim to the shore and join the others. And soon Panos—electrician in winter, boatman in summer—will emerge from the water, snorkel and mask in one hand, plastic bag bursting with sea urchins in the other. A little ouzo; the sweet-salt taste of urchin eggs; a squeeze of tart lemon.

It's a common notion among visitors here that spending summer in Spétses is like taking a colossal sleeping pill; that it makes you comatose for a couple of weeks. But I'm convinced the opposite is true. To be sure, one part of you—the clock-watching, cuticle-chewing, frenetic workaholic—shuts down. But another, neglected part—the carefree euphoric sensual-ist—springs to life. Spétses works like smelling salts; it's a corpse reviver, a spiritually renewing slap on the bottom. And every year, as the hydrofoil from Athens approaches the island and that first whiff of Aleppo pines comes blasting across the sea, some deep part of me starts to stretch and yawn and shake itself awake, happy to find itself back home.

I first arrived on the island in a basket—something I'm constantly reminded of by doting *yayas*, the Spétses "grannies." They seemed older than God then; now they're even more whiskered and toothless, and their ranks have been replenished by another generation of women in black. My earliest mem-ories are of being squeezed to an endless round of bosoms, my head stroked, my cheeks pinched, my knees squeezed—until, mercifully, my sister came along. With her fair hair and big blue eyes, she was like honey to the bees. It was the *yayas* who instructed my mother to tie a sprig of basil and a blue glass amulet painted with a white and yellow eye to my cot: one to repel mosquitoes; the other, the evil eye.

My parents had fallen in love with Spétses a decade before I was born. Every summer they rented the same house: a beautiful villa in the oldest part of town, near the mouth of the old harbor, right on the sea, overlooking the monastery of Agios Nicholaos—Saint Nicholas.

Like all the villas in the neighborhood, it was originally built by a merchant sea captain who'd earned his fortune blockade-running in the mid-nineteenth century. The house had walls several feet thick (whitewashed on the outside, so it was blessedly cool in the August heat); bare, painted floors inside; and stenciled borders round the ceilings, Venetian style. Off the sitting room there was a wrought-iron balcony that overhung the road and proved the perfect place from which my sister and I could flick pistachio shells onto passing carriage drivers when no one was looking. (Spétses then, as now, has no cars, only a bus, a couple of taxis, bikes and motorbikes, the odd donkey, and ranks of elegant horse-drawn carriages.)

The plumbing in the villa was a noisy, temperamental, twentieth-century addition—one single lavatory that failed spectacularly to live up to the trade name emblazoned on the inside of its bowl: Best Niagra.

My sister and I slept in the basement storeroom where the merchant would have kept his sacks of grain, casks of oil, and bolts of expensive cloth. The floor was uneven, of beaten earth; and light showers of dust fell from between the boards of the ceiling when the grown-ups walked around upstairs. At night the lighthouse at the entrance to the harbor would poke its beam through the bars of the window at the end of the room in three-second bursts, hypnotically—one hippopotamus, two hippopotamus, three hippopotamus, flash! One hippopotamus, two hippopotamus…I was asleep long before the rats ventured out to continue their gnawing on the legs of my bed.

When my bed finally collapsed one night, landing with a resounding crash on the floor, the *yayas* in the household were triumphant. Never keen on the unconventional idea of children sleeping in the basement, they'd scored a moral victory, and my mother lost considerable ground in her battle against their old wives' tales about things that go bump in the night.

The house belonged to the Bouboulis family, descendants of the great Spetsiot heroine, Lakkarina Bouboulina. It was she who captained the Spetsiot fleet in 1821, so the story goes, when Spétses won the first naval victory for the Greeks against the Turks in the war for independence. Bouboulina loomed large in my childhood repertoire of myths and legends, an Amazonian figure in felt skirt, brocade bodice, and bare feet, as fierce and dashing and romantic as Boadicea or Joan of Arc.

Charging around the garden between the plumbago and the pots of basil, with fly swatters in the waistband of my shorts, I was Bouboulina marshaling my troops, boarding battleships, firing cannons, drawing cutlasses and pistols from my cummerbund. Pushing my sister into the geraniums, I launched my fire ships at the Ottoman galleons, and leapt with breathtaking bravado onto the garden wall, shouting, *"Eleftheria e thanatos!"*—Freedom or death!—the only words, apart from "please" and "thank you" and "good morning," that our patriotic cook had thought essential for my sister and me to learn.

Bouboulina's sea battle was a victory that was celebrated every year with bunting fireworks and Greek dancers in traditional costumes (including pom-poms on their shoes), and the burning of a mock Turkish galleon in the sea in front of the Dapia—the high defensive wall overlooking the new harbor in the commercial part of the town. Those Armata, or "Burning the Turk," celebrations fell in the second week of September, so, until secondary school rudely intruded and we had to return home earlier for the start of the autumn term, our holidays always ended with a bang, the thud of cannons.

I like to think that some of that Mediterranean fervor, that love of rebellion, was scored into my soul at an early age, the Armata lighting a little bonfire that even the interminable English winters and a thousand school dinners would fail to dampen. I didn't think directly of Bouboulina when I got myself expelled from school, but I remember pledging "Freedom or death" rather melodramatically as my best friend and I broke out down the fire escape and headed off for an ill-fated rendezvous with our boyfriends and a bottle of Southern Comfort.

The influence of Spétses on my education was not all negative. It compelled me to pursue the challenging subject of ancient Greek. My fellow classicists chose the subject for a variety of highbrow and commendable reasons: for the discipline of tackling a difficult ancient grammar, for a better command of the English language, to study the tongue of the birthplace of Western civilization, to read Herodotus (the grandfather of history) and Aristotle and Plato, for a better understanding of the politics and philosophy of the modern world, or at the very least because it gave even the dimmest of us a fighting chance of getting into a good university.

But I chose it flippantly and self-indulgently—because it allowed me to dream myself back to the halcyon days of summer. While my classmates were furrowing their brows over aorist optatives, I felt myself skimming like a flying fish across the waves, invoking "goddess of Song, teach me the story of a hero…" I knew how Odysseus felt when he stood on the bow of his ship heading for home. I'd seen dawn come up with its rosy fingers. I was intimate with that wine-dark sea. As I gazed at the blackboard I could smell the pine resin from Circe's wooded isle, and hear the waves turning over the pebbles on the beach in Ithaca, the adzes knocking in the boatbuilders' yards, the cicadas rasping in the silvery, long-leafed olive trees.

By the time I got to Sappho's teasing fragments of erotic, bisexual love poems, there was no holding me back. I was in my late teens, and the isles of Greece were synonymous with sex. Accustomed to propping up the wall at the local disco back at home, or endlessly reapplying eyeliner in the ladies' room, I knew Spétses would work unimaginable miracles on my love life. Provided I could bribe, cajole, or coerce my heartthrob onto the airplane at Heathrow, I would be assured of an amazing transformation at the other end. Spétses would make him as pliable and powerless as Menelaus, and I, throwing caution to the winds, would be able to indulge myself, for a few precious weeks, as Helen of Troy.

I was too conscious of Spétses' charms to become swollen-headed. I knew it was the cocktail of sunsets and retsina; the sensual overload of sounds and tastes and smells; the arching, impossibly blue canopy of sky; the aching, glittering depths of the sea—all that was irresistible, not me. But my husband seems still spellbound. He fell in love with Spétses when he fell in love with me, so with luck he'll never disassociate the two.

A couple of summers after we got together, he bought a house here—another Venetian-style villa right on the sea, just a few doors away from the Bouboulis house. "Spiti Charlie" has traditional painted floors, high stenciled ceilings, shuttered windows, and thick walls, and a sitting room the most perfect powder blue.

Our first summer in the house we were so consumed with restoration that we almost failed to notice that a gem had fallen into our hands. We turned the tiles on the roof, repaired doors and windows, replaced hinges and panes of glass, buried electric cables, and battled with characteristically rebellious plumbing. The furniture we inherited—bedsteads and armoires, brass spice grinders and samovars, porcelain pitchers for water, the odd musket—were from the time of Bouboulina. In the storeroom under the house we found a Spetsiot war of independence flag emblazoned with ELEFTHE-RIA E THANTOS and a snake entwined around an anchor; the banner flew from the terrace as the fireworks burst on our first Armata party.

The following summer we came back to find that a squadron of bees had built a home in a niche above the bathroom window and the walls were dripping with honey. We set bowls on the floor, and dribbled the nectar onto our bread and yogurt at breakfast. Irini, our housekeeper, pronounced it a wonderful omen, a blessing.

Not everyone was so optimistic. The *yayas* (the new generation of them, that is) were horrified when we planted a fig tree just meters from the house. "It's no good for babies," they said, shaking their heads, ruefully warning that fig trees make men sterile.

Two babies later, I'm glad to have proved them wrong—though they would never bring themselves to concede it. But every year I brace myself, just as my mother did, for a torrent of matriarchal advice and more trinkets to ward off the evil eye. My son and daughter are pinched and squeezed and petted and teased and transported off for secret treats—honeyed pastries and moped rides and visits to newborn lambs—just as my sister and I were.

And at night, when I tuck them into their—thank goodness, rat-free—beds upstairs, we listen to the sound of the sea on the pebbles and the *ding-dong* of the carriage bells, and count "one hippopotamus, two hippopotamus, three hippopotamus, flash!" as the beam from the lighthouse floods the room and fills their dreams with the mesmeric, permeating sorcery of the island.

Isabella Tree writes about travel for the Sunday Times, Evening Standard, *and the* Observer. *Her writing has also appeared in* Reader's Digest, Today's Best Non-Fiction, Rough Guides Women Travel, *and* The Best American Travel Writing 2002. *She is the author of three books and is at work on her fourth, a novel set in Kathmandu.*

✳ ✳ ✳

Embracing the Dark

Sometimes the blues need to be met head on.

I NEVER EXPECTED CALIFORNIA WEATHER ON MY JANUARY trip to Brighton, but neither did I expect hurricane conditions. There I sat, in my oceanfront room as the wind shrieked and the rain smashed against my window. O.K., not hurricane conditions. But far from a civilized London drizzle. The irony was that this trip was supposed to help take away the winter blues I was caught up in, make me feel less lonely while my husband Peter was out of the country.

I'd needed to get away, do something special for myself. Something in me felt broken and I wasn't sure how to fix it. Winter was affecting me, the monotony of the dark, gray days that followed the excitement of the holidays. It was most decidedly winter in London, where my husband and I were living as expatriates, and the short dark days and drizzly weather made me feel draggy and sad. Slogging down the Putney high street past Boots Chemists, BHS clothing store, and Marks and Spencer, I'd numbly make my daily purchases. Faces of the people in dark coats hurrying past me were drawn, unsmiling, gray, reflecting the weather. The raucous noise of the red double-decker buses that boomed and heaved down the streets, battling with the ear-piercing squeal of taxis' brakes made me cringe, retreating further inside myself, grieving something I couldn't name.

When Peter went back to San Francisco on business for two weeks, I decided to take a weekend trip to spoil myself. I settled on Brighton, a seaside resort town that for centuries had been a tiny fishing village. The brochures and travel guides showed sunshine, happy people, arcades, and amusement rides—the Londoner's Atlantic City or Santa Cruz Boardwalk. I splurged and booked a pricey oceanview room in a posh Georgian-style mansion hotel. Perusing the brochure in the afternoons prior to my departure, I felt my spirits lift.

Arriving in Brighton, I checked into my mansion hotel and promptly headed out. Passing the narrow, winding, pedestrian-only streets of The Lanes that positively oozed charm, ignoring the eccentric Indian-style Royal Pavilion, I found my way to the epicenter of cheer and happiness: the Palace Pier, where the boardwalk attractions were shoved onto a pier that jutted more than 1,500 feet into the water. Tourists milled about as music blared from the loudspeakers. I strolled up and down the pier, checked out rides that elicited happy shrieks from passengers, and arcades that blasted out bells, clangs, electronic shrieks, and testosterone of the fevered teenage boys inside. Shivering in the chilly, damp wind, I worked my way through some sickly-sweet candy floss (that turned out to be plain old cotton candy) and tried to feel euphoric. But the loneliness, the numb, trapped feeling had followed me from London. I could *see* people around me laughing and having fun, but something wasn't letting me in.

After an hour of wandering around in the drizzle, worsening weather forced me back to my hotel. Fortunately, I had a pretty room—spacious with high ceilings, a sumptuous bed topped with a nest of pillows and a duvet of tasteful pastels that matched the room's chintz armchairs. The chairs and a mahogany table set between them were angled for maximum enjoyment of the room's crowning glory: an enormous picture window facing the ocean just across the street, a window that now rattled and shook as the wind picked up and rain started pounding horizontally against the pane.

I curled up with a cup of tea, studied the gilt-framed paintings adorning the walls, then tried to read as the wind shrieked. The storm worsened as night fell. Hunger pangs began to gnaw at my stomach, and I considered staying in the hotel for dinner, but the thought of English hotel food (could there be a worse combination?) depressed me unutterably. I'd picked out a cozy restaurant in The Lanes, tucked amid the picturesque shops, sure to cheer me up. Reluctantly, I picked up my raincoat and umbrella and headed out.

The rain was a brutal slap against my face. It became immediately evident that the umbrella was going to be more of a liability than a help. The battering wind turned it inside out within minutes and nearly wrested it from my hand. After five minutes of continued tug of war, I finally gave up and closed the umbrella. A block later, still far from my destination, I was drenched. *To hell with The Lanes*, I decided. I saw an Indian restaurant a few steps away and dove into it.

The owner of the restaurant seemed startled, as if he weren't planning on seeing anyone that evening. He shook my hand vigorously, his eyes brimming with gratitude, and showed me to a table. I took off my sopping London Fog, handed the dripping bundle and vanquished umbrella to the waiter, and sat.

The room had red leatherette booths, red tablecloths on the center tables, and dim lighting. Portraits of dancing Hindu goddesses graced the rose-colored, gold-trimmed walls. It felt like a womb. It wasn't what I'd planned. But it was warm and comforting, the air fragrant with cumin, cardamom and baking bread. I was the only customer. A busboy hovered in the corner, watching me sip my water. After every third sip, he'd rush over and fill it up. "Thank you," he'd say.

"Oh, thank *you*." I'd reply. I quickly caught on that this thank-you business was crucial. My food arrived. "Thank you," the waiter said, set down my chicken *tikka masala*.

"Thank you," I replied.

He returned with rice and *naan*. "Thank you," he said, before placing them alongside the chicken.

"Thank you," I parroted. This continued as he brought out the *raita*, the heated plate, the bread plate, the chutney, until finally he disappeared behind the red kitchen door and I was free to eat. The owner stood near the front door, hands clasped behind his back. He stared out the window and periodically turned to me, smiled and asked how my dinner was. At my enthusiastic response, he would give a little bow before resuming his gaze out the front window. I felt the sadness hovering in the shadows, like a leering gremlin. As long as I stayed in the light however, it would leave me alone.

I ate my dinner slowly, dreading my eventual departure back out into the storm. The wind continued to shriek. "Is the wind often this bad?" I asked the next time the owner turned back toward me to check if my food was still excellent.

He nodded sadly. "Winters are the worst. The bad weather is terrible for business." This I'd already surmised. He gave a philosophical shrug. "But it is a fact of life here. It is simply the season for these storms."

After lingering over a steaming cup of *masala chai* and paying, I pulled myself up with reluctance. The waiter fetched my soggy raincoat and umbrella and I bundled back up for the walk home. The owner shook my hand and the three of us regarded each other for a wistful moment, knowing the evening was only headed downhill from here.

My room back at the hotel was freezing. I called down to the front desk to complain. "Dreadfully sorry," the clerk apologized, "it's the wind from this wretched storm." He sent a bellboy up with a space heater to augment the heating system. When it arrived ten minutes later, I studied the narrow, white, three-foot panel shaped like a wall radiator.

"*This* will heat the room?" I asked, and the bellboy hastened to reassure me.

"Oh, these are *brilliant*. But," he added with less confidence, "if it doesn't work, call back down and I'll bring up another. We keep a lot of them in storage."

As expected, the panel's weak source of heat did little to offset the chill, emanating from the oversized windows. An hour later, the tip of my nose felt as cold and damp as a dog's. I called the reception desk again. Fifteen minutes later, I had twin white-panel space heaters standing sentry by my bed. Thus protected, I went to sleep.

I was having a dream. I was all alone in some frozen landscape that seemed to resemble my native Kansas. It was growing colder, darker, and I only had a nightshirt on. I was walking on and on, past the glacial hills and glittery trees. Snow animals, a cross between cats and wolves, sat off the side of the road, and howled at me. As I passed too close to one of them, he let out a yowl that made me jump away in fear.

I kept walking, and they kept howling, until I woke with a start. It was daylight and the howling noise was the wind. The room was even colder than the previous night. I called back down to the reception desk. "Perhaps another space heater?"

the clerk proposed, and soon, another space heater joined the party. "We're having quite a storm," the new bellboy offered as he turned on the heater. "Not a very good weekend to be out."

No kidding. And to think I'd left my comfortable home, driven two hours and was shelling out a considerable sum to be stuck inside a howling room that felt like a refrigerator. A wave of self-pity engulfed me.

After breakfast, I returned to my room, which was, if anything, colder. I peered outside. Rain slapped at the windows—there was no way I was going outside. The gloominess that had been flirting with me all weekend settled in my heart for good. I dropped in an armchair to read, but was soon distracted by a burbling noise. Looking up, I discovered the rain was coming in through the cracks of the side windows. Then I heard a distinct *splat.* I glanced up higher—water was leaking from the corner of the ceiling. Within five minutes, a second leak sprouted and began to drip onto the television. I called down to my good friends at the reception desk. "Another space heater?" the clerk inquired.

"Uh, no—buckets."

When the bellboy arrived, we planted one bucket on the TV and one next to the wall. "I don't believe it's any warmer in here, is it?" he asked hesitantly. I shook my head. "I'll bring you another space heater," he proposed, his face brightening. He scurried off and returned ten minutes later with yet another white paneled heater. Hunting down an available plug in the corner of the room, he got the heater going, and beamed up at me. Clearly my problems were solved.

After he departed, I went to the window to look out. Through the fog of rain and sea spray on my window, I could make out angry, white-capped waves plowing into shore. I turned around and regarded my deluxe, ocean-view hotel room—my supposed escape from the real world. Three buckets and four space heaters looked mournfully back at me. The gloom, the lurking sadness, the loneliness, the dark muck all came to the surface in a burst of cleansing rage. *Screw this*, I thought, *I'm facing this storm full-on.*

Zipping up my still-damp London Fog raincoat, I stomped out into the storm. The numb feeling had disappeared, replaced by wild grief, coming from a dark place inside me that didn't want to calm down. Rain and cold slapped at me as I headed down to the beach.

Like monsters full of fury, the frothy blue-white waves thundered down and attacked the sand. The little beach was devoured time and time again. With a hiss, the angry water would pull away, clattering on the pebbled sand. Attack and retreat, swell and bleed, ebb and fade, sighing with regret—the waves were alive and utterly indifferent to the people who scurried along their periphery.

I stood and watched, mesmerized. The ocean was *me*, it was the way winter was making me feel. And the storm was life, just as the dark, gloomy days of rain were. I thought of the restaurant owner's words last night: *It is a fact of life—it is simply the season for these storms.*

I knew all about inner storms—they'd tormented me in my adolescence, especially during the long, cold Kansas winters. As an adult, I'd polished the art of running from the winter blues. Keeping busy with work and social life had helped, as had California's sunny and mild winters. Now, however, I had the time, space, solitude, and increased darkness of the northern latitude to dwell inside the soul, to observe the murky depth, the grieflike yearning for something intensely primal, that weighed heavily on me each winter.

Standing there on the Brighton beach, watching the ocean batter and get battered, it dawned on me that this dark, weepy feeling was natural, organic—something I should embrace, not shun. Life, I sensed, wasn't about always running from the turbulence, rain and gloom. In pausing to mull this over, the dark feelings caught up with me and suddenly I was sobbing, unearthing what felt like an endless supply of tears and emotions. The ocean was roaring so loudly, none of the equally foolish people out walking the beach one could hear me, so I howled (never really sure *why*), shuddered, and snuffled. Finally the tears subsided, leaving me still sad, but paradoxically, feeling better. *"It's O.K., honey,"* I could almost hear my mom say, the way she did when I was a kid. *"Go ahead and cry—it gets the cobwebs out."* I thought of the other sayings she used to throw out, like, "This too will pass" or "Into each life some rain must fall." They were always folksy, timeless, and true. The latter seemed particularly fitting this weekend.

And the rain did fall. And fall. There was no clearing of the clouds and triumphant burst of the sun's rays after my moment of enlightenment. Calmer, I trudged back in the wind and rain to the hotel for a cup of hot tea with my buckets and space heaters. The winds died, the storm abated, but it rained all night and the next day on my way back to London. In fact, it rained for the next seven days. And every evening, still alone in London, I'd curl up in a blanket in the dimly-lit living room and read soppy romance novels. I'd cry and cry before reading more, emitting little hiccups of grief. But it was all O.K., because something inside me now recognized the importance of this darkness my psyche seemed to crave. Accepting this, my sadness became lighter, almost soothing.

I told my sisters later about embracing the dark, about acknowledging and honoring the grief that creeps over me every winter. One told me that she'd pray for me, that it was such a sad, terrible state. Another suggested trying out the antidepressants she used and swore by. Only one understood that this downward pilgrimage of sorts was what we were all intended to do. She could appreciate how *right* it felt to stop fighting and simply settle into that soothing darkness, the soul's form of hibernating. And when the season passes, just like in Brighton, the sun comes out, the ocean sparkles, and life once again blooms and thrives. Such are the seasons.

An insatiable appetite for foreign adventures led Terez Rose first to Africa for two years, then to Europe, where she and her husband took fifty-six trips in twenty-two months. She now writes about her adventures from her sunny home in the Santa Cruz Mountains. Her stories have appeared in the San Jose Mercury-News, Milwaukee Journal-Sentinel, *Peace Corps Online, and in the anthology,* Women Who Eat: A New Generation on the Glory of Food. *She recently completed her first novel, set in Central Africa.*

✱ ✱ ✱

Living in Two Languages

…allows you to choose who you want to be.

WHEN I MARRIED PIERRE AND MOVED TO FRANCE, I slowly slipped into a French-speaking pattern—thinking, dreaming, and raising children in French. Only when the children grew up and left home, did I have the time and space to venture back to an English-speaking pattern.

We were living then in Switzerland. Geneva with its lake and mountains was to become our permanent home. It is a neutral country, for the world and also for us, neither France nor America.

It took a while to adjust anew to English, to make the edges fit and flatten the seams. Then one day I found myself American once again. I was thinking and dreaming in English. Pierre appreciates the variable metamorphosis, like having both wife and mistress. And I have the choice: Will I live the coming day in French or in English?

If I decide for French, I'll greet my husband with, "*Bonjour, mon cheri, as-tu bien dormi?*" There will follow an intimate exchange about whether we slept soundly or less soundly, if we were too hot or too cold, how many times we woke, if we feel rested and so forth.

I will dress in a dark skirt and lighter blouse, with a silk scarf perhaps. We'll go downstairs together. Our breakfast will be short and precise—coffee, bread, and butter. I'll question him about his day, he'll question me about mine, it will all be quite rational, one subject after another, well constructed, with an introduction, development, and a conclusion, like a dissertation.

My day will continue as such. In my head I'll make lists of things to do and I'll go about my morning, proceeding methodically, not losing time. I'll refrain from any fantasy in my housekeeping. And when I do my errands I'll avoid odds and ends of conversation with people I meet, especially with people I don't know and therefore never shall.

At the same time I'll be unfailingly polite, *"Bonjour Madame,"* *"Au revoir Monsieur,"* *"Vous êtes très aimable, Madame,"* *"Je vous remercie, Monsieur."* I'll use the same salutation and the same tone of voice, be it with my neighbor, an old acquaintance, the mailman, or the butcher.

Back home, in the afternoon, when working at my desk, I may loosen up and temporarily slide out of this strict French speaking pattern. But if the telephone rings, I'll sit up straight, pick up the receiver and reply, *"Allô?"* without the slightest encouragement to whomever is at the other end of the line.

In the evening, I will relate my day to Pierre and ask about his. During dinner—the table will be formally set, linen tablecloth and napkins, the serving dishes will be hot—we will talk seriously about something in the news, politics, a book or movie, about our grown children, our friends, the people we should invite.

If we are planning a large dinner party, Pierre will suggest that I send invitations rather than phone everyone, "It's less familiar," he'll say. And I will explain that I prefer to call. "It's more personal," I will reply. And I will try to not confuse the "*tu*" and the "*vous*." Still today, we have certain close friends whom we address with the formal "*vous*." As well as Pierre's parents, aunts, and uncles.

Now, however, if I decide to live my day in English, I will greet my French husband with something like, "Good morning, dear, time to get up," pulling off the covers to make sure he's heard me. I'll dress in a purple track suit and go squeeze some oranges which will perhaps awaken our appetites for eggs and bacon or pancakes.

I'll take my time, talking to Pierre about whatever comes into my mind. He'll try to get up from the table once or twice, but I'll ask him not to rush off, reminding him how much I used to love long breakfasts when we lived years ago in the States.

And when he's gone, I'll stay right there and reread yesterday's English newspaper, making myself a second or third cup of coffee, sometimes adding more hot water. Before doing my work, I'll maybe call and invite a friend for lunch. I'll spend more time than I should arranging a book on a shelf, a bouquet of flowers.

When I go shopping, I'll meet somebody I haven't seen for weeks and I'll stop and chat. By the time I get to the post office, there'll be long lines of people waiting. I'll smile and talk with the clerk who's been there for as long as I can remember. Finally I'll skip the shopping and serve whatever I have in the refrigerator. My friend won't mind, she's used to my improvised meals.

In the afternoon I'll work at my desk. When the phone rings, I'll lean back in my chair—or better, I'll take the phone and go lie down on my bed—and answer, "Hi, this is Susan." And I won't look at my watch.

If the weather's good, I'll go for a walk, down the road opposite our house, near the empty fields that remind me of where I grew up in New York. I'll find a stone and kick it along for company. I'll say hello to the people I meet, they'll look startled and most likely won't answer. I'll smile at the woman who walks her cocker spaniel, every afternoon. I'll even try to pet the dog.

In the evening, I'll tell Pierre about my friend who came for lunch, the people who telephoned, and I'll tell him about my walk and the woman who was walking her dog and wouldn't look at me. But the dog did, it wagged its tail. I'll laugh and make him laugh.

I'll serve supper in the kitchen, we'll carry our plates to the dining table. He'll tell me about his day and what he did in the morning and what he did in the afternoon. I'll interrupt him and ask him questions that won't have much to do with what he was saying. He'll try to follow and reply. Then I'll go telephone our guests for Saturday evening, and I won't give a hoot about "*tu*" and "*vous.*"

Bilingualism or split personality? Once the two patterns fit, the choice is mine. I wake up and write down my dreams in whatever language I dreamed them. I read the newspapers in both. I say either "*tu*" or "*vous,*" whichever one seems natural. And I make "I love you" sound just as beautiful as "*Je t'aime.*"

Susan Tiberghien has been living in two languages ever since she fell in love with a Frenchman. Author of two memoirs, Looking for Gold *and* Circling to the Center, *she has a recently released collection of essays,* Footsteps, A European Album. *She lives in Geneva where she directs the Geneva Writers Conference, gives workshops, and edits* Offshoots, Writing from Geneva.

LISA ANNE AUERBACH

✦ ✦ ✦

Pope on a Rope Tow

She's searching for the heart of Poland
on the trail of the pontiff.

I'M SNOOPING AROUND THE POPE'S OLD BEDROOM IN Kraków, Poland, checking out the gouges on his skis. I confess: I've been in a lot of bro-dorms, but none nearly as holy. Usually the décor consists of empty beer cans, a PlayStation, and smelly Capilene underwear. But in the tidy one-room pope pad—now part of the Archdiocesan Museum, located near Wawel Royal Cathedral, where Father Karol Wojtyla hung his skullcap from 1952 to 1958—there's a dainty café table, three chairs, a neat bunk with purple cushions, and an armoire filled with colorful priestly garb.

But right now I'm more interested in the two pairs of skis leaning in the corner. One's an old hickory set with spring bindings and pointy tips, the kind you see hanging over bars in ski towns. The others, retired more recently, are the 105-centimeter Head Pros with Tyrolia bindings. I can't help myself—I have to touch them. The undersides are grooved with deep cuts and scratches. The skis don't quite qualify as sacred relics, but they do serve notice that when he got away from it all, up in the mountains, Father Wojtyla wasn't just sticking to the corduroy and cruising green runs, like Gerald Ford at Beaver Creek. No—*he skied over rocks!* He was out there, off-piste. The man who became pope in 1978 might, in fact, have been a bad-ass. As I clutch the skis, the docent stares, then quietly reminds me not to take a photograph.

Pope John Paul II is widely known and revered by millions the world over as the spiritual guide and shepherd of the Roman Catholic Church. What is less well known is his history as a trailblazing two-planker. The Man in White ripped the Polish pow from the time the papacy was just a gleam in his eye until his mature years as the toast of the Vatican. In his younger days, JP2 was known as a megahiker, an avid kayaker, and a camper nonpareil. He preached in the woods, ate watery pudding for sustenance while surfing the backcountry, and re-peatedly lost his prayer book in the wild. When asked, "Is it befitting a cardinal to ski?" his reply was, "What is unbefitting a cardinal is to ski badly."

One day I heard a tale from a gentleman I met in my neighborhood in Los Angeles. A draftsman who emigrated to the United States during World War II, he insisted he'd once skied with the pontiff back when His Holiness was a seminary student. As evidence, he produced an out-of-focus photo he claimed was him and a grinning Karol Wojtyla. He pointed to a city park on a map of Kraków and mentioned something about reveling in the outdoors.

Not being a student of papal extracurricular activities, this beta came as a shock. Up to this point, my interest in Catholicism had been limited to the idle thoughts about sin and the Inquisition, but as a skier I was intrigued by the no-tion of a sportive pope. So I went to Poland on my own sec-ular quest, to see the holy trail.

★

It may come as a surprise to the bourgeois Western skier, raised on a diet of fresh powder in the Rockies or the Alps, but southern Poland is carpeted with mountains, chairlifts, and après-ski huts full of sausages and beer. There are four major ski areas and all have names that would garner triple-digit Scrabble scores: Szczyrk. Zakopane. Szklarska Poreba. The Bieszczady Mountains.

Zakopane (the easiest to pronounce: Zock-o-pah-nay) is situated in the Tatra Mountains, a gnarly spur of the Carpathians that crowds the border with Slovakia. Thanks to the mounds of fresh snow that pile up there every year, it is known as the winter sports capital of Poland and a former stomping ground of JP2. Accessible via a well-marked two-lane road, the town lies just a couple of hours south of Kraków, unless you're stuck behind a horse-drawn vehicle, in which case it takes much longer. Joining me on my journey is Witold Krassowski, a dry-witted photographer with a bushy mustache. Wirold's usual assignments take him to war zones. He can't understand why anyone would be interested in the pope's sporting past, but he's happy to play along, and as a translator he's invaluable.

As we creep along in our rented Renault, Witold reads aloud from *Paiez, Jakiego Nie Znamy* (roughly "The Pope in Nature"), a paperback we found among the kitschy glow-in-the-dark Jesuses and cards depicting Catholic saints in 3-D at the apartment in Wadowice (thirty miles southwest of Kraków) where the pope was born in 1920. Now, of course, it too is a museum. Young Karol was studious, serious, and re-ligious, but he also dug the outdoors, and it was in Wadowice that he first strapped hickory sticks to his feet and felt the wind whistle through his hair as he slid down farm hills, past chickens and cows. Later, the freedom of downhilling would take on immense spiritual importance. "In the mountains," says Witold, quoting the more mature, philosophical pope, "the ugly hubbub of the city disappears and the quiet of immeasurable distances prevails, which allows a person to more clearly hear the inner echo of the voice of God." Sounds like some hippie telemarketers I know. And yet, JP2 has tapped his ecological veins to add a little more green to a typically anthropocentric religion. He's gone so far as to declare the worldwide environmental crisis an urgent moral problem and has called on Catholics and all humans to show respect for "the hidden, yet perceivable requirements of the order and harmony which govern nature itself." Could it be that the foundations he laid for his own brand of peace-and-earth-loving Catholicism as pope are rooted in his powder-loving past?

Well, it seems totally obvious to me. After he was elected to Rome, enough skis arrived from well-wishers to outfit half the Vatican, but the pontiff resisted the call of the backcountry. "I pray to God to lead me from this temptation," he said in 1979 to an Italian mountain sports club that had presented him with a pair of custom white boards. "I might yet slide into a ravine, and then what?" (Though he did think to add, "God bless skiers and their legs." Amen.) Eight years later he proved he was a regular guy by caving in to that temptation. He donned dark glasses, jumped in an Alfa, and sneaked up to a resort in the Rhaetian Alps. It was the last time he was healthy enough to ski. (Since the early nineties, JP2 has had his gallbladder removed, a hip replaced, and has battled what the Vatican calls "symptoms" of Parkinson's disease.) Still, it certainly lends credence to the Papal Powder Linkage Theory.

Like a lot of post–Cold War Poland, Zakopane is a mélange of communist-era concrete hotels and shops mixed in with traditional wooden buildings. Since the fall of communism, the culture seems to have grown more jumbled in appearance, if not in demeanor. Enterprising locals set up tables in the streets to sell football-shaped lumps of smoked sheep's cheese, which tastes surprisingly like rubber. But the main drag is also packed with restaurants, and a loud Internet café adjacent to a skateboard boutique—two sure signs that capitalist tomfoolery is on the rise—is crammed with malcontent punk rockers playing on-line killing games and kibitzing in chat rooms. These kids, spiky-haired and fashion-conscious, are the closest thing to ski bums I see the whole time I'm in Poland.

From the center of town it's a short taxi ride to the burg of Kuznice, where you can catch the cable car to the summit of Kasprowy Wierch, the most popular lift-served peak in the country. Crammed inside the cable car on our first morning in Zakopane, the "inner echo of the voice of God" is drowned out by the complex garbled consonants of tightly sandwiched Poles.

In photos, the Tatra Mountains are breathtakingly beautiful; in person, they're gray and fog-bound, magically deep and hobbit-sultry. When we crack through the cloud layer and reach the ski station at the top, the sky is blue, and rocky, snowcapped peaks stretch in every direction.

We pile out of the cable car, 6,500 feet up. Skiers are everywhere, fashionably dressed in understated Eastern European style and carrying the latest equipment. Right out the doors of the station, a modern quad is dropping people off at the top of a gargantuan treeless bowl. The slope is wide open and the icy terrain is crammed with skiers of all levels, though there are no snowboarders in sight. Being a powder-obsessed American, I traverse as far as possible along the ridge, which also happens to be the Poland-Slovakia border. Shuffling past gun-toting, camo-clad guards, I reach the far edge of the bowl,

where last night's two centimeters of fresh hasn't been decimated. Then I shove off.

It's a tough crowd on Kaprowy; people take their skiing
very seriously. There's no whooping or heckling, even when
there's a total crashing yard sale. I've learned that wearing colors other than dark neutrals is a fashion faux pas, but I can't
help feeling that people are looking at me suspiciously. Witold
claims it's the scrap of pink lining on my navy blue Patagonia
jacket—the bright color makes me look freakish and foreign.
By the time I reach the bottom, my wave of paranoia has
passed. Strange vibes and muted slope excitement are just
something else to get used to in this reserved culture.

When Karol Wojtyla was the bishop, and later cardinal, of
Kraków, he was still a ripper, and he spent two weeks each
winter from 1962 to 1978 with the Sisters of St. Ursula Grey,
in their convent just down the road from Kasprowy. Witold,
who has had to deal with nuns a lot over the years, says they
are incorrigible gossips. Don't believe anything they say, he ad-
vises, but I believe it all anyhow.

The day after our trip up Kasprowy, we comb our hair and
knock on the convent door. We are greeted by two nuns, both
named Sister Theresa. Sister Theresa No. 1, pleasant and brisk,
introduces us to Sister Theresa No. 2, an older woman eager
to talk about the pope. ST2 takes us upstairs to view the pope's
old lodgings. It's less of a museum than the other museums,
but it's still set up exactly as he left it. The desk, chairs, and
table have that behind-the-Iron-Curtain institutional look, all
blond wood and modular. Standing here, I realize that at this
point, I've been in more bedrooms belonging to the pope
than to any other man.

In the corner is a black-and-white shot of the then-bishop,

skis on his shoulder, wool hat pulled down over his ears. He's
wearing a nylon jacket with a broken zipper. ST2 tells Witold
that the skiing bishop was a fashion disaster—his goggles were
outdated, his clothes mismatched. She tells him this confiden-
tially, in Polish, giggling, saying it's not to be translated. Witold
immediately translates for me, happy to prove his point about
nuns with wagging tongues.

ST2 is full of dope on the pope, most of which supports my
vision of him as a hard-core downhiller. He skied Kasprowy,
she says, but preferred the solitude of the Chocholowska
Valley, about ten miles to the west. He would drive into the
valley, park, climb a mountain, and carve his way to the bottom. "He was critical of skiing as a sport," ST2 opines. "And
he didn't think taking a cable car up a hill and then going
down was sport. The only way he'd go skiing was to carry skis
up the mountain and ski down."

Visible through the convent's windows are the slopes of
Nosal, a small Zakopane ski hill with poma lifts and a rope
tow. ST2 tells me that one night long ago, the bishop arrived
at the convent at midnight, couldn't resist the allure of fresh
powder, and took off for a run. But then, she adds, he would
rarely go into the mountains alone. When I asked why, ST2
explains that to be a prominent Catholic clergyman in a communist country in the midst of the Cold War was dangerous.
Police would dress up as sheep in nearby fields as he frolicked,
she says. It's hard to tell what she means—were the police
masquerading as sheep to spy on him or to protect him?—but
I love the idea of fuzzy *baaing* cops hunched in meadows
wearing heavy woolen costumes. Witold doesn't believe a
word of it.

As we're about to leave, I ask the sisters if they have a pair
of the pope's old boards around. No, all his skis are in the museum in Kraków, they say. "We have his boots, though," ST1

offers. She leaves and comes back with a well-worn pair of leather ski boots, laces up both the front and back. She handles these relics lovingly, setting them on a desk for us to admire. The pope, it turns out, has average-size feet.

In Poland, Pope John Paul II is everywhere—on plaques and posters, in sculptural simulacra, and as the namesake of the Szlak Papieski, a.k.a. the Papal Trail, a hiking and ski route that stretches for three miles in the spruce forests of the Chocholowska Valley. I expected the official Papal Trail to ascend dramatically heavenward, but no dice. In fact, it moseys for most of its length along a creek that meanders through the valley. Trees are marked with the colors of the Vatican, yellow and white, and the trail is dotted with small crosses adorned with tired-looking Jesuses, shivering in the Carpathian wind.

We leave the Renault behind at a Tatra National Park kiosk and jump into a horse-drawn sleigh, the traditional method of accessing the Papal Trail if you're not hiking or skiing. As we plod along, snow starts falling in clumps. Soon it's as misty and atmospheric as a Zeppelin box set. Visibility is so low we can't even make out 6,165-foot Mount Rakon, another of the pope's old haunts. After a mile, our carriage reaches the Papal Trail; we get out and start to walk. Hikers pass us going the other way, and some are on downhill skis, which seems odd, given that the trail is nearly flat. One man trudges by alone. I ask where he's coming from and he replies, sullenly, "From up to down." I brace myself for an uphill rally, but the trail peters out at a makeshift shrine of candles and crosses. It's a bit of a letdown.

The day after, I say good-bye to Witold and decide to follow the pope's footsteps on my own. This means going deeper into the Tatras, to a "refuge," or inn, that lies on the banks of a small alpine lake called Morskie Oko, "Eye of the Sea."

There are eight refuges in Tatra National Park, and they're open year-round. In summer they're often filled to capacity, but in winter the trans-Tatra trails get a lot of snow, leaving only the most hardy souls to trek in.

After an hour's drive east to the village of Lysa Polana, I park again and hoof the six-mile trail to Morskie Oko solo. The refuge looks a bit more rickety than I'd been led to expect. On my map there's a photo of a spiffier building perched beside emerald-green waters and surrounded by mountains, but today everything is uniformly white. I walk toward where I think the lake might be until I hear ice creaking beneath my feet. I'm on it.

I turn around and make my way back to the refuge. Downstairs, in a wood-paneled dining room, the proprietress brings out a photo album and shows me snapshots of a surprise visit the pope made in 1997. When she was a little girl, the future pope would visit Morskie Oko for one or two nights at a time during July and August, bringing youth groups to the mountains. She points to a picture of JP2 in '97, standing on the shore. He's wearing white robes and a matching windbreaker. "He remembered my parents," she says in halting English. "Nice man, very nice man."

After the sun sets, the bright white landscape turns to gray and then black. I'm served chicken and cabbage salad, which I eat alone in the dining room. There are three other people spending the night, but they are nowhere to be seen.

Outside, the "quiet of immeasurable distances" fills the crisp night air and the Tatras breathe with the solitude and wonderment that nourished the pope during campouts, ski trips, and kayaking adventures. It's my last night in Poland, so I take another walk atop the lake he's paddled across and delivered sermons beside. It's dark, but I can just make out a cross nailed up on a nearby tree—a reminder, I'm guessing, in case visitors become so distracted by the splendor that they forget about the nuts and bolts of the equation. I listen again for that inner echo of the voice of God, but hear only muffled voices, nothing more mystical than my three fellow refugees, out for a late-night smoke.

Lisa Anne Auerbach is an artist and writer living in Los Angeles, where she teaches at University of Southern California and Los Angeles City College. Although her words and images have appeared in legitimate publications such as Outside Magazine, Freeze, Skiing, Knitknit, *and others, most of her effort goes into the production of obscure, limited-run publications like* The Casual Observer, American Homebody, *and the* High Desert Test Sites *publication. Her current project,* Saddlesore, *chronicles bicycling in Los Angeles.*

ANDREA CARLISLE

* ✳ *

The Full Brontë

She went in search of Heathcliff, and others.

I AWOKE, MY NOSE PRESSED INTO A HEART-SHAPED ROSE sachet, and groped across the bedside table for the remote control. A hobbity man wearing green boots appeared on the television screen across the room. He addressed a couple seated next to the corpse of an aged collie curled up in a box, and described the process of the collie's internment, from tender combing to cremation. The middle-aged, intelligent-looking couple, dressed in good but well-worn clothing, looked as if they might go on to tea with Virginia and Leonard Woolf later in the day, sorrow permitting. Through a window behind them, viewers could see the crematorium owner's two dogs peeing on the stubby headstones in the pet cemetery. "Oh my God," I realized, yawning. "I'm in England."

The trip to Yorkshire took twenty hours. When the B&B owner saw me creeping slug-like up her front steps in mid-afternoon, a roller-wheeled suitcase flopping behind me, she'd put me to bed, swept the curtains shut and…well, that's all I remember about my arrival in what the brochures called Brontë Country, a place I had longed to visit since my first reading of *Wuthering Heights* at thirteen.

Awake, I ventured outside. The locals were closing up shops and heading home for dinner. Or, I thought jovially, *suppertime* here in Brontë Country. Puffing up Haworth's steep main street against a stiff wind, suddenly hungry, I felt like the aging, tired English major I was, back aching from an uncomfortable plane seat and a year in a cubicle inside a gray building. Editing computer manuals had made me starved for real literature. But now, thanks to that income, I found myself in Charlotte, Emily, and Anne Brontë's hometown.

When I entered an empty café, my young waitress nodded at the darkening window. "T'weather gets war un war," she said. "And nobbut round tuh neeght but you. Wenting sup?"

While arranging vacation time, ordering tickets, and packing, I'd overlooked revisiting *Wuthering Heights* to take notes on the old servant Joseph's vocabulary. I may have set out for Brontë Country but had arrived in *Joseph* Country. I needed a Berlitz course in Yorkshire.

In my first reading of the book, I'd puzzled over Joseph's speeches: "Here's a rahm," he (Joseph) said at last, flinging back a cranky board on hinges. "It's weel eneugh tuh ate a few porridge in…" I'd sorted it out then, but in the Haworth café I was back at the beginning.

"I'm sorry?" I asked idiotically. Old Joseph's descendant stared, then dropped a menu near my plate. "Take yer time."

After eating an almost frozen lasagna supper, I over-tipped and rushed into the gusty twilight. At the top of the hill stood the Brontë parsonage, closed and dark. A graveyard crept ominously close to it. How many coffins—especially of children like themselves in those high mortality days—had Charlotte,

Emily, and Anne watched being deposited into this bleak resting place? Nearby, tavern lights beckoned. I gladly turned toward them.

The Black Bull, a welcoming pub, still contains Branwell Brontë's favorite chair. Steep-backed, with widespread arms and a peculiar wooden seat—the point of a square where your legs would want to go—it hardly invites you to sit and relax. To become an alcoholic with that chair as your hoisting place, you'd have to be determined. Brontë biographers had agreed: Branwell, the only brother, possessed the required devotion.

While nursing a hot rum drink, I brooded about writing as I often do, but so near the Brontë parsonage and within spitting distance of Branwell's chair, this was passionate brooding. The sisters had depended on Branwell, who was supposed to become an artist or writer or, dammit, *something* to keep the wolf from the door. He'd failed them (and himself). They became writers out of need, managing to be geniuses besides.

The menu, posted at the end of the bar, made me smile. "The Full Brontë" included both steak *and* scampi, potatoes and assorted vegetables. Too bad I'd already eaten, but I'd save this meal to share with my friend Annie, a fellow writer, who was to join me in Haworth in a week.

It turns out there is little to do *but* eat in Brontë country. After you've visited Patrick Brontë's church and the museum several times (the docent finally offered with stern practicality, "It'd be cheaper for you to become a member, dear"), there's nothing left but the shops, which are pretty much all Brontë all the time. The faces of Charlotte, Emily, and Anne adorn everything from bath salts to scented soaps to place mats.

Discouraged, you sit in tea shops with friendly cats and try to imagine your own face emblazoned on a place mat. Who would be dropping muffin crumbs onto your forehead, occasionally wiping you off with a gray dishrag, and finally setting you out on the curb in a garage sale FREE box five years from now? Increasingly depressed as day follows day, you find yourself avoiding frozen lasagna in favor of puddings, scones, tarts, gingerbread, soda bread, truffles, fairy cakes and lemon cakes, and don't forget crumpets. Plus jam, jam, jam, butter, butter, butter, and clotted cream and Devon cream and buckets of plain cream dumped into gallons of tea. Soon you are waddling up and down the steep street like an aging, disillusioned, and quite *hefty* English major, pondering how the Brontës managed to live here, yet fit into those teensy dresses displayed in the museum.

After I viewed their shoes, gloves, bonnets, and dogs' collars, Charlotte, Emily, and Anne were now real people to me. I wished I'd let them remain in books. When had the purveyor of the bath salts last read *Jane Eyre*? Should I feel put out with her because she'd probably never read it, or try to understand, like a good American capitalist pawn currently paying her own way by placing commas correctly in computer manuals, that people who are not geniuses need to make a living, too?

Now would have been a good time to leave Haworth and travel around Yorkshire but, stuffed and lethargic, I didn't really *want* to go anywhere. A few locals asked if I were writing a Brontë biography, explaining no one ever stuck around for more than a day. When I said no, they seemed to accept me as a kind of non-threatening Brontë lunatic. In my favorite teashop, my favorite cat and I watched parades of tourists come to absorb some literary color. Most didn't even hang around for a snack though, if asked, I could have served as their cake and crumpet guide.

Annie finally arrived. We toured Haworth. I pointed out the cemetery, the church, the museum, the museum shop, the pony who lived next door, the apple tree the pony liked to eat from, the moors, and the sheep on the moors. I taught Annie that here in Brontë country, Keighley (a neighboring town) was correctly pronounced "Keethly," and she congratulated me on learning the local dialect in such short order.

One night we stopped in at the Black Bull and Annie smiled, as I had, at the "Full Brontë," but I couldn't stand to read the description of the meal again. By that time, I *was* the full Brontë. "You can order it," I said, eyeing Branwell's intolerable chair. "I'll just have a glass of water."

Andrea Carlisle's short stories, poems, and essays have appeared in Northwest Review, Calyx, Chicago Tribune, Texas Observer, Willow Springs, Seattle Weekly, Mountain Living, Funny Times, *and other publications. She is a recipient of the Oregon Arts Commission Individual Artist's Fellowship (for fiction), a fellowship from the Oregon Institute of Literary Arts (for nonfiction), and she was cited as an "outstanding writer" by the Pushcart Awards. An occasional commentator for National Public Radio and Oregon Public Radio, she lives in Portland, Oregon.*

ETHEL F. MUSSEN

⁺

The Repairman

It's all in a day's work.

A FURIOUS KNOCKING ON THE DOOR INTERRUPTED MY breakfast. Mme. Bondil usually tapped politely and called my name, so this must herald an emergency. I was not prepared for the muscular little man I saw when I opened the door. He crossed the stoop into the entryway and glanced up at the furniture in the living-dining room where I was eating. He introduced himself quickly in a rapid French dialect. I hesitated a moment, trying to translate and determine who he was. He continued talking and I caught only something about his coming for the chairs as he swept upstairs past me to examine them.

One of the four bentwood chairs had a mended leg at the seat, and the black paint had chipped away. "Yes, I'll take care of that and have it back this evening," he declared. That much was clear. He was husky, dressed neatly in work clothes, and fingered each chair expertly, checking for weak spots. I had never seen him before, but assumed he was a handyman around the ateliers. After all, I had been away for some years and couldn't know everyone who worked in the village.

"Did the Bondils send you?" I asked, as he hoisted the chair on his shoulder and went down the short stairway. He nodded and muttered. I heard "*ce soir*" as I closed the door after him. I assumed my friends were maintaining the apartment equipment and furniture since they often rented it now. Puzzled only that they hadn't warned me, I returned to my croissant and coffee.

Once I'd tidied up the tiny kitchen, I leaned out the window of the studio to breathe in the valley morning air and see if anyone was out yet on the main avenue of the village. One man hurried by carrying a baguette, his small son skipping alongside. The white-haired neighbor to my left swept her courtyard under the watchful eyes of the calico cat. The salesgirl at Lallier's shop had dusted the display table and was putting out an array of pitchers, bowls, and small plates. I could not see if Françoise had yet opened the Bondil shop Number One since it was recessed a bit and directly below me. Pigeons in the plane trees cooed a soprano chorus against the roar of the cascade, crashing and splashing in the ravine. As soon as the street sweeper appeared on his small green tractor, stirring up the dust and leaves at the curbing, I was assured that the normal life of Moustiers had begun.

The "studio" was my own special favor from the Bondils who urged me to visit Provence yearly and furnished me free housing when the space was available. It filled the two floors above one of their four shops, but the hilly terrain of the avenues was such that the store opened on the main street, the Avenue des Lerins, and the entry to the studio was on La Bourgade, the street above. A bedroom and bath below completed the apartment. Just large enough to provide me with space and facilities for living and writing, I set up housekeeping for however long I stayed and became serenely established in the life of the village. I became known again to the grocers, the baker, and the garage man. Mostly, I prided myself that although I missed some phrases and unfamiliar idioms, my French was fluent enough for my conversations with the potters in the ateliers (workshops) in the valley and the women who sold their *faience* in the village.

For twenty years I had been studying the history, art and commercial health of this small center of *faience*. Once these red cliffs had housed a *moustier* or monastery of monks from the Isle of Lerins surrounded by a stone village. Villagers and the farmers below scratched out meager crops in clay soil and pastured sheep and goats in the sandy scrub. In Provence, Moustiers was famous for its golden star, suspended across a ravine and hung there by a knight who was grateful for returning from the Crusades in 1283. In 1689, an enterprising potter and a knowledgeable Italian abbot took advantage of Louis XIV's royal confiscation of gold and silver tableware throughout France. The clay in the bed of the rushing Beauvoir was admirably suited to meet the sudden fashionable demand for fine earthenware. Like the abbot, designs and technique for manufacture had come from Faenza in Italy and the French wares were deferentially termed *faience*. Once artists joined the growing workshops, the fame of the *faience de Moustiers* spread rapidly and, for a century, the village prospered as one of the great "Five" producers. The competing popularity of porcelain in the mid-eighteenth century was then capped by the Revolution. The resulting turmoil led to the demise of both *faience* and Moustiers until after the two World Wars.

An upsurge in Provençal nationalism led to a revived recognition of Moustier's history and interest in the old craft, even as Vallauris and Biot in Provence were producing contemporary pottery and glass. As trained potters and decorators moved south in the postwar decades, some converged in the abandoned factories and ateliers to reestablish the old forms and designs according to the old expensive standards. By 1970, the community had grown and new European affluence had developed a luxury market for eighteenth century decors. It was this phenomenon I chanced upon in the early '80s and, as an American, did not fully understand. I wanted to chronicle its people, processes and products and educate my own countrymen even as I learned more about the present Moustiers, now dubbed Moustiers Ste. Marie.

Regular visits had made me known to most of the families, hoteliers, and restaurateurs. I liked to think that I melted into the pattern of the residents when I came, unlike the summer tourists and sportsmen who passed through. Although I was closest to the Bondil family, others made me welcome in their shops and ateliers and confided bits about their business, lives, and accomplishments. Like my friend, Bernadette, the *conservateur* or curator of the Museum, I maintained an interested neutrality. I did my best to learn and observe without being obtrusive.

When I left the studio this morning, like every other morning, I went uphill to Madame Bondil's specialty boutique of Provençal crafts to say "*Bonjour*" and pay my respects. She was unwrapping some new Occitane scents for the shelves and invited me to sniff. I approved and then duly reported, "The man came by for the chair this morning." She glanced at me a moment, then nodded and returned to her chores. I assumed she knew of the transaction.

My appointment that day was with Marcel Beaudey at his atelier. On this trip I was trying to document production and decoration at each of the workshops and make sure that I had good clear photographs of the faiencier himself. The Provençal preference for privacy and secrecy forbade photographs in the shops, and only a few of the sixteen ateliers permitted visitors. Since everyone knew that I was writing about the village, they accorded me unusual privileges but I usually had only one photo opportunity. My portfolio of pictures taken over the years had several omissions or fuzzy details, since I'd always had to wait for developing. My new digital camera was more forgiving of the contrasts in the light and dark spaces than my previous instruments and enabled me to reshoot any image that was incomplete or unflattering.

Marcel was a cordial contrast to his stern mother-in-law who governed his shops and marketing. Twice he had arranged special visits for me, once to the man who mixed the clay used by all the potters and later to a computer technician in the next town when my camera had a problem. Not intimate, but always friendly, today he demonstrated all his techniques of rolling, pressing and molding, showed me his latest projects and designs, and introduced me to his wife who was decorating a bowl. The German shepherd dog that had so vigorously announced my arrival at the gate escorted me amiably up the driveway and I left with the pleasure of having done a good day's work among friends.

The rest of the day I wandered through town taking pictures of tourists, funky art installations, radiant clumps of flowers, the broad landscape, and the trademark golden star, gleaming above the ravine near the chapel. Late in the afternoon, I returned to the studio to write my notes and to download a particularly satisfying array of pictures—a comprehensive portrait of village and valley.

I happily reviewed the images, editing those I would record on CD, when a pounding at the door reminded me that the chair was to be delivered. I opened the door to the same swarthy man who thrust the chair before him and carried it upstairs, placed it at the table and stood back. "*Voyez, comme nouveau!*" He turned the chair to show off his expert mending, "like new," and how he'd sanded and painted the scarred areas. I nodded and murmured my admiration of his work. As we spoke, a woman and small girl came in behind him and filled the room. Both were blonde, thin, and birdlike, and stood timidly near the top of the stairs. "*Ma femme,*" he said, gesturing to his wife.

"*Bonsoir,*" I greeted her, and smiled at the solemn child. I remembered I had downloaded pictures of people carrying dogs. "*Venez*. Come look," and I escorted the daughter to the computer and ran though a small slide show. She smiled wanly, then moved back to her mother's side. I thanked them for bringing back the chair so promptly and again noted the good work. I commented that Monsieur Bondil would be satisfied for I knew Jean-Pierre was a particular taskmaster. In fact, I was surprised that he hadn't done this small job himself, since he did so many construction jobs with his own hands. Perhaps, since his recent illness, he delegated more. With finality, I smiled and started to lead the child downstairs.

The parents didn't follow. The workman stood beside the table, his arms folded, his feet firmly planted. His wife remained behind him and gestured to her daughter to come to her side. The girl turned back and clutched her mother's dress. I searched their faces and saw only implacability on his, wideeyed timidity on hers. "*Soixante-quinze euros!*"

Seventy-five euros! I was aghast. I could not believe the Bondils would spend so much on a chore that M. Bondil could have done himself. He held out his hand, obviously expecting me to pay him. I protested, for I was sure that the Bondils would have insisted on a more reasonable price and would not reimburse such extravagance. "*Non, non! Demandez a Madame Bondil!*" My voice rose in desperation, but he did not move.

"I don't know anything about Bondil; you are here," he growled.

"But this is not my house, I am only a guest." Ever shriller, I mentally counted my supply of euros, fearful that if I didn't have enough, the whole family would sit on my couch until I secured more at the ATM. Or worse. He seemed so fierce. "Madame Bondil is the owner! You must ask her."

"I don't know Mme. Bondil. You answered the door." He frowned at me. "You ask her. Seventy-five euros!" And he held out his hand.

Reluctantly, I gave him seventy-five of my eighty euros and stared with mixed feelings of relief and fury at the family's departing backs as they marched down the stairs and into the street. I replayed that morning in my head and recalled only that there were some words I hadn't understood. Had he really explained that he was sent by the Bondils or had I assumed it? Who else would come and demand a chair to be mended unless he knew it existed? Had I been conned because my language wasn't adequate?

I turned back to recording the pictures on the CD, but suddenly the sunny pictures looked garish, the workshop pictures seemed pedestrian, and the valley views like vague postcards of any Mediterranean landscape. Even the little dogs hoisted by stout European matrons looked neither charming nor amusing. I felt ashamed, gullible, and that worst of French sins, imprudent. I tried to console myself with clichés, "Chalk it up to experience, it's only money, you'd pay that for a night's lodging at Le Relais, consider it an expensive lesson and move on." I was miserable. I would never tell the Bondils, for they must not know how foolish I had been.

It was time for dinner, but I had no energy for cooking and little appetite. I walked down the street to Le Relais to see if the chef had a light menu that night. Martine, the owner, was busy serving the first dinner guests but I confided that I wasn't hungry. One salad and glass of wine later, after being tended by Martine and the smiling summer waiters, I'd regained some composure. I lingered over my coffee until the dining room was full, then rose to free the table. Martine's husband, Pierre, the person I'd known longest in the village, was at the register.

"Tonight I must pay by credit card, Pierre," I confessed. "A terrible thing happened to me today and I don't have enough euros."

He was concerned and I was compelled to share my misfortune with someone, so I related the whole tale. "I don't want the Bondils to know," I ended. "I don't know where the man came from, or why."

"*Un gitane!*" he declared, shaking his head in amused sympathy. "They come through looking for work." My memory suddenly switched to stories I'd read in my childhood where gypsy tinkers, searching for fix-it jobs, appeared in tales of country life. Of course! He had probably asked if I had work, and seeing my hesitation took it upon himself to find it. Though I was somewhat mollified, I still wanted my gullibility to be secret. "Don't tell anyone," I pleaded again.

The next morning, I heard Reine Bondil's familiar knock at the door. As usual, she called my name before I answered, and as I opened the door, she immediately warned me that I must ask who was there and keep the door locked when I was inside.

"Did Pierre tell you what happened?"

"But of course! We must know about these people coming through the village. The shopkeepers must look out. Tomorrow is market day and we must all be alert!" In my own shame, I had forgotten that the village had to be protected

from light-fingered strangers. Pierre had not so much be-
trayed a confidence as broadcast a warning. That day the gen-
darme patrolled with a sharper eye but still missed the
blonde, birdlike woman as she stole a girl's dress from one of
the outdoor clothing racks. Eventually caught and identified
by the owner, she claimed to be from another village over the
hill beyond our valley. She and the child were alone at the
time, but everyone assumed she was the same woman I'd met
with the repairman.

Jean-Pierre Bondil came to inspect the chair. "Well enough
done," he snorted, "but it wasn't the only one that needed
painting. They're all scratched. And how much did he
charge?" He shook his head in dismay when I told him.

Bernadette clucked sympathetically when I saw her later at
the Museum and asked me to tell the story again. Pierre
laughed and waved from the bar when I walked by the hotel.
"Any *gitanes* today?" he called. By the next day, every villager
nodded knowingly when I passed—Madame the Sucker. It
took a week before no one mentioned my gypsy anymore, yet
the mayor continued to touch his hat, even though we had
met only once previously. At last, I sank back into the normal
pattern of village greetings and exchanges.

My last morning, the Bondils came to the door to make
sure I left early enough to reach the Nice airport in time.
Reine checked the studio with me and turned off the propane
for the stove. Jean-Pierre helped pack the trunk so my baggage
wouldn't slip. Some cars were blocking the road out and he
directed me through the narrow spaces. Just before I turned
up the steep exit from the village, he leaned through the open
window and thrust a wad of folded euros in my left hand.
"Stay away from *gitanes*," he admonished and smiled, waving
me on. Of course, there were seventy-five.

Ethel F. Mussen is a peripatetic octogenarian and retired health care professional whose years of international travel have resulted in a collection of typical arts and crafts, especially ceramics. Over the last twenty years she has been documenting the fortunes, misfortunes, and history of the people and art of Moustiers Ste. Marie in Provence. A brief description appeared in Travelers' Tales Provence, *and her adventures and misadventures in other countries have appeared in other anthologies. She lives in Berkeley, California.*

⋆ ⋆ ⋆

After Midnight

Comfort goes both ways
across the Atlantic.

IT WAS JUST AFTER MIDNIGHT. KANDY AND I HAD TAKEN the last train of the evening and the Metro babushka locked the station's carved wooden doors behind us. We'd been out celebrating the end of our first month in Moscow, and it was the latest we'd ever returned. Two things we failed to take into consideration: the darkness and the cold. Shivering spastically, we wondered how to get home to our dormitory.

We usually walked along the kiosks that stretched two city blocks, but they had closed for the night and turned off their lights. The drunks and ice patches that lurked along that path were hard enough to avoid in daylight: how could we navigate them in total blackness? The other option was to walk along the street, but that would add at least five minutes to the journey—and my teeth were already chattering so violently, I had to roll up my tongue so it wouldn't get bitten.

While we could condemn the city's dearth of street lamps for the darkness, we could only blame vanity for our skimpy attire. Having spent our entire lives in tank tops and sandals down in Texas, the frumpy layers of long johns, undershirts, overshirts, sweaters, scarves, mittens, boots, hats, fleece, and Gore-Tex we now had to don before so much as opening a window had become a serious affront to our femininity. Reasoning that our dorm and the Taganka Theatre were so close to linking Metros, we'd only be exposed to winter's elements "ten minutes max," we seized that evening's performance of Mikhail Bulgakov's *Master i Margarita* as an opportunity to reassert our womanhood, stripping off the thermals and sliding on the hose. But that miniskirt and navy peacoat I'd so happily put on a few hours ago now felt as insulated as cheesecloth, while a swarm of hornets seemed to be sucking on my toes straight through my cute leather shoes.

Erring on the side of safety, Kandy and I shuffled through the snow toward the street, where the occasional passing car cast a wan light through the icy sleet. It couldn't have been more than 10 degrees and the temperature seemed to drop every minute. I was so focused on retaining body heat, I didn't even notice the tinny gray Lada trailing behind us until it pulled right up beside me. The window rolled down and a man poked his head out. "*De-vu-shka,*" he called out.

That was the name I'd acquired in Russia. It means "young, presumably unmarried woman" and is actually quite handy. Rather than saying, "Excuse me!" and hoping the right person in a crowd turns around, it is perfectly polite to be specific in Russian, as in *"Dedushka!"* (Hey you, old man) or *"Devochka!"* (Yo, little girl, I'm talking to you).

In this context, however, *devushka* sounded sinister.

"It's too cold to be out on the street, *devushka,*" the man slurred. "Come inside, where it's nice and warm."

"*Ne nada,*" I said brusquely. That was the second mistake of the evening: he could tell by my accent and word choice that I wasn't Russian.

"*Amerikanskie devushki!*" he exclaimed triumphantly. American girls! Laughter erupted from inside the car as more windows rolled down. There were four men altogether. I could smell the vodka on their breath.

Fuck.

Kandy and I quickened our pace, but the Lada followed so closely behind, its heat singed the backs of our legs. We soon reached a video store that had also closed for the night. A thigh-high snowbank loomed behind it.

"Let's lose them in there," I whispered to Kandy.

"Go for it."

On the count of three, we darted behind the store and promptly sunk into the snowbank, which soaked our hose and filled our shoes with slush. The Lada, however, sped on down the street as we tromped through the snow toward the kiosks. The dorm was still a block away, with only the glimmering steeples of the distant Church of St. Nicholas of the Weavers to guide us. Back on the icy kiosk trail, we hurried in silence. My worries shifted from the men back to the cold. What happened to my feminist virtues? I resolved never to compromise body heat for fashion again.

Suddenly, two bright lights pierced through the darkness. It was the same Lada as before, only now it was in front of us, and rapidly approaching. "*A-mer-i-kan-skie devushki!*" they called out.

We were so astonished, we could only stand and gape— until a hunchbacked man staggered into the Lada's light. He was one of those kiosk bums we'd been trying to avoid, but it simultaneously occurred to us that we might be safer with him, if only because he was male and we were not. We darted over to either side of him, grabbed an arm, and held on tight.

"Could you walk us back to the dorm?" Kandy asked in as conversational a tone as possible.

"*Kuda?*" he inquired, spraying us with toxic spittle.

Using the drunk as a shield, we approached the car blocking our way home. When we got within a few feet of it, the
doors opened and all four men climbed out. The car's inner
light spilled onto the snow as the stench of vodka, leather, and
cigarette smoke thickened the air. I watched in disbelief as the
driver's shoes sauntered toward me. My eyes ran up from his
socks to his jeans, his black leather coat, his jutting chin, and
finally his glassy eyes, peering hard at me. When invited, the
stare of a man feels so warm and wet. It turns your insides out,
quickening your breath, swelling your breasts, parting your
thighs. But a predatory stare feels cold and dry. Muscles lock,
hairs stand, lips dissolve, thighs press tightly together.

"*Amerikanskaya devushka,*" he said, then reached out for me.

"Leave us alone!" I hollered in English, backing up.

Kandy and I exchanged a final glance. We'd seen enough
movies to know that women in these situations had only one
recourse.

RUN!

*Down the dark alley, across the glittering snow, in little black heels
designed to make me feel like a woman. (They were doing their job
tonight). Don't slip, don't fall, don't look back, never look back. You're
already going to be haunted by their sound, their smell, their pursuit,
your fear. Don't add the sight of them chasing you, too. Focus on those
steeples of St. Nicholas, gleaming golden in the distance. SCREAM!
(How do you call for help in Russian? They didn't teach us that!)
Remember that ice patch that has wiped you out so many times before. JUMP! Feel the solid concrete beneath your feet. You're almost
there. The security guards! They're probably drinking on the couch in
front of the TV. They need to open the locks before you get there.
SCREAM!*

As I rounded the final corner, two guards miraculously appeared. I slid right into them. "Men—in the street!" I cried.

Understanding immediately, they took off running.

Kandy. WHERE'S KANDY? I screamed out her name, panic riddling my body. And then she, too, appeared—silky blouse soaked, hair tangled, mascara everywhere. We exchanged wide-eyed looks before she beelined through the foyer and up the stairs. But I couldn't make it through the doorway just yet, electing instead to stand and shiver.

After some time, the *komandanka*—the dorm's superintendent—appeared, ostensibly to shut the door. She gasped at the sight of me. "*Idi syuda!*" she demanded, grabbing me by the arm and yanking me inside. "You're wearing a skirt? In this weather? Do you want to catch a cold? *Uzhasno!*"

My suitemates sat up with me in shifts that night, holding me as I contemplated the horrible fates we had narrowly escaped. Of course, drunk men chase women down dark alleys the world over. I just hated being reminded of the universal vulnerability of my sex so soon after my arrival to an exciting new place.

When the sun rose the following morning, I placed a collect call to my parents at a phone downstairs. Mom answered on the first ring. She immediately asked what was wrong, as I normally called during their Sunday mornings—not early Thursday evenings. I couldn't tell her the truth though: my parents already worried so much about me. Instead, I mumbled about homesickness and she promptly began to soothe me with peaceful, calming words. Then she passed the phone to my father, who continued where she left off before handing it to my sister, her husband, and a succession of *m'hijita*—crooning aunts and uncles. I was so caught up in my own life, I didn't even question the occasion that had brought them all together. I just assumed fate had gathered them to field my call, never fathoming they'd have their own traumas to tend to.

It was a Friday night, two weeks later, around seven. Not yet knowing the best places to shop, Kandy and I had spent hours tramping through the snow for dinner, only to return with pasta, onions, a kilo of walnuts, and some mealy red apples. Our suitemates, however, had found sour cream, raspberry jam, and a kilo of mutant mushrooms that the vendor swore hadn't been gathered in Chernobyl. Our mood lifted considerably when Katie popped some Irish tunes in our cassette recorder. She hacked away at the onions while Kandy buttered some bread and Karen and I improvised a walnut-butter-cream sauce. We had just set the table when David, the grad student our university shipped over to be our "group leader," came in with the mail he had retrieved from the embassy. Only soldiers huddled in foxholes could have been happier to see that bundle of letters. Kandy pried them away and launched them one by one across the room. "Katie, Karen, Stesha, Stesha, Karen—oy! *Moya!*"

Six letters, all for me. My hands quivered with excitement as I thrust my thumb under the first flap and unsheathed its precious contents. So much news from my housemates back in Austin! Jason's band lined up a new gig, Arthur was rebuilding a keyboard he found in a garage sale, Joy bought an iguana and named it Ayla, Michelle and Ari finally hooked up. For a moment, I was swinging my legs from our communal kitchen's countertop while Tyra filled me in on the past month's gossip.

Then Karen started sobbing.

"Sometimes I miss you so much, I just go and sit in your room and cry," she read her best friend's letter aloud as tears streamed down her face. The rest of us dutifully put down our mail and went over to console her. Then Katie started sniffling over her boyfriend's card. We walked over to rub her shoulders.

Kandy also received upsetting news and retreated to the hallway for a smoke.

Finally, I returned to my cot, where I'd saved the biggest and thickest letter from my parents for last. I paused for a moment, savoring the anticipation, before unfastening its metal clasp and spilling its contents onto my blanket. My eyes landed first on an image of the Virgin Mary in mourning. This was death's calling card for Catholics, but it couldn't have been anyone close to me: I'd just shared a pleasant conversation with my mother a few days before. Must have been some long-lost uncle or twice-removed aunt (I had lots of those). I flipped it over to read the fine gold print.

"In memory of Nicole Elizondo."

Nicole. Elizondo. Nikki? My cousin? My beautiful, twenty-three-year-old cousin? She can't be dead. I just saw her at Christmas. My whole family went to that barbecue place where she waits tables. She bought us cheesecake and ice cream. Called my parents Aunt Irene and Uncle Dick. She's not dead. She wants to be an airline stewardess.

What else is in this envelope? Newspaper clippings. Black-and-white mugshots of Nikki everywhere. Here's a letter. Folded twice. Written by my mother. So many words that make no sense. The sentences just dance together. But then the first one stands still: "It is with a sad, sad heart that I write you about Nicole..."

It was late. The manager of a nightclub offered her a ride home on his motorcycle. He was drunk. Had only one helmet, and he wore it. Rammed right into his own jeep. Nikki was thrown thirty feet. That shattered her spine, punctured her lungs, and incapacitated her brain, but her heart continued to beat a whole extra week while my family kept vigil by her side and I, back in Russia, conjugated verbs of motion.

That's why everyone had gathered at my house that night—so they could pray for Nikki. But instead, I'd made them comfort me.

Images. Thanksgiving at *tía's* house. Playing "Bloody Mary" in the shed while our fathers dealt poker chips and drank beer and our mothers basted turkeys and gossiped. Easter at the King Ranch. Nikki showing me where she'd hidden a whole crate of *cascarones* (painted eggs filled with confetti) for us to use once the tradition of cracking them over everyone's head began. Junior high. Nikki sticking up for me, the nerdy little cousin relegated to the sidelines.

Of my several dozen cousins, I had always related to Nikki best—probably because she, like me, spoke little Spanish and was blue-eyed and fair-skinned in a dark-eyed, caramel-skinned, r-rolling family. But while my racial loyalties used to fluctuate with my company, Nikki always claimed a Mexican heritage.

"You don't look Mexican," people would tell her.

"Well I am!" she would say.

I admired her for that. I wouldn't take that sort of pride in my culture until college, where it was more acceptable—even cool—to be Chicana.

Suddenly I was screaming and then I was crying as arms wrapped around my body and squeezed me tight. More hushed words, more sweet soothing.

A long time later, the four of us stumbled back to the table. Our pot of cold stroganoff and loaf of buttered bread were now coated with flies.

"What have we done to ourselves?" Kandy gloomily asked.

"Well," Katie surmised, "the countries with beaches were just too expensive."

We looked at her and then each other before breaking

down once more, this time in laughter. After picking at the mushrooms, I retreated downstairs to call my parents.

"I got the letter," I said when they picked up.

"Oh, hon," my mother said, heavy with grief. "We were afraid you would have wanted to come back home, and there was nothing you could have done. It's better you're there in Russia. We know we should have told you when it happened, honey, but we just couldn't bear to....."

When I packed my bags for Moscow, I somehow thought I was simultaneously wrapping twenty-one years of personal relationships into a box, tying it neatly with a ribbon, and setting it off to the side so that nothing would change in my absence. I didn't fathom that Nikki would die, or that one of my best friends would sink into a manic depression, or that my mother's hair would further gray. I didn't consider what it might feel like to know my sister was giving birth to her first child and I wasn't there to greet him.

That's because true travel, the kind with no predetermined end, is one of the most selfish endeavors we can undertake— an act in which we focus solely on our own fulfillment, with little regard for those we leave behind. After all, *we're* the ones venturing out into the big crazy world, filling up journals, growing like weeds. And we have the gall to think *they're* just sitting at home, soaking in security and stability.

It is only when we re-open these wrapped and ribboned boxes, upon our triumphant return home, that we discover nothing is like we had left it before.

Stephanie Elizondo Griest has belly danced with Cuban rumba queens, mingled with the Russian Mafiya, and edited the propaganda of the Chinese Communist Party. These adventures are the subject of her first book: Around the Bloc: My Life in Moscow, Beijing, and Havana. *She has also written for* The New York Times, Washington Post, Latina Magazine*, and* Traveler's Tales: Cuba, Turkey, China, Her Fork in the Road, Hyenas Laughed At Me and Now I Know Why, *and* The Best Travelers' Tales 2004. *She once drove 45,000 miles across the nation in a beat-up Honda, documenting alternative U.S. history for a web site for kids on a $15 daily budget. Visit her web site at www.aroundthebloc.com.*

JAN MORRIS

* * *

Vienna at Christmas

It's a magical place, and time.

CHRISTMAS AND VIENNA GO TOGETHER, DO THEY NOT?
Like waltzes and cream cake, like snow and steepled churches,
like Mozart and the baroque. We can all see in our minds' eyes
the city's gilded domes beneath a clear night sky, and hear the
strains of Austria's very own Christmas anthem, "*Stille Nacht,
Heilige Nacht,*" sung perhaps by the Vienna Boys Choir in the
chapel of the Hofburg, the old imperial palace, while
Lippizaner stallions steam the air with their breath and paw
the ground in splendid loyalty in their stables across the way.

But Vienna, one of the most compelling of all the capitals
of Europe, is far more than mere *gemütlichkeit*. It is a city of
antithesis: merry-neurotic, charming-surly, liberal-reactionary,
the disturbing questions of Freud beside the easy answers of
Johann Strauss, the homely memory of the Emperor Franz
Josef, Father of his People, next to the equivocal presence of
Kurt Waldheim.

It is the city that buried Mozart in a pauper's grave, and
drove Mahler in despair from its opera house. Beyond the

quaint rooftops of its old quarters lie the vast communal housing projects that have spawned, across the world, so many derivative miseries of tower block and tenement. It was Adolf Hitler himself who, remembering from his youth the grandiloquent Ringstrasse, Vienna's ceremonial highway, likened it ecstatically to a dream out of the Arabian Nights.

Christmas in Vienna, then? Perfectly proper: for after all Christmas is itself an ambivalent festival, by no means all *gemütlich*. It foreshadows in its happiness the tragedy of Christ, and it reminds us in its goodwill that the Christian message has not yet been fulfilled. We were right the first time: Vienna and Christmas go together—like life and death, like up and down.

In many ways, during the days before the festival, the city satisfies all one's fondest preconceptions. Vienna is likely to be white with snow then, but even if it isn't there blows through its streets the authentic Christmas cold of Wenceslas—a bitter bracing cold gusting out of Bohemia in the north or stealing in from the wide Danube plain that stretches away from the city limits to Hungary and the east. Vienna is the epitome of Central Europe, where Santa Claus was born, and its evening crowds of scarfed, top-coated and tight-buttoned citizens, sauntering with their children among the bright lights of the city, are truly Christmassy crowds, like crowds on Christmas cards.

This is partly because they appear to have come not just from many places, but from many times. During Christmas week there is an evening crafts fair in a narrow pedestrian street of the Seventh District—once a red-light area, now delicately restored to politesse. Scores of stalls are set up along the dimly lighted thoroughfare, selling anything from wooden toys to jewelry, rugs to mulled red wine, and there are rich Christmas smells and cheerful Christmas sounds upon the frosty air. The faces of the stall-holders, though, are still more seasonally suggestive. Some are high-boned and Slav, some fair and blue-eyed, some Turkish-looking, some Latinate. Lit from below by the lamps of their stalls they have a universal, timeless look, like figures in a Nativity painting—tinged, amid all that hubbub, as the faces in old paintings so often are, with wistful melancholy.

Or at least with reserve. Vienna is a profoundly introspective place. It is inhabited by people of many strains, many faces, but at Christmas especially it emits a potent sense of civic collusion. The festival brings out in its rather elderly populace all those Viennese tastes, values, and preferences long ago given the name of Biedermeier (after a nineteenth-century fictional character). They are expressed not only in decorous Biedermeier furniture and agreeable Biedermeier pictures, but in an unquestioning Biedermeier respect for order and tradition—knowing one's place, watching one's manners, doing one's duty to God, to Country, to Society, and to Family.

So a Viennese Christmas is still a homespun and domestic festivity. Mercifully rare in the shopping malls are canned carols and ho-ho-ing Santa Clauses. Even the decorations are restrained, and the pace of expenditure seems to an outside eye distinctly relaxed—free of the frenzied competitive buying, the goaded extravagance, that disfigures this holiday time in cities farther west. Vienna is an uncrowded city (its population is actually declining), and even in the last days before Christmas, so madcap and vulgar in London or New York, it remains its essentially dignified self. In the coffeehouses solitary elderly gentlemen are still bent, as always, hour after hour over their newspapers, while cheerful *fraus* in fur hats and galoshes tuck into the chocolate cakes. From the misted windows of the streetcars trundling round and round the

Ringstrasses, citizens look out with a calm complacency, as they do every day of the year, upon the parade of their beloved capital.

Of course there is no mistaking that Christmas is coming. For one thing the street musicians are out in force, attended always at a wary distance by solemn knots of citizens. A couple of Chinese students play "Silent Night" on trumpet and tuba, very slowly, as though they are sight-reading. An elderly woman in trousers plays Strauss vigorously on her accordion. Outside the great gate of the Hofburg a bemused young man with a barrel organ churns out a procession of familiar old melodies, simultaneously working with his left hand the arrangement of cords and levers that animates his mechanical monkey.

Christmas-tree sellers are all over the place, squeezing their trees through cylindrical packing-devices on the sidewalks. On the Ringstrasse the Burgtheater looms refulgent in the streetlights, and farther along the way, Pallas Athene stands triumphantly outside the classical Parliament building. The pinnacles of the Gothic Rathaus (City Hall) tower romantically against the night sky, and in the park in front of it the trees have been dressed up for Christmas. One is all aglow with golden hearts. Another is loaded with metallic stars and ladders, showing the way to Heaven. Professor Hutter, says a plaque, is responsible for the tree covered all over with red, blue, and yellow sprites, and toward the Ringstrasse a tree is alive with a cascade of electric bulbs, as though somebody were hosing it down with light.

There is, I think, a faint strain of recorded music somewhere, but it is almost drowned out by the traffic. Otherwise everything in this fairy forest is altogether suitable to the place and the moment. No louts have thrown rubbish about, or carved graffiti on the tree trunks. No raucous drumbeat sounds. The families who walk sedate and tight-bundled along the shadowy paths, explaining to the children the Herr Professor's symbolism, or pausing to look back admiringly at the silhouette of their civic headquarters, are like images from a Vienna album.

Yet it is impossible in Vienna, even at this moment of family dedication, to forget that it has been in its time an imperial capital, one of earth's seminal cities, whose writ ran across half of Europe. On one of its most consequential tombs, that of the Emperor Frederick III, the cryptic letters AEIOU are inscribed. They stand, it is thought, for AUSTRIAE EST IMPERARE OMNI UNIVERSO, "It is for Austria to Rule the Whole World." And the suggestion of tacit arrogance, tempered perhaps by historical resentment and expressed in a kind of family cipher, to my mind, hauntingly represents the deeper sensations of the city. An old, grand, regretful memory is instinct in Vienna, and even in these festive days, even to one strolling only with gifts of self-indulgence in mind, it constantly surfaces.

It might show itself in the ornate headquarters of Julius Meinl, once grocers and bankers to a continent, whose façade above the Fleischmarkt still flaunts the city crests of Paris and of Hamburg, or in the black tourist *fiacres* that clip-clop around the city center like hallucinatory relics of imperial times. It might be manifest in the sudden appearance of Waluliso, the city's best-known eccentric, who dresses in spotless white like a Roman, smiles graciously on one and all as he swaggers down the street, and carries with him in this now bourgeois town an air of aristocratic license, like some crazed archduke.

In the pretty little street called Schönlaterngasse, the Lane of the Beautiful Lantern, Enrico Panigl's Café claims to this day to have branches in Trieste and Marienbad, long lost outposts of the Habsburg dominion. In the Peterskirche visitors are offered pamphlets in Czech, Slovak, Croatian, Hungarian and Slovene (but not in English, French, or Spanish). Step inside Café Hawelka, and there the young intelligentsia of Vienna sits bleary-eyed and hung over in the morning, argumentative after dark, just as it did in the days when a spectacular stream of ideas, from atonalism to psychoanalysis, was springing from the minds of this citizenry.

And most tellingly of all, the open door of the Capuchin crypt will lead you almost against your will, almost mesmerically, directly out of the street into the cold vaults where 138 members of the Habsburg dynasty lie side by side in their sarcophagi: the tremendous Maria Theresa, mother of sixteen and mistress of her age; the unfortunate Maximilian, shot by a Mexican firing squad in 1867; and Franz Josef himself, gone to his reward after sixty-eight years upon the imperial throne. There they all lie, in the crypt of the Capuchin monks, attended still by the glory—or the vainglory—of old Vienna.

It is more than mere nostalgia. I sometimes think Vienna the most complete of all cities, the place where all the civilized appurtenances of urban life—theater and café, bookshop and nightclub, grand hotel and museum and opera house and cathedral—are most readily to hand. Though it is now the capital only of a minor republic, about 8 million souls in all, Vienna remains, somewhat incongruously, the Big Time. Leftover from its vastly more important past, when those monarchs in the crypt proclaimed themselves rulers of Dalmatia, Galicia, Tuscany, Transylvania, and Kings of Jerusalem, too—leftover from those heady days of the double-headed eagle—are the institutions of a great metropolis.

At many times Vienna's pretensions can be insufferable, so sycophantic of manner, so smug of attitude. But at Christmas, when people grow sentimental as a matter of habit, this anachronistic grandeur acquires a moving poignancy. All is subsumed in geniality, the gush seems more like kindness, the formality is diffused into diffident bonhomie. Actually I know of no great city where Christmas seems more properly honored, and "*Stille Nacht*" seems less cruelly anomalous.

Last Christmas I sang the carol myself, with a few thousand other people, in the nave of St. Stephen's Cathedral, the central church of Vienna, of Austria, of all that spectral empire of the past. The genius of the city seemed to surround me. The music of the choral Mass was by Mozart, and Schubert himself, I swear, in steel spectacles and student scarf, was singing in the choir. After the service I walked over to thank the conductor for the exquisite music, but he dismissed me with a perfunctory nod, as a tutor might dismiss an overfamiliar student.

For even at this joyful, generous season, when the fairy lights blaze in the Rathaus trees, and the mulled wine flows, one feels that in its heart of hearts Vienna does not welcome outsiders—or at least, does not greatly value their compliments. More than most cities, Vienna lives to its own standards, and as Christmas draws near one can sense it drawing in upon itself, preparing the family hearth and the family Christmas tree, lighting the parlor candles, barring the front door not only against strangers, or even against friends and neighbors, but actually, I am told, against insufficiently intimate relatives.

It is on Christmas Eve, not Christmas Day, that the Viennese have their celebratory dinner. It is then, Vienna being what it is, that the women withdraw from sight to prepare, if not the stuffed blue carp of tradition, at least the supermarket turkey or the yogurt-based soufflé. Banished from the house during the long preparatory afternoon, husbands and children promenade the cold zoo or wander in a desultory way through the Prater amusement park, whose great

slow wheel, that prime emblem of the city, has privacy to un-
wonted extremes by living all alone.

Last Christmas Eve I treated myself to my own old times:
dinner at Sacher's, that most homelike of Vienna's great hotels,
which I have known on and off since it stood as an oasis of reassurance (it was a British officers' club) in the battered Vienna
of 1946. There avuncular waiters kindly guided me through
an unexpected menu: salmon cake with roe, consommé, turbot with shrimp sauce, and a punch-soaked pear with ice
cream, accompanied by a delightful white wine from the
Wachau, the region just beyond the Vienna Woods, and served
with an immaculate gleam of silver and starched table linen.

But I did not feel to the manner born. For all the Sacher
charm, for all my own memories, that evening I felt superflu-
ous even there. I thought all the tables should be occupied by
high ministry functionaries, postimpressionist artists, professors
from the university, and perhaps the odd colonel of Hussars—
all eating, not turbot in shrimp sauce, but *Tafelspitz*, the boiled
beef with dumplings that Franz Josef himself preferred.

However, the stranger can become part of Christmas in
Vienna by going to the Staatsoper, which even has a performance on Christmas Day. Last year it was *La Traviata*, and I sat
in a front seat of a box, cheered when the audience cheered,
hissed once or twice when it didn't, and felt myself at last, if
only momentarily, an honorary Viennese.

We were not a very grand audience. We were not the
Diamond Horseshoe. We were nicely rather than spectacularly
dressed. We paid close attention to the music, we did not
cough or drop our programs or ask each other what was hap-
pening in the plot or make unthoughtful rustling noises with
chocolate boxes. To say that we were familiar with the per-
formers is an understatement. Half of us, it seemed to me,
were related to one singer or another, and the rest of us had

establish semifamilial connections with conductor, orchestra, soloists, and chorus alike. It was a very cozy evening. Violetta died without too many spasms, and throughout the opera the principal baritone carried his silver-knobbed walking stick with Viennese decorum, as if it were a staff or office.

The applause at the end, if not thunderous, was appropriate. The soloists took many curtain calls. The conductor elegantly bowed. But long before the clapping ended, I noticed with approval, the gentlemen of the orchestra (there were no ladies) had one and all crept out of the pit and vanished, leaving only their music stands behind. They had gone to catch the U-Bahn or the streetcar home—turning their backs on Verdi and the great world, going home to *Frau, Kinder,* the last of the Christmas cake and all the consolations of Biedermeier.

Jan Morris has been wandering the world and writing about her experiences for more than forty years. She is the author of numerous books and her essays on travel are among the classics of the genre. She lives in Wales, where she is helping to found a Welsh-language newspaper, Y Byd—The World.

$\star$ $\star$ $\star$

Walking in No Man's Land

Humanity is alive and well in a place
that saw unspeakable horrors.

"VERDUN?" I LOOK UP THE STEPS AT THE BUS DRIVER, intimidated. My French is not up to snuff.

"*Oui*," he waves me on with a jolly smile.

I climb the steps. The bus is nearly empty, a few women sit in the back. The driver gestures to the seat behind him and I sit.

He drives with his round body hunched over, his elbows resting on the steering wheel. Underneath his cap I catch a glimpse of thinning, gray hair. He maneuvers the bus smoothly through the narrow, busy causeways, leaving bustling Metz behind.

"*Woher kommen Sie?*" He turns his head, but keeps his eyes on the road.

German. Good. I am better at German than French. "*Ich komme aus den USA.*"

"Ah," he laughs, "I thought you German," he struggles with a thick accent.

"No, but my German is better than my French."

The driver shakes his head, not understanding so I repeat it in German, adding that *his* German is very precise.

"I went to German school." He turns back to the front, suddenly quiet.

Verdant hills speed by the picture windows. The sky is gray. I hope my trip to the battlefield will not be a wet one.

"Do you know Alsace-Lorraine?" the driver asks, without turning.

I did. Metz is part of the border provinces of Alsace-Lorraine, a territorial sore spot of nineteenth- and twentieth-century European history. Alsace-Lorraine was the knot in the middle of a tug-of-war rope between France and Germany, resulting in one of the most devastating battles in history, Verdun. Two times (1870-1918 and 1940-1944) the German Empire annexed the province only to lose it back to France at the end of World War I and World War II. But, both annexations lasted for a combined total of fifty years, leaving a distinct German mark on the French provinces.

"You visit Verdun?"

"*Oui, je visite Verdun aujourd'hui.*"

The driver nods grimly, satisfied. "You will see what Germans have done."

In a conversation, broken into bits of French, German and English, the driver proceeds to tell his story—the likes of which I may never encounter again.

"I live all my life in Metz." He was born French, but before he finished grade school he would be declared a German citizen, his town, a German burg.

Nazi Germany annexed Alsace-Lorraine in September of 1939. The new government declared High German to be the only permissible language. Children spoke German at school, used German textbooks, and learned Nazi propaganda and theory. The Nazis drafted 140,000 Frenchmen and forced them to fight for the Fatherland on the eastern front.

"*Malgre-nous*," the bus driver speaks quickly now. His words come, urgent, important. "My brother was sixteen. He fought Russians for Nazis. He never came back. *Malgre-nous*—against our will." He strikes his fist on the steering wheel and withdraws into silence.

I want to ask questions, but this is not the impersonal, cold search for information in a history book. It is a personal tragedy, with real feelings, memories and nightmares. What can I say? I say nothing, but keep my eyes on him. I will listen, if he will talk.

"My grandson studies to be a doctor. How old are you?" He glances in the rearview mirror at me, a slight smile on his face.

I laugh and point to my engagement ring.

"You know the battle Verdun is outside city? Ten kilometers."

I didn't, and find out when we arrive in the city of Verdun, that there is no public transportation out to the memorial. I meet the bus driver back at the station, unsure of what to do. I really want to see the memorial.

"I drop you off. You must walk back. Be back on road at three o'clock. I be there to pick you up." He looks at me sternly and shakes his finger. "Be on time! I can't wait."

I want to hug him, but don't. He drops me at the entrance of the park and points up the lonely road, "You walk. But be back here at three o'clock." He taps the three on his watch, to make sure that I understand.

I wave and begin up the road. It winds through a pine forest, black-laden branches shading the barren ground below. The road is quiet and long. I begin to wonder if I will reach somewhere, or if the road is a twilight zone. I notice the silence, only the shuffle of my feet along the gravel shoulder. No birds. No squirrels rustling in the dead needles below the trees. No whistling mortars. No wounded, moaning from their injuries. No hearts pounding in fear.

Ranks of rich brown pine trunks line both sides of the road, like old souls waiting, waiting. And then I see a darkened crevice in the shade below the old souls. It skirts about, in and around, as if ambivalent to show itself. A trench. An approaching car startles me out of my trance. It is mildly comforting, but I cannot shake the feeling of thousands of eyes watching me, mourning and lonely.

I've heard stories about Verdun. The air laden with the weight of the near-two-hundred- thousand lives lost in the ten month battle. The eyes. The utter sorrow blanketed to earth by heavy clouds, unable to accept, unable to move on. I didn't believe it. It was just some emotional sap's reaction to encountering the reality of history. And now here I was, growing more disturbed with each step at this unwelcome sixth sense. Is it true? Or am I becoming an emotional sap myself?

I finally round a bend to see the missile-like tower of the Verdun Memorial, L'Ossuaire, in the distance. I am almost five kilometers into my walk. I pick up my step, energized by the knowledge that there is an end to this road.

The trees fall back to reveal a barren waste. The ground swells and dips like ashen-green waves in a turbulent ocean. The pits in between the swells are filled with water. The derelict wall of a bunker gapes from underneath a mound of wild vine. It is unlike anything I have ever seen before. They are shell scars of the most brutal battle of World War I.

The memorial building sits aside, meticulously groomed with formal rows of what I think are arborvitae—the tree of life. A lush green carpet spreads before the memorial, *covered* with thousands of white crosses, each with its own bush of blazing red roses.

I enter the Memorial Hall. Orange stained-glass windows and glowing candles remind me of a cathedral. Engraved names of MIA's adorn the walls and ceiling. Their unidentified bones are entombed below. I see them. There is a row of windows at the rear of the memorial through which I can see. Skulls, femurs, ribs strewn in no order. I feel the sheer waste and disrespect of life then. I also feel like an intruder.

I walk down the cross-strewn lawn back to the road. I follow it towards Fort Douaumont. A trench runs right up to the road and continues on the other side. It marches back into the trees, not shy or proud. Just there. The hard-packed path winds around a rise out of view, at one time muddy, swampy, full of stench, the sleepless, the frightened, the dead. I feel the pull to jump down and follow it. And then a shudder quakes my entire body. No.

What once was a state-of-the-art fortress, protected by eight feet of concrete, three feet of dirt, retractable gun turrets, a moat and barbed wire now appears as a monstrous cave. Fort Douaumont is dark, cold, and damp. It *was* dark, cold, and damp for them, too. A huge underground cavern. A city. Stalactites stab like bayonets hung from the ceiling. Its corridors and rooms are empty but for the skeletons of machine guns, stoves, beds. The rusty brown color bleeds into everything. The bed frames grow into the ground. Earth to earth. It is hard to believe that anything but nature herself created this place.

I emerge, squinting in the cloudy light. I walk on top of the Fort. Green hills undulate all around. They are inviting, but guarded by a sign. "Terrain Interdit." Shells, thousands of them, unexploded, volatile, buried in mud. Forever barring visitors to this land. It is ironic, I think. We did it. We fought over the land. We killed thousands of men for the land. And now, we must let it be. The land itself is forbidden territory. For the French. For the Germans. For everyone.

I look at my watch. I have to walk back to make the bus. I walk a little faster this time, for I know there is another end to the road. Ten months of fighting. Almost one million casualties. Two-hundred thousand dead. German and French. For nothing. Neither France nor Germany made any strategic gain. I can feel the eyes, the sorrow of lost youth and sanity, the appalling tragedy, the weight of my heart. For all that, it isn't frightening. It is an unsettling feeling for a place such as this.

It is peace.

I emerge from the trees just in time to see the bus hurtling towards me. My friend stops and waves me on. It is starting to rain. The gray clouds have finally caught up with me.

The bus driver smiles, glances at me in the rear view mirror and says, "How long you be in Metz? I want you to meet my grandson."

Julie Crea lives in Colorado with her two sons. She has published numerous essays and recently completed a historical novel. She hasn't decided what she wants to be when she grows up yet, except that it must involve traveling, hiking, massages, and chocolate.

* * *

The Road to Balbriggan

Tracing roots leads to an unexpected conclusion.

BALBRIGGAN IS NOT A TOURIST DESTINATION. FORTY-five minutes from Dublin, it is possibly the only town in Ireland that does not have a quaint pub or a house with a thatched roof.

Instead of Aran sweaters and keychains made of old Guinness advertisements, its shops sell pork chops and discontinued shoe styles. It has a beach, but the only thing that appears to go near it is the train up from Dublin. We were the only people to get off that train at Balbriggan station. My father and his second wife, Ellie. My husband, Ken, and our two-year-old son, Alex. Me. American tourists with new sneakers and money belts that made our sweaters bulge out in odd places. We had come to Balbriggan in search of family.

At least those of us with Irish blood had. Ellie was German by way of Kentucky, Ken was a Jew whose ancestors had come from a small town near the Polish border, and Alex was a little Russian boy who'd spent the first fifteen months of his life in a Moscow orphanage.

My father looked over the concrete wall of the train station and took a deep breath of Balbriggan's foggy air, as if it might awaken some forgotten genetic memory. His mostly black hair was squashed down into the shape of the Irish tweed cap he'd bought almost as soon as he'd gotten off the plane. The same cap that was now on Alex's blond head, floating around his ears. Ellie was singing to Alex, a country and western song about a lonesome train, while Ken tried to open the stroller without damaging the print, slide, and video cameras he had slung around his neck like the bandoliers of a Mexican bandit. I, too, tried to wake a sleeping genetic memory with a deep breath of Balbriggan's damp air. It smelled mostly of car exhaust.

My father spoke to the stationmaster. "We're from the United States," he said, as if he thought the man might find the news surprising.

"Tony McCormick," the stationmaster said, reaching up to shake my father's hand. He was a small man with white hair and a blue uniform.

"My family came from this town," my father said, "name of Harford."

"And would you be knowing old Freddy Harford then?" stationmaster McCormick asked. "He'd be living just up the road next to the hairdresser's."

"Freddy, huh?" my father said. "We should invite him to the pub."

"You'll not be wanting to do that," the stationmaster told him. "Freddy's a pioneer."

"A pioneer?" my father asked.

"Have you not heard of the pioneers? They never take a drink."

"Freddy doesn't drink?" My father sounded as if the stationmaster had just told him that our new-found relation had been born with three legs. "Are you sure he's a Harford?"

"Oh, is it Harford you're saying? I thought it was Harper. Old Freddy Harper's the one lives next to the hairdresser's. I guess he wouldn't be a relation of yours then, would he?"

We decided to ask stationmaster McCormick for directions out to the old cemetery, where we'd been told we would find a family grave, and leave it at that. Like all Irish directions, they were as dense, as beautiful, as baffling as a page of *Ulysses*.

"What you'll be wanting is the road that bends and leads off the main road, past the video store where the wall is painted a yellow-gold like sun shining and sends you down past the old factory where there's been no work for a good long time now, to the butcher shop on the corner where the Benson and Hedges advert's been painted over the old kiln bricks," he told us. We set off walking, Ken pushing the videocamera in the stroller, Ellie looking in the windows of Balbriggan's stationery shops and newstands for an Irish sweater.

Up ahead, my father had taken Alex's hand, and it made me think of the things we'd done together when I was a child. How he would lie in my bed at night and tell me stories until he fell asleep, how he'd put on his plaid bathing trunks and join me in the bathtub, how one time we'd stayed up all night filming pictures of World War I battlefields with an eight millimeter camera for my history project.

The old cemetery was perched on a green hill off the main road to Dublin. An ancient church stood at the top, and the white headstones of the graves marched up in neat rows like a small army. My father and I walked through wet grass looking for a headstone with an inscription that matched the one his mother had recited from memory before she'd died. It was her grandparent's grave.

My father found it almost immediately.

It was a rectangular stone with a large Celtic cross on top, and the family history carved into it. Listed among those who had died in America, was Marianne, my father's grandmother.

My father ran his fingers over the carved letters on the headstone. "In a few more years," he said, "you won't be able to read it at all."

I found drawing paper and a green crayon in Alex's diaperbag. I put the paper over the rough stone and rubbed with the crayon. The words *Erected in loving memory* appeared.

As I rubbed, the words came letter by letter, the way they do on a Ouija board. I felt as if I were receiving a message from the grave.

When I reached the last line, it started to rain, and I gave the crayoned rubbing to my father, who rolled it up and tucked it under his jacket as if it were a rare and valuable parchment. Then we crossed the road to a modern pub that had a sign advertising conference rooms.

The pub was paneled and carpeted and had two color televisions tuned to the same soccer match. We sat in a corner booth and ate oxtail soup, while Alex walked behind us and made animal sounds into the backs of our necks.

"If it's living relations you're looking for," the bartender, a tall man with red hair and a pink face said, "you should be talking to Sean McNally the Undertaker. He knows everybody."

We took a taxi to McNally's Drapery Shop, an old-fashioned clothing store, with racks of men's sports coats with plastic covers over the shoulders.

"You'll be finding Sean at home," the man behind the counter told us. "Just go back up the road away from Dublin, past the Church of our Savior, and look for the tallest of three tall houses all in a row." His shirt still had creases where it had been folded in its package.

My father and I wanted to go off in search of the undertaker, but the last train back to Dublin was leaving in fifteen minutes, so we headed back to station.

"Did you have any luck?" stationmaster McCormick asked when we returned.

"Not really," my father told him.

"This might be of some help to you then." He was holding a small white piece of paper. "It's the phone number of Monica Harford. She reckons her husband Patrick might be a relation."

Two days later, the five of us returned to Balbriggan in a rented car to have lunch with Monica Harford at the Mile Stone pub.

The Mile Stone smelled like old cigarette smoke and gravy. There were dead flies caught between the screen and the window behind our table, and a small color television set tuned to the sheep dog trials above the bar.

Monica arrived in a flurry of face powder and conversation. "I'm expecting a fax from the Fingal Heritage Group," she said. "I've a friend over there looking up Harfords in their database. They'll send it round about three-thirty." She pronounced it *tree-turty*.

"Would you like a drink, Monica?" my father asked.

"Vodka and white lemonade," she said.

"Just white lemonade?" my father repeated, not having heard the rest.

"Now what good would that do me?" Monica told him.

Her hair was standing straight up on one side of her head, as if that was the side she slept on.

Between bites of the turkey and ham special, Monica told us about the Harfords who were still in Balbriggan.

"Of course, there's my Patrick, and Patrick's three brothers," she said. "And Christy Harford, the bomb maker, sure and he's dead now."

"The bomb maker?" my father said.

"Have you not heard of Christy Harford?" she asked. "Made up bombs for the IRA, he did. Made them right in his basement." A large drop of brown gravy fell onto the front of Monica's pink blouse. "The Gardai arrested him ten years ago. A pub owner in town paid his bail, and sure and if Christy didn't disappear right after."

"How did he die?" my father asked.

"One night, about five years after, men in *balaclavas* brought his body back to his house. He'd died of natural causes," she said. "Sure and there's still bombs today they call a Harford, after Christy."

The fax from the heritage society arrived, a document that traced the Harfords back to my great-great-grandmother's baptism in 1847. My father poured over it.

"It's grand what you Americans do," Monica said. "Tracing your ancestry. It's important to know who you belong to." She smoothed the curled pages of the fax flat on the table. "Not like some. A school teacher and his wife here adopted a baby girl from Romania. Now that child will never know who her real family is, will she?"

I looked over at Alex who was sitting at the bar with Ken and Ellie, watching a horse race on the small television. He was wearing a little Irish tweed cap my father had spent the morning searching Dublin's shops for.

My Irish father, his wife who wasn't my mother, my Jewish husband, my Russian son. The day before, we'd stood and listened to a soft-voiced Irish actor recite from Beckett, and I could sense them standing around me. It had made me feel the way you do when you discover that someone who loves you has been watching you sleep.

I folded my copy of the Harford database, and put it away. I could feel no real connection to the Richard Harford who

was married in 1870, or the Christy Harford who manufactured bombs in his basement. Real family was not found in
Heritage databases or carved on headstones. It was found in
the man heading to the bar to get Monica another vodka and
white lemonade, the woman explaining what that thing on
the jockey's head was to Alex, the little boy dropping a plastic
hippopotamus into a glass of Guinness.

When lunch was over, we stood in front of the Mile Stone
and Ken took pictures of us with Monica. Then we walked
back to the rented car, Alex and my father up ahead, moving
past Balbriggan's used furniture stores and ladies' dress shops in
their matching Irish tweed caps.

*Janis Cooke Newman is a writer who lives in Northern California
with her husband and their son Alex, who has recently added
Mexico, Italy, and the Jersey Shore to his list of travels. Janis's memoir
about Alex's adoption,* The Russian Word for Snow, *was
published in 2001.*

✦ ✦ ✦

Sleeping Beauties

In Germany, fairy tales
come to life.

I STAND ON MY HOTEL BALCONY IN THE BAVARIAN DUSK as the jagged mountain peaks blur across the valley. The light fades, and laughter floats up from the restaurant downstairs. Suddenly floodlights snap on, and there, on a massive promontory before a backdrop of black peaks, stands Neuschwanstein, white parapets and crenellated towers aglow in the blue twilight. I'm caught between a gasp and a laugh. King Ludwig II's wild, romantic nineteenth-century fantasy of a medieval castle looks exactly like a child's toy perched on a papier-mâché crag.

It's been a long time since I believed in fairy tales, but I'm rooted, shivering in my nightgown as I gaze across the valley. Something deep in my soul responds to Ludwig's self-indulgent whimsy and yearning for a time gone by, a time of chivalry, of lion-hearted kings, noble knights, wandering minstrels, and virtuous ladies.

My awe, I learn, was shared by Walt Disney, who used Neuschwanstein as his template for Sleeping Beauty's castle, both in the cartoon and at Disneyland. That may be why at first sight of the castle many people experience déjà vu. Like the reflections of reflections in a hall of mirrors, Neuschwanstein, itself an extravagant interpretation of the past, became what postwar generations of Americans think of when they hear the word "castle."

Germany has hundreds of castles, in part because of its long history as a collection of separate city-states governed by war-ring electors and dukes, most of their fortress-castles fell into disuse and ruin in the fifteenth century, after gunpowder, can-nons, and firearms meant even the thickest stone walls were no longer impregnable.

Today the most famous have become popular destinations in western Germany, so popular, in fact, that visitors can wait hours to get in. Getting up with the sun to be at the head of the line to enter Neuschwanstein cures me of braving the crowds, but having a fairy tale come to life unexpectedly is be-witching. As I read over the brochures and materials I col-lected on my morning visit, I discover Neuschwanstein owes its farfetched proportions to several medieval castles that lie in what was formerly the German Democratic Republic. All long forgotten by Westerners, these castles wait, I imagine, deep in enchanted forests or towering on top of majestic cliffs, to be woken from their spell. Now I have a quest: to uncover the sources of Ludwig's inspiration.

After exploring for a few days, I realize that my journey won't end by discovering an 800-year-old version of Neusch-wanstein. Ludwig's castle ended up more a homage to the Middle Ages than anything else. The king felt he'd been born in the wrong era, but his version of the past borrowed more from nineteenth-century Romanticism than historical fact. Like his mentor Richard Wagner, he occupied an imaginary world somewhere between idealized Germanic history and

Grimm Brothers' fairly tales. "You've heard the word kitsch," a young archaeologist told me, shrugging. "We Germans have our own version of Disney, and its roots go back to the eighteenth- and nineteenth-century Romanticism." It's no wonder that in 1868, after he'd visited the eleventh-century fortress-castle of Wartburg in Thuringias, Ludwig decided he had to have a medieval castle of his own and in an inspired moment hired a theater set designer named Christian Jank to draw up the fantastic plans.

Ludwig's chief inspiration is one of the best-preserved Romanesque buildings in northern Europe, as well as a striking example of a mountaintop fortress-castle. Religion, not architecture, has made Wartburg a pilgrimage site ever since Martin Luther translated the Bible there into the vernacular in 1522 while in hiding from the pope. At the edge of the mountainous Thuringer Forest, Wartburg looks down from a steep hill onto the city of Eisenach. The road that winds up to the main gate is now only for energetic pedestrians, and there's something especially humbling about approaching the castle on foot, as peasants and servants did long ago.

In spite of its historical significance, the castle was allowed to deteriorate until Goethe began to visit it in the late eighteenth century. His interest prompted a reconstruction. By the time Ludwig arrived in 1867, the interior had been covered with Pre-Raphaelite frescoes of the castle's legendary events, including the War of the Troubadours, a contest in the twelfth century that inspired Wagner's *Tannhäuser*, which is set in Wartburg. The great hall received a new two-story-high coffered ceiling and windows far larger than the originals. With its gilded details and marble fireplaces, it's easy to see why Ludwig went to so much trouble to copy it, even though it has little to do with the Age of Chivalry. But much of the castle is still intact, including the plastered half-timbered facades, a key feature in German castle architecture, and the squat towers, although predictably, these aspects interested Ludwig the least.

The next morning I leave Thuringia, which calls itself Germany's green heart, and drive east to explore Saxony's castles. My first is Burg Kriebstein, built in the fourteenth century on a rocky promontory overlooking a river and sweeping valley. At a distance, it truly seems like a miniature Neuschwanstein. The castle was built as one of a series of fortresses on the silver route from the mines to Dresden, and it's spectacularly beautiful. Soaring vaults with delicate Gothic tracery make the castle keep's interior seem anything but martial. On a wall are the crests of all the families that owned the castle, ending in 1945, when East Germany's communist government expropriated private property. Once a year, in a medieval festival at the castle, a local legend is reenacted in which invading outlaw knights tell the vanquished owner's wife she may keep what she can carry out of the castle on her back and she chooses to carry her husband. Nearly all the castles I visit stage this sort of festival, with jugglers, ladies in flowing dresses, authentic banquets—be prepared to use your hands—and the Deutschland equivalent of Morris dancing.

If you fall in love with this sanitized version of castle life, consider buying one. A visit to Rochsburg will give you an idea of what's on the market. Approximately fifty castles are for sale in Saxony, starting for as little as $1,000,000, a result of eastern Germany's still-weak economy. Rochsburg dates back to the twelfth century and sits on a hill in the midst of a park that has meandering trails, glades of trees, and pretty vistas of the town below. You reach the castle by a tree-shaded stone bridge that leads to an arched sandstone gateway. Inside, the castle's architecture ranges from Romanesque to Gothic to

Baroque. With all its renovations and additions, Rochsburg seems like a pastiche of every epoch's stylistic flourishes. Luckily, it comes decorated with suitably imposing furnishings. Massive tapestries and antlers from the early seventeenth century hang on the castle walls, mementos of a time when Rochsburg's lords displayed their prowess in hunting rather than fighting.

Another hour's drive east brings you to Meissen, a porcelain-manufacturing town on the river Elbe that has preserved its medieval center intact. Half-timbered houses with steeply slanted red gables line the labyrinth of streets in the old town. More than a thousand years ago, a fortress-castle was built on a rocky hill—now the centerpiece of the town. By the early fifteenth century, the ruling duke, Albrecht, wanted to rebuild what remained of the original in the latest style. From the castle hill visitors look over the rooftops of the old town to the meadows and vineyards of the fertile Elbe valley, conjuring up a time when a man might literally be lord of all he surveyed.

The result of Albrecht's commission, the late Gothic masterpiece of Albrechtsburg, dominates Meissen's skyline. It marked the transition from castles built for defense to those meant to demonstrate their owner's wealth and power. Renowned architect Arnold of Westphalia created arched windows and many-groined vaulted ceilings that resembled beehives. His crowning achievement is the tower-encased circular stairway. Windows, vaulted ceilings, and fluted curving stone railings give an illusion of delicacy and fluidity as the stone steps curve around sandstone columns.

In the nineteenth century, artists from the Academy of Arts in nearby Dresden set to work gilding and painting the walls with historic scenes. The results detract from the stark beauty of Arnold's engineering feats only a little. While Ludwig claimed Wartburg as his chief inspiration, Albrechtsburg's steepled towers and parapets may well have played their part.

A short drive east of Meissen stands the grand hunting lodge of Moritzburg. Built in the sixteenth century as a Renaissance-style pleasure castle, Moritzburg paved the way for the palaces and manors that were to replace castles entirely by the eighteenth century. In fact, the ochre castle underwent a total renovation in the eighteenth century to give it a suitably Baroque façade and the air of a chateau. Moritzburg sits on an island in a placid lake, complete with swans. A wide, tree-lined gravel causeway fit for Cinderella's coach sweeps up to the entrance. Despite its formal gardens and studied beauty, or perhaps because of it, Moritzburg seems nearly as much a fairy-tale castle as Neuschwanstein. That may be because it's nearly as artificial. Once marshland, the grounds around Moritzburg were drained centuries ago to create fishing ponds for the members of the Wettin dynasty. Even the lake is artificial. By the time the walls went up, the landscape was a level stretch of countryside punctuated by ponds and meadows.

There are so many castles in Saxony and Thuringia that it's difficult to choose which to visit even if you have a specific purpose in mind. Some, like Burg Kriebstein, have never seen the likes of a tour bus, and others, like Wartburg, are on everyone's list. But while other people stand in line waiting to get into castles on the Rhine, in Eastern Germany you may find yourself alone on a parapet dreaming of knights in clanking armor and maidens in fluttering silk.

Ann Johnson wrote this story for Travel Holiday.

KRISTIN JACKSON

Bambina, Bambina!

When in Rome, a child is a bonus.

THE FRUIT VENDOR AT THE OUTDOOR MARKET IN THE heart of Rome stared at me as I picked up one of his little baskets of strawberries.

"Those for her?" he asked gruffly, pointing to my six-year-old daughter who was smiling up at him. Yes, I nodded.

"Don't buy them. They taste bad," he barked, waving us away from his fruit and vegetable stall.

Dumbfounded, I put down the strawberries and stammered my thanks. *"Ciao, Ciao,"* chanted my daughter, waving good-bye and practicing one of her few newly learned words of Italian as we headed down the narrow, cobbled street. The grizzled fruit-seller grinned.

During the eight years I lived in Rome, and in frequent return visits, I had never met a vendor who told me not to buy his produce. Quite the opposite; unless you're a regular customer, many vendors will slip in some crummy produce or overcharge.

But on a recent visit to Rome with my daughter, Stephanie, we encountered kindness at every turn.

In the little food stores where we shopped for our picnic lunches, the grocers frequently slipped her a free chunk of Parmesan cheese. At the ice cream shop where we often stopped, her serving grew more massive each time, great spoonfuls of homemade strawberry, lemon, and chocolate draping the cone.

At the restaurant where we became evening regulars, the waiters took her into the kitchen to watch the chefs cooking pasta. On our last night each waiter gave her a little gift—a necklace, a pen holder—and hugs and the biggest plate of seafood I have ever seen served in a Roman restaurant.

In Rome, the importance of eating is matched, barely, by the importance of religion. And again, traveling with a child opened doors. Just down the block from where we stayed was a convent. Each morning, a nun, in her long gray and white habit, swept the outdoor steps and sidewalk.

"*Ciao*," chirped my daughter cheerfully as we walked past. A conversation began, and soon we were invited through the tall wood door that seals off the convent from the world.

One thing led to another. We were asked to stay for lunch, then two smiling young nuns whisked Stephanie through marble corridors to introduce her to other nuns.

Traveling with a child also got me the closest I've ever been to the Pope.

We'd gone to St. Peter's to see the church and the Pope, who was scheduled to hold an audience that day outdoors in the basilica's vast square.

He sat under a burgundy canopy on the steps of the church; the square teemed with thousands of people cheering as he addressed them in a dozen different languages.

We wormed our way forward to a barricade where police

checked credentials, admitting only dignitaries and parish groups who had prearranged their seating in rows of folding chairs near the Pope.

I asked a stern-faced policeman if we could go through, just for a moment. He impatiently shook his head no, then saw my daughter looking beseechingly up at him. He took her hand, ushered her through the crowd, and pointed us to seats a dozen rows from the Pope.

Our days weren't always so sweet. There were times when my daughter was overwhelmed by the urban bustle of Rome, when the manic traffic and jammed buses were frightening, when she longed for some green space to play in this park-poor city.

Not understanding me when I spoke Italian confused her; not being able to speak with children she met frustrated her. But she soon found she could play without words.

At one of central Rome's few playgrounds, she shrieked and climbed and played tag for hours with three Roman children. And at almost every piazza we found a soccer game she could join.

One day, after watching shyly from the sidelines, she was invited into a soccer game in Piazza Navona. Soon she was part of the pack, chasing the ball around a centuries-old foundation in the majestic square.

The tough Roman boys, fierce and devoted players twice her age and size, slowed the game to her pace. And I sat on the steps of a church and watched, marveling how a child brings out kindnesses that drown the differences of culture and language.

Kristin Jackson is a travel writer and editor for the Seattle Times. *She has lived and traveled extensively overseas, with and without her daughter.*

JENNIFER COLVIN

✦ ✦ ✦

Full Circle on Mont Blanc

Notions of wilderness give way to inner peace.

LATE IN THE DAY, BOB AND I RODE OUR BICYCLES INTO the campground across the river from Avignon in southern France. We were sweaty and tired, and all we wanted was a bare patch of dirt where we could pitch our tent for the night. I knew better than to hope for a spot with a view of the Palace of the Popes rising above the city walls. Privacy was completely out of the question. It was August, when flocks of Europeans traditionally migrate south. Everyone, it seemed, was on holiday, which meant that our holiday had become less like vacation, and more like work. The crowds of people made everything from finding a place to camp, to buying groceries, to sightseeing, a test of patience as we stood in line after line.

"There!" Bob said, pointing to an opening near the bathrooms.

I looked over to see a young guy eyeing the same place. "I've got it," I said to Bob as I moved quickly to stand in the area just big enough for our tent, staking our claim. As Bob unpacked the tent, the German told us about the fight that took place yesterday between two campers over that very spot.

"He's stoned," I whispered to Bob as I knelt on the ground, pushing in tent stakes.

I kept a close eye on the bag that contained my camera, journal, and wallet. Beer bottles were scattered on the ground nearby. Dismayed, I realized the tent just a few feet away belonged to our new friend. It was going to be a long night.

I'd had enough. We'd been cycling for four months in western Europe and northern Africa, and we'd dealt with lightning, flash floods, speeding trucks, drug dealers, and dehydration, but this was just too much. While the boys partied in the tent next to us, we planned our escape. If we caught the first train out the next morning, we could be in Chamonix in the French Alps that night, far from the overcrowded campgrounds and towns we'd been staying in.

I pictured myself and Bob hiking through flower-filled meadows and camping in remote mountain valleys with no one else in sight, just like we did at home in the Pacific Northwest. But hiking in Europe would be better than hiking at home because it would be exotic: we'd get to see chamois and ibexes, instead of boring old deer. It would be a perfect break.

The next day, we schlepped our bicycles and gear onto three different trains, and finally arrived in the cool mountain air of Chamonix that night. Groups of people bundled in waterproof jackets walked through narrow streets lined with restaurants and mountaineering shops. You could tell which ones were tourists and which ones were the outdoorsy types because the climbers, mountaineers, and hikers all walked with a sense of purpose. I could feel the mountains rising up around us, even though I couldn't see them through the fog. The wood chalets and creamy, green-shuttered hotels looked saturated, but the black cobblestones at my feet and the trees on the slopes of the mountains glistened in the rain. I smiled at the thought of being in the mountains high above the bustle of Chamonix as Bob and I walked our bikes briskly through town.

Our plan was to circle the base of Mont Blanc, Europe's highest mountain, by hiking 120 miles through France, Italy, and Switzerland. We figured we could complete the Tour du Mont Blanc circuit in about ten days. After spending a couple of days buying maps, renting hiking poles, and organizing gear, we started our hike up the valley at Les Houches.

The clouds had lifted, and in the warm sun, surrounded by the snow-capped mountains, my footsteps felt light even though I shouldered a backpack full of camping gear. Although we could have stayed in the mountain chalets and refuges along our route, we were willing to pay the price of carrying extra gear so we could have the solitude and peace of camping along the trail.

After several hours of hiking, we crested a hill and were confronted by a mountain chalet and a group of people. My heart sank when I saw what the local railway had brought up here. Families were lounging in swimsuits, drinking wine, and watching their children play with toys. I had spent all afternoon hiking up a hill that, it was now apparent, was just a short train ride from the village below. All that effort seemed pointless.

"Well, so much for escaping to the outdoors," I joked.

Bob didn't care so much about the people, but he was worried when we saw the cows near the trail, ripping up mouthfuls of grass and dropping steaming cow pies.

"What do we do?" Bob asked me nervously.

Bob expected that I'd know how to deal with the situation because I grew up on a cattle ranch. The cows I knew at home were domesticated in the sense that they were confined by a fence that surrounded the property, but they were generally wild and mean, and it was mutually understood that both parties would keep their distances. But here, the cows had broad sets of pointed horns, and they weren't moving. Bob was worried about getting gored, and so was I.

"Keep an eye on them, and walk slowly," I instructed Bob with fake confidence.

When I imagined seeing wildlife in the Alps, this wasn't what I had pictured. Now I wasn't sure if this whole thing was such a good idea. We would be ascending and descending a total of 32,808 feet the next week on our route, which would be like climbing to the summit of Mont Blanc—more than twice. All of that work, and now I feared I wouldn't even get the pure outdoors experience I had envisioned.

At the end of the day, my feet hurt and my pack felt heavy. In the valley below, we saw the trail lead to the dots of a few buildings, the Chalets de Mirage. The descending path was steep and difficult, and without the aid of switchbacks to make downhill walking easier, my legs were soon shaking with fatigue.

At the refuge, we stopped to fill our water bottles at a standpipe, where cold mountain water spilled from a gargoyle's mouth into a hollowed-out log trough, but I was distracted by the large berry tart a woman brought to some hikers sitting at picnic tables.

"Bob! Look!" I called, pointing at the tart. "I have to have one."

"Want to share?" he asked.

"Nope," I said happily as I walked over to the picnic tables.

Minutes later, as I ate my own berry tart (topped with fresh cream provided by the cows grazing nearby), I watched the snowfields on Mont Blanc turn pink as the sun set.

"This isn't so bad, now is it?" Bob asked. I had to admit, it was a pretty good way to end a day of hiking.

The next day, our route took us along a Roman road outside of Contamines. Large slabs of smooth rock jutted unevenly from the earth, paving the way straight up the mountain. It seemed the Romans didn't believe in switchbacks, either. When our route left the ancient pathway, we began to follow a trail of toilet paper. The sight of each pile rubbed against the serenity I had been feeling like an ill-fitting boot, until my content was marred by a festering blister. I mumbled about "leave no trace" wilderness ethics.

As we continued hiking, Bob and I fell into a comfortable routine. I complained about how there was no real wilderness in the Alps, while shopping for fresh food in the towns we passed through each day, a luxury we'd never have on a backpacking trip at home. Bob marveled at the scenery, but he moaned about how we'd spend hours hiking up thousands of feet of elevation, just to descend the same amount at the end of the day. We walked for long stretches of time in comfortable silence, following the red and white blazes on rocks that marked our route through flower-filled meadows.

One night in Italy, we decided to set up our tent in a small saddle. Green hills rose up on one side, and gray mountains and glaciers bordered us on the other. The moment we stepped off the trail, a horse appeared over the crest and ran straight for us, head held high. I stopped in my tracks. The horse slowed, then walked straight up to me and whinnied. As I reached out to pet his nose, he stuck out his tongue.

"He's looking for handouts," I told Bob.

As we set up our tent, the horse kept us company. I understood how it could get a little lonely up here by yourself. The horse halfheartedly tried to nibble my pack, and gave the tent a hopeful lick.

"Hey!" I yelled.

The horse looked up at me. When he finally realized he wasn't getting any goodies, he snorted, dropped a load in the middle of our camp, and cantered off. I was about to complain again about how there was no real wilderness in the Alps, but it seemed that I kept getting shit on for having that attitude. I giggled. Bob looked at me, and we started to laugh.

The next morning the weather turned cold, and I gave myself over completely to the European style of hiking. This meant that we hiked from one refuge to the next, stopping for hot coffee or food each time. At the Hotel La Vachey, we had a lunch of ham and cheese crepes, followed by creamy polenta with mushrooms and sausage. Dessert was apple pie with fresh cream, eaten on the deck of the Elena refuge facing the Pre de Bar glacier. Instead of eating energy bars like we would at home, we filled up on ice cream bars in the villages before tackling yet another ascent.

Now, as we continued hiking, I talked soothingly to the horned cows along the trail, "nice cow, that's a good, nice cow," and Bob waved to the shepherds. I thought about the ancient Roman road we had walked on a few days earlier. How many thousands of feet had followed this same route? People had been living in these mountains for hundreds of years. Their lives were just as much a part of this place as the wilderness I had hoped to find here.

Farther away from the villages and mountain refuges, we often had the trail to ourselves. When I got dizzy taking in the 360-degree mountain views in places where the trail dropped off sharply, almost vertically, to the valley below, I'd look closely at the bright alpine flowers blooming in pinks and purples and reds at my feet.

On the day we walked down a road to the small town of La Fouley, I could tell without a doubt we had entered Switzerland. Even though we had just left Italy, the wood chalets with firewood stacked carefully under the eaves, red geraniums decorating the balconies, and neat yards made it clear we'd crossed into a more ordered land. So did the rules—camping was only allowed in the two official campsites along the route. This was fine with us. After a week of hiking by ourselves, Bob and I longed for some company.

At the campground near Lac Champex, a friendly English sheep dog wandered over to our tent. I have a soft spot for large dogs, and when the woman in the tent nearby apologized and called her dog over, Bob introduced us. Henk and Sylvia were vacationing from the Netherlands. We offered them some of our Swiss chocolate, they offered us their potent Dutch alcohol, and we spent hours talking about our travels and our lives at home. Henk and Sylvia told us about their trip to the U.S. and the national parks they visited. Bob and I talked about our plans to travel to the Netherlands and spend the last month of our trip living there. We all went to bed late.

The next morning, as Bob and I finished packing, Sylvia offered us coffee.

"No thanks," I said. "We have to get on the trail."

We had a full day of hiking ahead of us, and I was ready to finish the route and get back to Chamonix. Sylvia insisted.

"Oh, come on," she said, and looked at Henk.

Henk brought out his guitar, knowing that Bob would be tempted to stay and play music.

"We really should get going," I repeated.

I was glad we had their company for the evening, but I was puzzled that they were so insistent about having coffee. It was the type of friendship that travelers make easily, and leave behind once they move on. Finally, Sylvia just came out and said it.

"We have a proposal for you."

Now, we couldn't leave. I dropped my pack.

"We would like to make you an offer," Sylvia continued. "We want to give you our keys so you can stay at our house when you arrive in the Netherlands."

Immediately, I politely declined. They couldn't just give their house keys to strangers, I thought. Henk and Sylvia explained how it made sense for us to stay in their house while they were on vacation for the rest of the month. They insisted we take their keys. I wouldn't trust strangers the same way Henk and Sylvia were willing to trust me, so I didn't feel like I could accept such a generous offer.

Then I realized that Sylvia probably saw a little of herself in me. She told us about how she had hitchhiked through Canada when she was younger. She understood what it's like to be young and to travel, how you discover the importance of trusting yourself, and learn to accept kindness from others. Bob looked at me, and we agreed.

Henk and Sylvia gave us a crash course in their neighborhood and their neighbors (everyone knows everyone and looks out for each other, they explained), and Sylvia wrote us a letter of introduction that we were to give to the friend who was watching their house. As we started hiking that day, the mountains seemed to shrink around us, and I felt more awed by Henk and Sylvia's generosity than by anything else we'd seen on our journey.

Our last night back in France, we hiked late into the day, trying to get through the wilderness preserve where camping was illegal. Dusk fell, and as my eyes slowly adjusted to the growing darkness, I saw something move out of the corner of my eye. There, behind a boulder, was an animal. It darted straight up the mountain like a cross between a nimble goat and a small deer.

"It's a chamois!" I called to Bob.

After all of the cows, sheep, horses, and people, I had a fleeting glimpse of wildlife. My heart beat faster as I looked for more of the animals. Soon, we were surrounded by them. Their eyes glowed in our headlamps. At least a dozen delicate-boned chamois grazed around us on the trail, tails twitching. Slowly, I walked just a few feet from the pointed horns of one. My trip was complete.

After completing a six-month bicycle trip through Europe and Africa, Jennifer Colvin and her husband Bob settled in the San Francisco Bay Area. Her stories have appeared in the Travelers' Tales anthology Sand in My Bra and Other Misadventures, *as well as other print and online publications.*

KAREN CUMMINGS

⋆ ✶ ⋆

Forgiveness

It took crossing an ocean for a daughter
to leave her pain behind.

FOR AS LONG AS I CAN REMEMBER, EVEN AS A TINY
child, I always felt I was the mother to my mother. She'd call
for an Anacin and a half-glass of water when one of her "sick
headaches" would come on. She'd curl up into a ball on the
couch. I'd deliver the medicine, then go back to the business
of childhood. Or try. It wasn't easy or simple. The child in me
ached for a real mommy who'd smile lovingly and tell me
what a good girl I was. Who'd hold me close when I was hurt-
ing and help me feel everything would be all right. Who'd
take care of me instead of forcing me to take care of her.

On the surface of our lives, everything looked fine. I was
fed and clothed and sent to school. We appeared to the outside world as if we were the perfect family. Knowing that the
socially visible didn't match the truth only intensified my confusion and loneliness. My little girl heart was broken. Why
didn't Mommy love me? Why didn't she ever touch me—
except to yank my hair in a rage? What was wrong with me?

By the time I was thirteen, I had emotionally divorced

myself from her. I was civil, but detached. I pretended things were fine. But they weren't. When her stinging criticism and biting sarcasm were whirled at me, I felt numb. It was the only way to keep the peace.

As soon as I could, I left. Went to college and then moved to New York City—about as far from the upstate New York farm as I could get. I aggressively abdicated Mom-care.

Occasionally, I'd visit. Spend a few hours. But her cutting remarks were constant. Crying and ranting on the way back to the city, I felt a hard, mean anger growing inside. I was beginning to hate my mother. She made it so difficult to love her.

And this was painful, too. Because, in spite of all I had been through, I had a conflicting need to be a good daughter.

After my first year of independence in New York, my army-officer brother was stationed in Germany. My mom hinted that she'd like to visit him. Then hinted again. Like many women of her generation, she hadn't traveled much. I knew I was being manipulated into taking her.

I landed us two seats on a military transport plane. In the window seat, I was cramped and miserable. "God," I wondered over and over again, "What have I gotten myself into? Will I ever be free of her demands?"

My mother, in the middle seat—boxed in by a young mother and her baby, was oblivious to my discomfort. That didn't surprise me. What did startle me was how she kept her good cheer. I couldn't believe my eyes or ears. Flying across the Atlantic was a different woman than the one I grew up with: she was softer, lighter. "I have to pinch myself to believe we're really going," she said several times.

Our first day trip was to go, by train, to Stuttgart, the bright city set in a golden-green valley forty miles or so east of Schwäbisch Gmund. We arrived, late morning, at the train station, the Haupbahnhof. Glancing up at its soaring ceiling, my mother looked in my eyes and smiled broadly. It was an unguarded moment. And I felt as though we were a far, far distance from the farm—and all its sad memories.

We strolled the Konigstrasse, exploring the historical buildings. My mother commented pleasantly on the wide streets and verdant parks, so clean and obviously cherished. Even the sky looked pristine—blue with little white puffs of cottonball clouds scudding across. I told myself to loosen up.

My brother's wife gave us a long list of must-do's. But before we could find a single spot, we stumbled on Altes Schloss (Old Castle). Inside this museum, we moved effortlessly among four floors of galleries—filled with rare tapestries, ceramic craftwork, silver tableware, old costumes—all things we both coincidentally adored. Each time we entered a gallery that looked out over the Renaissance Courtyard, we stopped to admire together its beauty, and to share our great good fortune in stumbling on this place. We were genuinely agreeing.

Last stop was the exquisite clocks gallery. We had several treasured antique timepieces at home, but we'd never seen anything like these. We were the only people in the room. Listening to the thrum, tick, and chunk of the different clocks, we grew quiet. These instruments were created hundred of years ago to monitor lives. I felt the ancient owners' spirits, and sensed that I, too, was merely a fleeting visitor on Earth. I could measure my time, but like those nameless clockmakers, could do no more to control it than I could control the weather.

My mother then made a solo circuit of the room. I stood in the corner of the gallery, near the window now bathed in the early afternoon light, and watched her move. Most certainly, I felt it wasn't the twenty-first century anymore. It could have been the nineteenth or eighteenth.

Moments like these, the ones that take us out of our own worries and concerns, are crossroads. Choices get made, seeds planted. Out of time, out of familiar surroundings, freed from the bonds of our former life, I saw my mother in a new way. As she exclaimed over the delicate miniature clocks, I got a glimpse of her own fragility, her—I gulped—humanity. My mother's childhood hadn't been wonderful either. She had faced disappointment and tragedy—a mother who beat her with a belt, a beloved sister who died young of cancer.

The hard place in my heart began to soften. As the sun warmed my shoulders, this trip's medicine, already making such a difference in my mother, began to work on me as well. Like the gong of a grandfather clock that moved a large brass hand from one hour to the next, I dared to look at her, and my life, with a deep breath.

It was possible to heal from a childhood that was unhappy, I heard myself say quietly. I could open my heart to forgiveness. Of course, forgiveness of this magnitude isn't an event—it's a process that can take years. But that day, in that lovely museum that took us out of our present time, our space, and even our own history, I made the most important choice of my life—to begin again.

Karen Cummings is a pseudonym for a New York City writer. She's the mother of three children, with whom she shares great happiness.

JUDY WOLF

★ ★ ★

Vagabond Love

Two free spirits converge and connect.

I FIRST CAUGHT SIGHT OF HIM IN THE VIENNA TRAIN station. Surrounded by four strangers I'd seduced into taking an overnight train across the newly opened border to Prague, I sat on my backpack and observed the passing crowds.

I didn't know I was looking for him, but there he was. He sauntered across the polished floor, long limbs bronzed beneath well-worn flannel, his boots still muddy from a solo excursion in the Alps. Reclining against a marble column, I watched him stroll past, and didn't say a word.

Then there he was again, hours later, in the last compartment that still had empty seats. I settled into the corner across from him, this man with the sun-bleached hair. He looked at me as though he'd been waiting for me to sit there, met my gaze with eyes a color of blue I'd never before imagined, and we began to speak.

Our conversation flowed, words tumbling as if between us ran a river, a torrent, a mutual urgency. My traveling companions forgotten, our minds leapt and played along similar paths, and we delighted in shared humor and instant shorthand as our banter snaked through stories full of parallels. It was as if we were both affirming, in rhythm with the train wheels, "Yes, yes, yes."

He was going only as far as the Breclav border stop. Once his passport was stamped, he would hitchhike from there, see what came next. The congruence with my own hunger for leaving the beaten path left me breathless, and I longed to be so bold. But I said nothing.

We talked through the night, smiles flickering between us like moth shadows in candle flame. Toward midnight, knowing I would never see him again, I leaned closer, looked him in those marvelous eyes, and said, "I've taken an immediate liking to you in case you haven't noticed." His placid expression hid an interior smile, and I sat back, fully aware that the feeling was mutual.

At the border, we parted. No point in hanging about. I rejoined my companions, noticing that they seemed a bit less interesting than they had mere hours before.

The train to Prague arrived, sidling up to the station as if exhausted by its journey, and there beside me appeared Wolfgang. "I hope you don't mind me hanging about for a bit longer," he said.

Within a few days, my traveling companions had returned to their standard European tour. I had turned down the invitation to join them, opting instead to follow Wolfgang deeper into Czechoslovakia, down into Hungary. "I can go to Germany any time," I said to my departing companions. "How often do I get to explore the Eastern Bloc?"

The Berlin Wall had only just come down, and countries like Czechoslovakia and Hungary were opening their borders to the West for the first time in decades. Already cities like

Prague had become tourist destinations, and I wanted to go farther afield, test myself in areas not yet so exposed.

Little did I realize the true challenge that lay before me, though already I could feel the panic rising like a premonition. In my life, I strove above all else for transience. People came and went, and I liked it that way. I found relationships messy, entangling, and tended to avoid connection. Being alone in a crowd was so much easier, and the less I knew about people, the less likely they were to bore me or make demands.

So I was aware from the beginning that what scared me most about this man was the fact that I had no urge to walk away from him. I wrote in my journal, "Be careful what you wish for..." The more I learned of Wolfgang, the more he fascinated me. It was as though I'd met my twin, my doppelganger.

"So much for opposites attract," he said when I offered this thought out loud.

That which passes, passes, I reassured myself.

Sitting side by side in the train station, he arched his left eyebrow and said, "It's interesting to watch you become more sure of your position with me."

I raised an eyebrow. "You've been pretty sure of your position with me from the start."

"You were very aggressive."

"I thought I was talking to someone who was getting lost at Breclav."

"I thought so, too. I'm glad I came to Prague."

"I'm glad and I'm angry."

"I can disappear tomorrow and you'll never see me again."

"I don't want you to."

"That's why you're angry." He laughed. The look he gave me then cut past my ersatz smile and left me exposed, vulnerable, wanting something.

My walls began to crumble then, and I scrambled to reconstruct them. *Never let them down,* said one voice, while another laughed and sobbed with relief. My journal replied, "Oh, yes, be careful what you wish for. He has stepped out of my head, and I must let him go within a matter of days. Reality can be heartbreaking. The subtle humor of the cosmic joke."

Our overnight train dumped us in Banská Bystica, where we found an $8 hotel and slept away the afternoon. We ordered our evening meal from a menu we couldn't read ("Point and pray," whispered Wolfgang, grinning) and ate slowly in the high-ceilinged red dining room of a restaurant crowded with resplendently-clad locals.

We caught a bus to Zvolen, where we ate goulash standing up next to the street vendor's corner trolley, then spent the night on a train to Sahy. There, we left the train station and walked in the 2 A.M. darkness to the border, intending to hitchhike to Budapest.

My heart beat loud in my ears as the armed border guards held up their hands to halt our progress. Where were we going? Why not on a train? Were we alone? What were we thinking?

Earlier that night, my throat had started to hurt when I swallowed, and now my head was pounding. Did I have a fever? I raised my hand to my forehead, trying to appear casual.

One of the guards spoke enough English to let us know that this was a strange and suspicious thing we were doing. I smiled, a friendly and harmless American, and tried to think of the right answers. My sinuses ached, and dizziness threatened to topple me. Wolfgang took over. He was self-assured, jovial. Finally, they let us pass.

And there we were, on the other side of the miniature toll booth that was the Czecho-Hungarian border. *Not much different,* I thought. The weeds were the same, the darkness still complete, and behind us, yes, there were the guards with their drab olive fatigues and semi-automatic weapons. This was a mirror image of where we'd been a few moments before, and I reflected momentarily on the arbitrary nature of boundaries. Now we just needed to find a ride.

Not certain hitchhiking was even legal, we walked a few hundred yards down the road before attracting attention to ourselves. The few cars that passed us—waving our sign for Budapest—ignored us. An hour later, after handing me a throat lozenge, Wolfgang headed into the bushes to set up his tent, while I sat on the backpacks, holding my throbbing head and smiling occasionally in the direction of the border guards.

When the next car stopped at the booth, the English-speaking guard wandered down the road to me. "Where is your friend?" Thinking we might be in trouble, I indicated the shadowy bushes, and he nodded, understanding that this was a bathroom break. "Tell him we get you a ride." When I didn't move right away, he repeated, gesturing toward the car, "A ride. To Budapest. Tell him."

The Fiat pulled up next to me just as Wolfgang was stuffing the tent into his bag. Its drivers seemed reluctant—and why wouldn't they?—but in the shadow of the guard station had little choice. Wolfgang and I climbed into the back seat, and the Fiat sped off into the Hungarian night. By then, I had given myself over to whatever illness was upon me, and lay curled with my head in Wolfgang's lap, hoping he could protect us both from whatever came next.

In Budapest, we walked from where they dropped us to the central train station. There we slept on the floor for two hours before being kicked awake by a passing guard, a woman with a harsh voice and pickled face above her featureless brown uniform.

What is the significance, I wondered in a nearby café over a cup of hot tea, *of meeting the man of your dreams in Czechoslovakia and never saying—though thinking constantly— "I've been expecting you..."? Because I have. Where do I go from here? I knew I'd meet him, knew he was coming, but I didn't really think about the life beyond. Oh well, he'll be gone soon. Yes, keep that distance. Plans don't work, don't make them.*

"Would it bother you if I came to visit?" he said. It was a test. I felt exposed, ready to run, but it seemed needless. I looked around me at the gray dawn of this ex-Eastern Bloc country, and realized it was not the land itself that was gray, but the buildings and the faces of the people, the manmade conditions. The land was land, like any land, and goes on. Perhaps love was like this, and we manufactured our own fears.

We seethed through the streets of Budapest, exploring the steamy underbelly of this city formed from the merging of two distinct towns, two separate sides of the river: the hilly, intellectual Buda and walled, industrial Pest. We wandered the pedestrian centers and soot-clogged streets, passed masses of city people on their way to work, stayed in the back room of a woman's apartment far outside of the Nagykörút, witnessed brawls in smoke-filled basement dance clubs, and bought each other yellow roses edged with blood-red hints of tenderness.

Back at the station, we waited for another train. Days had passed, and we now had a rhythm together: easy, unaffected.

A photograph of the waiting area would capture women selling flowers, their broad bottoms and empty faces speaking eloquently of daily endurance. One-legged, a man moved on crutches near the base of tall windows. Details leapt forward as if viewed through a telephoto lens, and I realized suddenly that I was not afraid anymore. Having thus defined myself in a Budapest train station, I could do anything.

"Do you want to catch the next train out?" he said.

"Where to?"

"Does it matter?"

We found ourselves in Füsezabony, Hungary, on a red park bench with a bag full of poppy seed breakfast pastries. We'd arrived at night and walked out of town along empty country roads. Picking a spot that looked good by night, we'd set up the tent and fallen asleep. Awakened by a pack of barking dogs, we discovered we'd stopped in a farmer's field, and moved swiftly back to town, but not before Wolfgang plucked a morning glory and placed it behind my ear.

From Füsezabony, we wandered through towns with names that satisfied my tongue, like Miskolc and Kosice. We returned to Prague on an overnight CCCP (USSR) train, where an "intercity supplement," we were informed by the red-faced, bellowing conductor, was payable directly to him. After this altercation, I splashed stale train water on my face, curled my toes inside dirty socks, stared out the window.

"We just passed Vychod," I said.

Amused, Wolfgang responded, "Vychod means exit."

"Does it? Well, we just passed a place with exits."

That evening, in one of Prague's ubiquitous fountain parks, we stumbled upon an orchestrated light show. A symphony played over loudspeakers as colored lights illuminated the water, which rose and fell, switching patterns with the pulse of the music. We stood at the edge of the crowd and intertwined our fingers.

Finding a cheap hotel room with faux figurines painted on the ceiling, we opened our window to the warm night air and read curled together, propped on pillows. Casual and comfortable, we had now slipped through multiple stages of relationship on the compressed timetable of intimate travelers. Each of us was reserved in our own way, for our own reasons, and we did not say aloud that we still wanted to move together. Instead, it just happened, day after day. Wolfgang, inscrutable, had once again changed his plans to continue with me, and I, reticent, did not say to him that I was glad.

Two people with nothing to prove, we relaxed at the edge of a landscaped pedestrian square. Wolfgang slept with his head in my lap, and I was struck by his vulnerability. One booted foot lay sideways on a brown carpet of needles and dirt beneath the low bushes that edged our platform. I ran gentle fingers through his hair. Awake and watchful, I took my turn standing guard over this entrusted sleep.

My gaze caressed his features, beautiful to me in their imperfection. His eyes were closed, body twitching now and again in response to whatever he saw behind his lids. Flannel worn and washed, bandana twisted around his neck, hands limp, his thumb still marked the place in his book where time was suspended when his eyes closed.

We were surrounded by warm sun and milling people. Horses moved past us in pairs, magnificent creatures of curvaceous, bridled movement, twitching their ears in dislike at being held in slow-paced check.

A seed pod floated toward me, a downy and weightless wish, mine for the taking. I looked down at the accepting, kind, gentle, intelligent man that had been emerging before my eyes these past weeks, and I let it pass, uncaptured. I had no more wishes.

Standing at last on the train platform in Bruges, I looked at Wolfgang and thought, *The only way to let you go is with a whole heart.*

Ironically enough, we shared a platform, essentially taking the same train in two opposite directions. We sat quietly, arms touching, on a bench. There was no summing up. We made no promises. He had my only permanent phone number, my mother's. I did not ask for his—I was afraid that I would want to call—nor did I expect to hear from him.

As his train heaved a sigh of relief beside us, he reached out a hand to touch my cheek. "I'll call you."

"It's O.K.," I said, knowing he wouldn't. He laughed at me and boarded his train.

I had told him in the beginning that for me, fear disallowed loneliness: I was more afraid than I was lonely. *Let him go,* I said to myself now.

It is impossible to lose oneself in another. There is no vacuum, no upsweep, no blind fall into sanctuary. For me, there was only the constant, pressing need for movement. I suddenly wished I'd grabbed the floating seed pod in the park, stopped time in that instant, clung to what I had.

But instead I boarded my own train and pondered this vagabond, this drifter, the best thing I'd ever seen. *I sing the same song,* I reminded myself. "Yes, yes, yes," chanted the wheels with a slow, reluctant groan. A gypsy moth alighted on the sill outside my window, then was blown off as the train picked up momentum.

Judy Wolf (www.judywolf.com) is a freelance writer, speaker, mountaineer, and whitewater kayak instructor. She's taken numerous, extended solo journeys around the world, traveling by foot, bus, jeep, camel, truck, boat, train, plane, elephant, and bicycle to over thirty countries on five continents. She's currently working on a book of travel essays about her most recent adventures. (And yes, Wolfgang did call her. He became one of the loves of her life, and is still numbered among her very favorite people.)

* * *

Cement Pole

*Meeting the family can be the most
important journey you ever take.*

WE'D LEFT PARIS ALMOST TWENTY-FOUR HOURS EARLIER, moving between planes, trains, and buses trying to get to Baba's (my grandmother's) house in Croatia. The rundown condition and slowness of these modes of transport combined with the dress of the locals confirmed for us that we were now in the shadow of Eastern Europe. Due to my father's thirty-year status as a political exile in what was still then Yugoslavia, this marked the first time anyone in my immediate family was visiting Croatia. It was 1989 and since Tito's death almost a decade before, assurances from our Croatian family that times were changing finally brought Catherine and me forward. Despite the fact that my sister and I had been traveling in Europe for several months (and thus considered ourselves veterans) and that we'd spent a good portion of our youth surrounded by Croats, we were experiencing fairly intense culture shock as we exited the train station in Split. Surprisingly, this would mark the beginning of one of the most profound experiences of my life.

Split is a beautiful and ancient city on the Adriatic coast. While our original plan had been to stay a night or two, visiting the city, beach, and surrounding area, these plans were abandoned once we realized the only hostel was booked and the beaches difficult to access. And so, reluctantly, we left for Sovici, a province which lay between Split and Mostar, earlier than anticipated. Within Sovici is a spot of a village called Bobanovadraga, not even on a map, where some houses were still without running water and the cows outnumbered humans. This is where Baba lived, where my father was born and raised and, unfortunately, where my sister and I were to spend the next two weeks.

Still the bus meandered. I opened my eyes and stared out of the window. I'd never seen anything quite like the landscape outside. Like a continuous loop, small rural villages rolled by, all reminiscent of images derived from Mother Goose stories. Perfect fairy-tale haystacks and pastures with women and men, both young and old, performing a variety of backbreaking tasks in these storybook fields. The elderly women wore dark scarves over their heads, tied either under their chins or at the nape of their necks, many with long, heavy skirts that reached mid-calf, despite the hot weather. And although the fieldwork was grueling, younger women still wore simple cotton short-sleeved dresses. Men, boys, and young girls, I noticed with no surprise, wore whatever they pleased. Surrounding these fields were old and new houses, barns, farm animals, children playing, horses, wagons, tractors. For urbanites like us, it seemed fantastical and otherworldly, as though we had traveled back in time.

Since my sister and I had boarded the bus in Split several hours prior, the landscape outside had slowly changed from seaside vegetation and sloping hills to harder and less forgiving, but still stunning, fields and rock-encrusted mountains. As the bus rambled farther inland, I was surprised by the absence of towns until I realized that the appearance of vineyards, a solitary café, and front-room stores meant that we had actually just driven through a village. Though it was a beautiful and surreal landscape, my only emotion was a mild sense of dread. Around me, I listened wearily to the heavy sighs, subdued coughs, and whispered conversations of the other passengers. Now, moments away from our destination, I was dreading our arrival.

It's not that Catherine and I didn't want to meet our family or that we weren't interested in exploring our father's place of birth. We just didn't want to do it now. For us, planning a traveling adventure did not include being constrained by family obligations. My sister was twenty-one and I was nineteen, and having planned, paid for, and (loosely) organized our European tour, we resented this forced detour.

Being raised within the confines of the Croatian community of San Francisco, Catherine and I were too aware of the many societal, cultural, and religious expectations, especially those placed on young women and girls, to naively believe that we would be having any type of mischievous fun once in Croatia. As it stood, we had spent our last days in Paris finding clothes that would hide our tattoos. While we loved our father and the community we were raised in, we were by and large California girls. The too-repressive gender roles and expectations we had witnessed being pushed on our Croatian-American female peers was not to be our reality, not now and not ever, despite our father's most ardent attempts. So, on that lazy late summer day as the bus ambled towards Sovici, my sister and I stared morosely ahead and, unbeknownst to the other, we both silently willed the bus to never reach its destination. I was already counting the days until I'd be sunning myself, topless of course, on the beaches of Greece.

My siblings and I had little tangible knowledge of my father's life before he became a political exile. We had heard stories, had met relatives who came on year-long tourist visas, had seen photos of Baba with the scarf on her head, but we weren't prepared to visit the "old country" alone. In my father's excitement that two of his children were finally able to visit his homeland, he decided that our visit should be a surprise to Baba. Normally, I would have thought this an exciting idea. However the fun of such a surprise was dampened by our not speaking the language, not knowing how to get to Bobanovadraga and having no idea who our grandmother was. So, working on memories over twenty years old my father, pencil in hand, excitedly drew us a map. This map charted the way from where he remembered the location of the bus stop to be on the main road all the way to our grandmother's house. The map included not only crudely drawn stick figure houses, but also such written directions as: "You'll see a cement telephone pole, the first one ever built in our village. Go past the pole about 300 meters…." Looking at the map, Catherine and I were skeptical that we'd ever find Baba. How far was 300 meters anyway?

The bus had slowed almost to a stop now. My sister called out to the bus driver, "Bobanovadraga?" He nodded indifferently. Nervously, we hoisted our packs onto our backs and made our way toward the front of the bus. As it stopped, we noticed ten or so people milling about, looking eagerly upwards into bus windows, searching for familiar and expected faces. Most were older men and women and here and there a few young mothers and children waiting for husbands and fathers. Younger men typically left home to find work in the cities.

Hesitating, I stood on the last step of the bus. I noticed an old, smallish woman with a scarf over her head and the dark clothes of a widow, looking fretful and teary-eyed, standing beside a teenage boy. She was anxiously searching all of the faces, both those still in bus windows and those of the few passengers who had already exited from the bus. As we made eye contact, I slowly began to wonder if she was Baba. I did not know my grandmother though I'd spoken with her several times on the telephone; stilted, formal conversations, with both of us struggling to understand one another. In addition, throughout the years I had seen numerous photos of her as she had seen of us. I looked at her. Taking that last step off the bus, I realized with some relief that this was my grandmother. My father never was good with secrets.

"Baba?" I said uncertainly as I examined her face trying to make sure she was the same woman I had seen in photographs. She came towards me, grabbed my hands and, crying and laughing, clung to both Catherine and me as we stepped onto the street.

Exhausted, hungry, dirty, and timid with our inability to fully speak our father's tongue, we finally had arrived. The teenage boy turned out to be our cousin, Vlado, my father's brother's son, visiting Baba for the summer. Fortunately for us, he spoke enough English to help fill in the gaps of our broken Croatian, thus creating a relatively seamless flow of communication.

For the short walk home, Baba insisted on wearing Catherine's small day pack (a strange addition to her traditional attire). As the four of us walked along the narrow path, my sister and I observed with amazement that my father's map had been uncannily accurate, the landmarks and landscape hardly changing over the last thirty years. People spilled slowly out of their homes to say hello to Baba while looking curiously at my sister and me, smiling and asking her who we were. Baba, glowing with pride and joy, told them we were

Milan's daughters. We were suddenly looked upon with smiling familiarity.

Along the way, Baba pointed out houses, being sure to tell us who lived there and how they were connected to my father's past. As we walked by the cement pole my father had drawn on his map, Baba pointed to it and with a smile told us that in 1956 my father had carved his initials and date on that very pole. Catherine and I walked to the pole followed closely by Vlado. Slightly above my eye level, I found "MB 1956" carved into the cement. I slowly traced my fingers over the now dull carving. This act brought on the first of what would be many peculiar sensations of glimpsing my phantom-father while in Bobanovadraga.

While we weren't the first American-born grandchildren to visit Bobanovadraga, we were the first of our father's children and in this village, our arrival was an event. The magnitude of our visit slowly dawned on Catherine and me as we made our way up that small incline, causing both of us to become self-conscious and overwhelmed during the short walk home. What had seemed to us to be a sleepy village closing down for dinner was now apparently alive and overpopulated. People came out of nooks, doorways, fields, and hidden paths to stare at us, making perfunctory comments to Baba. We were suddenly aware of the consequences of not learning more Croatian when we'd had the chance.

As we approached Baba's house, two women emerged and waited on the landing. One was older and dressed like Baba. The other, slightly younger woman was dressed in a sleeveless summer dress with the word "SURF" written colorfully all over it. I wondered if she knew what it meant. We soon learned that the younger woman was our aunt, my father's youngest sister, Matija. The older woman was a much-loved family friend. The day wore into evening and the open air courtyard, tucked in the center of Baba's house, slowly filled with locals. Everyone wanted to meet us and hear news of our father. As each new person arrived with a hug, it would prompt fresh tears from the *babas,* tears that fell fast but dried quickly. Catherine and I pulled out the photos we'd brought which helped to alleviate some of the awkwardness surrounding our inability to communicate. Evening turned into night and slowly the younger folks began to drift away leaving only the old men and women in Baba's courtyard. The elders had known one another for so long, they shared an ease and comfort only obtained with time and trust. I was unprepared for the zest for life exhibited by these rural seniors. Their quickness for laughter, endless teasing, and ability to drink Slivovic (homemade plum brandy) fresh out of the bottle without wincing made a lasting impression on my young mind. Exhausted, Catherine, Vlado, and I finally retired near midnight. I fell asleep to the voices and laughter of old men and women outside my bedroom door.

Catherine and I spent the next two weeks at Baba's house before leaving to visit our many other relatives in different parts of Croatia. During this time, we were often bored, often restless, and often surprised at how slowly time passed in this tucked away village. For two city girls, living hours away from the nearest traffic signal (and nightclub!) left us feeling somewhat undernourished for the urban and exciting. Despite this, these two weeks were among the most memorable of my life and proved to be instrumental in my ability, for the first time, to view my father not only as the man partially responsible for my birth, but also as an individual. My time there, even with my linguistic shortcomings, shed enormous light on the forces that shaped my father into the person I know today.

At that time I could see my father only through the eyes of the person I had been before I left home at the age of seventeen: an overly oppressed, powerless young woman living under the thumb of a strict, repressive, chauvinistic man. He was a controlling, demanding, driven, and often frightening person whose expectations I could never live up to. That he loved me, I knew, though my fear of him and my frustration with his strictness and old-fashioned ideals drove our relationship to be defined more by my ability to creatively avoid him while still carrying on an illusion of a loving father/daughter bond. I didn't understand him, his principles, or his values nor was I amused by his peculiar sense of humor. Furthermore, I didn't know how to begin to understand him and in my resentment at his strictness, I'd convinced myself that I didn't care to understand.

During those two weeks, Catherine and I spent our time bouncing back and forth between moments of severe boredom and a riveting tour through my father's youth. When we weren't being rushed from house to house to visit with people my parents' age or older (where we were offered more food and drink than we could possibly consume), we were swept away to see sights both near and far. We visited the muddy, murky pond-like basin where my father, against his parent's wishes, taught himself to swim. We climbed the woods behind my grandmother's house to visit the old well and traveler's den my father often talked of. He and his friends would come here to escape the farm work, drink *rakija,* and sing *ganga.* We learned how to get water out of the well, light a wood stove, and help our grandmother string tobacco. Vlado, acting as our tour guide, showed us the ins and outs of the village. He introduced us to the local kids, drank Turkish coffee with us at the only café in town, and took us to meet any adult worth his or her salt, including Mladin, the village

wonder. Mladin had never owned a watch yet without looking at the sky could always tell the correct time. This
prompted many conversations of whether his time-telling skill
would falter if he should find himself on a transatlantic airplane trip.

In all of these experiences, both those borne of pleasure and
those borne of necessity, a story slowly began to weave itself
around me. This was the story of my father, of how he came
to be who he is today and thus what helped make me who I
am. For the first time, I began to see my father as an individual. He was somebody's son, brother, buddy and best friend as
well as the town clown, the bully, the victim and the protec-
tor. He was somebody aside from and despite me.

With pain, surprise and sadness at my own selfishness and
inability to understand him, I was overcome with shame. I
began, selfishly, to gather the stories people told about my father. I found myself feeling jealous of their intimacy toward
him, an intimacy I couldn't remember having ever felt. I listened to the villagers intently and watched as memories
spilled out prompting yet more memories, amid laughter and
guffaws. I held these stories tightly, wrapped in the creases of
my mind. At night, in bed beside my sister, I reconstructed
him first as a boy, then as a teen, and finally as a young man
based on the fragments I had collected. I did this over and over
again. It wasn't so much that he had a remarkable life nor a life
so different from many others in his village, it was that he intrigued me as a man who *was not my father*. It was a sweet and
contemplative surprise to have met this individual during my
travels. Even the unpleasant recollections, while painful to
hear, shed light on many of his less favorable traits.

My father was one of six children, three boys and three girls
(seven others had died during childbirth or infancy). He was

the only one of his siblings to be pulled from school at age eight in order to work the farm. He had the unfortunate position of being neither the oldest son (which automatically presents such privileges as education) nor the youngest son (which ensures an allowance to be free of responsibility); he was the middle son. This position holds no special privilege. Although I already knew that he had not finished school, I didn't know that he was the only one among his siblings not to have done so. This knowledge shocked and confused me. I knew that he liked school and felt regret at never having finished. He was close to his siblings and I never heard my father speak unkindly about any of his family members. Years after I'd left home, my father's oldest sister was visiting us. She was an eccentric, strong-willed woman who could tease my father endlessly. After dinner one evening my aunt reminisced with my father about life "back home." Everyone seemed in good spirits, chuckling over memories. Suddenly, my father in a tense and choked voice, lips, jaw, fists tightly squeezed, said in anger so aged, "You all left me. You all got to go to school while I had to work! I had to work on the farm! I wanted to go to school! You all left me!" Angry, hot tears rolled down his face. My aunt rushed to his side after a brief moment of shock. "Oh Milan, Milan," she said, hugging his head against her breast trying to comfort him. But the moment was over. The "weakness" gone. He pushed her away and smiling tightly tried to pretend that his outbreak had not happened. My mother, sister, and I sat quietly at the table, tears stinging our eyes, apples in our throats. In all of our years, we had never seen our father cry nor suggest that his life was not what he had wanted it to be. He was from a time when men did not cry or show emotion or feel bitter or blame others for their lot. Catherine stood up and, putting her arms around him, made a comment about how it was O.K. to talk about it.

Unlike most American families we knew this "talking" phenomenon simply didn't apply to us. My father said there was
nothing to say and changed the subject. My mother said
nothing. She knew the extent of his pain and loss and regret
and anger and bitterness. My mother sometimes...often...
bore the brunt of these suppressed emotions. It was never
mentioned again.

When not stringing tobacco, lounging about bored, recon-
structing my father's youth, or eating *pura* (boiled cornmeal),
prsut (prosciutto), or homemade cheese, I spent my time
meeting my aunts, uncles, and cousins—so much family I
never knew and never thought I'd meet. Our lives were so
vastly different it was sometimes hard to believe we were of
the same blood. One of my aunts lived close to Baba giving
Catherine and me the opportunity to meet three of her sons
while we were in town. Two of them were our age. I can still
remember the awkwardness of that moment as we all stared at
one another while the adults talked nearby. These boys were
raised working the land and livestock in much the same way
their parents and their parent's parents had done for generations. As we struggled to find common ground, I was struck
with such clarity as to the privileges and freedom Catherine
and I had merely because we were American and they were
not. And it wasn't so much that we were American, it was
more that we simply weren't Croatian. Being two Western
girls with backpacks and no male chaperones traveling
through Europe was beyond the realm of anything our female
cousins could hope for. Even our male cousins could not
imagine having the time or money for such a vacation. It was
very humbling to meet these boys, these blood kin of ours,
and to experience through their eyes how lucky we were,
how privileged and luxurious our lives were despite the fact

that we had very little money and no help from our parents. This encounter has continued to shape my thoughts about how I choose to define "necessity" in my life.

The time passed and during the two weeks we spent in 'Bobanovadraga, the Croatian language slowly released itself from the confines of our minds where it had remained dormant for too long. By the time we left Baba's, our Croatian had improved to the extent that we were able to hold our own in most conversations. We also grew to both know and love Baba and Vlado. Furthermore, the disapproval we'd anticipated was met instead with love, acceptance, and enthusiasm. Shockingly, we learned how to survive without such modern conveniences as running water or air conditioning...again confirming for me the differences between "want" and "need." For those two weeks, we experienced the lifestyle of a mountain village where old widows gather routinely at dusk to drink *slivovica* and relive old times. Most importantly, we liked what we saw.

It was a special time for me, in some ways my most profound entry into an adult consciousness for it summarized that moment when I truly understood and appreciated the uniqueness of my parents as individuals irrespective of me. However, this isn't a fairy-tale story. Upon my return to the U.S., my relationship with my father did not undergo a sudden and dramatic transformation. No soul-baring conversations resulting in heartfelt "I love yous" and "I'm sorrys" ensued over the following weeks. In keeping with the tradition of my upbringing, I never told my parents about my experiences at Baba's house, how I was unwittingly introduced to this father/man along my journey. With that said, things between my father and me did improve. The power struggle that had previously defined our roles as "father" and "daughter" changed and evolved into something more manageable for both of us. With the information learned about my father while in Bobanovadraga, I had a newfound desire to know him as the person I'd met in his village. Thus, I found myself interacting with him in a completely different way. I was patient with him, I listened to his often-repeated stories, I asked him questions and even sought his opinion, I laughed at his jokes and, most importantly, I sometimes defended him from my siblings. I even felt slightly possessive of him. While this idealistic attitude towards my father did not last long, it did allow the smallest of shoots to take root, softening the armor we'd constructed against one another. Through this tiny sprout, he and I found a way of relating to one another without the constraints associated with the label of "father" or "daughter," labels we were never comfortable with anyway. Coming home and trying, for the first time, to meet the man inside my father made me want to be a better daughter despite his inability to ever be the fantasy father of my childhood desires. I am no longer just his child and he is no longer just my father. Finally, due to the time I spent in his world, we are friends.

I'll never forget the day we left Baba's house. We were leaving to visit our uncle, Vlado's father, who lived in a village several hours away. He'd arrived earlier that morning and busied himself stowing our packs in the car. Although there was a slight summer rain that would end soon, many of the local *babas* had come to say goodbye. While all of them shed intermittent tears throughout the morning, our Baba cried profusely. Her sadness perplexed me until I realized that she'd watched all of her children leave this way and she lived alone in a house that held memories of happier times. My uncle bundled my sister and me in the back seat, constantly reassuring his mother that we would be back. As he drove down the muddy path leading to the two-lane highway, I turned back to wave to Baba. Out of the corner of my eye I caught sight of the old cement telephone pole. There it loomed in the distance, standing tall, as if in defiance of the drab gray morning. It seemed like a lifetime ago that I'd first placed my fingers on that cool cement. In the shadow of that pole stood Baba. She was alone now, in the middle of the dirt road, kitchen aprons draped over her head in an effort to keep the rain from her hair, waving a limp and saddened wrist in our direction, tears slowly streaming down her time-battered face.

Drina Iva Boban was born and (mostly) raised in the San Francisco Bay Area. One of six children born to a French woman and Croatian father, her childhood was a strange blend of Croatian backyard pig roasts and snacking on Brie cheese and lemon-sugar crepes. She currently holds a joint position with the University of California, San Francisco and Kinemad, Incorporated as a clinical research manager. She lives in San Francisco with her partner, David, and their two Rottweilers, and she spends her free time attempting to balance a social life while training for and competing in triathlons.

ROBYN S. SHAW

✦ ✦ ✦

Flying with the Gulls

It was a dream come true.

SEAGULLS FLOAT OVER SCOTLAND'S TERRAIN LIKE GHOSTS that are seeking a lost ancestry. Their gentle forms are colored like the gray of clouds, while their piercing eyes tell stories of both fishing trawlers and farming tractors. The hazy hues of Scottish mists blend with their movements, yet the gleam of the sun also carefully delineates the clean line of their wings and the sharp markings of their faces. Throughout my childhood, envy would fill my body whenever I watched them flit over my homeland and as I imagined myself flying alongside them.

Now, many years later, fear filled my body as I ran across the frosty runway to the rusty two-cylinder plane that was waiting for me. The air was cold as the anxious faces of my two friends, Matt and Kevin, peered out through the gaping space where the plane's door should have been. In the next half hour the three of us would perform a parachute jump that would literally enable us to fly with the gulls. We were scared, we were petrified, yet still we eagerly anticipated the moment when our bodies would be free of this earth and its restrictions. Our longing for this freedom held us in place as we huddled within the metal body of the plane, as we felt the plane take off, and as the land below disappeared.

Watching the landing field, the training shed, the tumble-down farm, and the bodies of the other parachute students become smaller, I felt my heart lurch. I physically felt myself letting go of the elements that tied me to the ground and to my life's security. Human lives are framed by the land and its demands. Our minds are chained by the need for greed and opulence. That I was about to leap from a plane at two thousand feet was my signal to the world that I did not need to be bound by either wealth or physical belongings. For a second, I felt proud, I felt ready, but then, as my mind became again terrorized by fear, my thoughts returned to more humble beginnings.

The decision to throw myself out of a plane had actually come upon me as I stood with a group of friends staring at the wooden sign, advertising both the jump and training for only £75; this was propped against the bar from which we were ordering our night's first drinks. Matt had turned to me and, in his Belfast drawl, questioned whether I had ever wanted to do a parachute jump. My reply, as I reached for my freshly poured cider, provoked further conversation. "Actually, yeah, I have. I don't know why, but I've always thought it would be pretty cool." Now Kevin was interested and so his southern English accent interrupted my initial dreamily-expressed thoughts. "Well, I've always felt the same way, so why don't we all go and do a jump together?" Bravado turned to exhilaration as we faced each other, our excited faces warming to both the beer and the thought of shared adventure.

Now we were each inside this tin can of an airplane and, as it soared up through the sky, I felt as though part of my soul, part of my security, was being left behind on earth. Looking out of the grimy plastic window, I could see Scotland open up below me. The site of hundreds of years of history and of family-making lay below as my landing space. My hometown of Stirling had become a gray patch over which the dark castle resided. The great mountain, Dumyat, huddled around the town, seemed to protect its ancient walls from the same dark rain clouds through which I was about to float. Latched onto my back, the gray casing of my parachute bag similarly protected my body. The material contained within was about to be released in a manner akin to that when a butterfly first spreads its wings, but was I ready for such a transformation?

Somewhere down there was the white cross that I was supposed to land on, but (as I craned my neck) I was damned if I could see it. That frightened me. I was going to have to trust myself to maintain enough control to find a marked spot, twenty feet in diameter, that was somewhere out of sight two thousand feet below. I couldn't see the cross, but I knew that it was there waiting for me. The trees and the houses had become smaller, almost miniscule, but what was exciting me was that I could see as far away as Edinburgh and the North Sea. Once, as I'd traveled on a shambling train between Stirling and Edinburgh, I'd wondered what it would feel like to fly between the two cities. Sitting on that train, with the man in front of me snoring, I'd stared out of the window at the gray gulls as they'd flitted over the fields. Their white wings were twisting in the air as the somber light of the evening's clouds caught their beauty in their swift movement of uplift. I had remembered then my childhood dreams of flying with the gulls. Now, recalling both that train journey and earlier hopes of flight, I realized that much of my delight was derived from the precision of the gull's movements, of their curls and twists through the void that is this earth's atmosphere.

I'd seen gulls earlier as I'd donned my jumpsuit and tightened the buckles of my harness. Their freedom had mocked my unnaturally taut form yet it had also reawakened my sense of longing. There were no gulls now, we were too high, but their message remained with me. I should trust the movements of the wind to carry me through the air and over the land to my destination.

Now, anxiously crouching at the door of the plane, I could feel the material of my harness rub uncomfortably against my legs. The unopened bag of my parachute had locked my body in an unnatural position. Similarly, my mind was being held in an unnatural position as it fought to come to terms with the situation in which it had placed itself. In a matter of seconds, I was to eject my body out of the plane and downward. Matt and Kevin were nervously watching me as I clutched the cold metal framework and stared into the abyss.

As the two-cylinder plane began to circle at two thousand feet, my coach crept to my side and began counting me down. "Three, two…" I stared at my male counterparts—still snuggly in place within the plane—with horror. "One." I jumped and fell through the quicksilver blanket of clouds and dissolving fear. For five seconds I dropped, my arms and legs spread-eagled. "One thousand, two thousand, three thousand…check canopy." My head slammed back, full of fear, to check if my canopy had opened. Relief swept through me— I shouted a clear and resolute, "y e e e e s" out into the wild blue yonder. I screamed with exhilaration, for now I was attached to a psychedelic flower floating in the wind. I was more than glad that the petals of my canopy had stayed open, instead of slamming shut against the wind's harsh current. I had been warned of the terror that accompanied the failure of a parachute, and of the need to follow the subsequent safety procedures that never seemed entirely safe.

My hands clasped onto the metal grips that would direct me toward the ground. My body felt empowered as fear left and joy arrived: I was safe. Indeed, slowly drifting downward, I felt the landscape come into my soul. I was no longer an observer of the land; I was a part of its own wild structure. And, as part of that bargain, I was no longer in control, but at the mercy of the winds and also, in part, fate. Pulling the left cord down, my canopy drew me around in a circle. All of Scotland lay before me and, as I squinted, I could see the blue line of the North Sea off in the distance. I smiled to myself as all went quiet and I floated in the wind.

The intimacy of flight astounded me as I silently twisted in the air. The white mist embracing me danced in tune to my turns while its gentle cold particles pressed against my face. Every few moments I would pull down on one of my cords and draw the canopy in toward me, controlling my movement through the air. This ability to control my flight felt magical as I weaved through the mist, enjoying my newfound freedom. The descent took a little over three minutes but the experience will last me a lifetime. I discovered during my fall to earth that humans don't need to be bound to the earth's surface but that with a little help from technology they can become as free as the birds that twirl and dance in the wind.

High above my homeland I learned to read the landscape of Scotland, as my mind gently probed for meaning and as my memory conjured fantastical images of battles and bloodshed long past. I also learned to read my own flight patterns and to transform my fear into a positive energy. It was this positive energy that allowed my to make my landing in triumph. Initially, when I'd seen the chalky dust of the cross far beneath my feet, I'd been calm. Then, suddenly, as the ground started rushing up toward me, I began to panic. I felt as though I had no control over the irresistible force of gravity. Then, I felt the awesome power of trust pulse through my body, and my fear turned into exhilaration because I knew I could land properly. I pulled down both cords close to my body and drew my knees and legs together. My actions prepared me physically for the landing but, all the same, I was startled by the hearty *thump* with which I hit the ground and then by the *whoosh* as I was carried quickly from the ground back into the air. My parachute—as though itself exhilarated by the journey—had refilled with air as soon as I had touched down. The momentum carried me not only two or three feet off the ground, but also along the line of the white cross and farther out into the field. I had to think quickly, so I drew my cords so tightly into my side that they crossed over in front of my stomach while I ran my feet back down to earth and to a rather clumsy stop.

And so my dramatic flight ended in laughter as I gathered the folds of my parachute into my arms. The friends who had come to watch my jump had seen my body crumple on landing but they had also seen the huge smile on my face as I had drawn myself back up into the standing position. So, as we all walked back to the training shed, and as Matt and Kevin joined us equally exhilarated, we shared much laughter. Behind my laughter, though, was a quieter sense of pride. I had accomplished my dream; I had flown with the gulls.

Half an hour later, as a I drove home, I saw a seagull perched on the shiny metal of a barbed-wire fence. It seemed to be grinning at me, and I grinned back. Poised intently, it flew off as soon as the car had passed. My eyes followed the beat of its wings as it curved across the land and away to distant dreams.

Robyn Shaw left her home in Scotland seven years ago and has since been living in and learning about France and America. As a teacher of composition, she is constantly trying to find new ways to turn experiences into words.

CHELSEA BAUCH

✦ ✦ ✦

A Portrait of the Artist as a Bold Man

Florence speaks, and lives, through its art.

THE CHILD RISES. THE FRIARS KNEEL. THE WOMAN weeps. The crowd gathers. The saint hovers. The street darkens. And half-hidden by the crowd, yet still boldly recognizable, a young man stares out of the painting.

His name is Domenico Ghirlandaio, and among his many achievements, he is the man responsible for the dimly lit fresco before me. His hands rest confidently on his hips, and he wears a blue tunic and a red scarf. There is nothing discreet about his identity. Such audacity at first strikes me as strange, but the longer I stare the more I see the look of confidence in his eyes. Half-hidden by the crowd, yet unmistakably visible, this self-portrait is merely his signature.

I leave the church. The street before me looks no different than that in the fresco: the bridge of Santa Trinita, the Ferragamo Palace, the Arno River. This is the essence that Ghirlandaio saw in some damp plaster more than five hundred years ago. Something like nostalgia, or perhaps just hunger, tugs at my stomach. I cross the road, narrowly missed by a speeding moped.

The streets are made of heavy blocks, black and smooth from hundreds of years of use. I can't help but wonder who laid them, but there is no self-portrait, no signature, carved into the stones to tell me who it was. Eventually the narrow road opens into the square leading to the city's cathedral, the Duomo. Scores of tourists prowl the piazza, eagerly snapping pictures that have been painted or photographed thousands of times already. Inside the cathedral it is quieter but no less crowded as craned necks guide aimless bodies throughout the church. The dim walls are lined with nameless faces that peer out from dusty frames.

Along the left corridor hangs a painting of Dante Alighieri. Renouncing traditional Latin verse, Dante wrote his masterpiece, *The Divine Comedy*, in the common vernacular of his era. Although he was consequently expelled from Florence, centuries later it is that very brazenness for which he is still celebrated. Even in the fading picture his confidence remains unmistakable.

At the end of the wide nave, the ceiling opens up into Brunelleschi's dome, a structure considered at the time of its construction to be the greatest feat of engineering since antiquity. The interior is covered in frescoes and two narrow walkways cling to the circumference inviting closer examination. It is little wonder that this structure was also once the world's highest dome. I almost fall over from leaning backwards to stare up at it.

Outside again I walk toward the river. Sculls and rowboats slide along the water effortlessly as the pale yellow houses that line the banks watch in silence. Past the Ponte Vecchio, I turn left toward the entrance to the Uffizi. The most famous work of Ghirlandaio's most famous student becomes visible as I approach the museum. An imposing replica of Michelangelo's *David* marks the corner of Florence's vast Piazza di Signori where the original once stood. Although statues of nudes are no longer unique to the square, Michelangelo's work was the first of its kind to appear in a public area. From the way that he is standing, however, *David* is clearly not concerned with modesty.

The main corridor of the Uffizi is attended by an endless procession of anonymous busts and statues, which are surrounded by art students fervently copying their pallid forms. The ceiling is frescoed and lined by what appears as a type of "Who's Who in the Renaissance" array of portraits. Unfortunately I have no idea just *who* any of them were.

Entering Botticelli's room I am quickly overwhelmed by his artistic power. The feigned modesty of the Venus, the sallow cheeks of an old man lost in a background, the mere presence of *The Allegory for Spring*, and a daring suggestion of the Virgin Mary pushing away the angel Gabriel, all capture the essence of a man who was not afraid to paint as he willed.

Walking farther through the galleries, I am confronted by Bronzino, Da Vinci, and Caravaggio who greet me without acknowledgment. I see Michelangelo's *Sacra Famiglia,* a painting that resembles a sculpture more than it does reality. He painted the way that he sculpted, depicting muscular limbs and well studied nudes. Even the figures in the painting have that half-frozen movement that sculpted forms so often suggest.

I finally leave the museum and make my way back into the heat. The Piazza di Signori is more crowded than it was earlier so I head toward the narrow side streets to avoid the crowds.

Eventually I come to a small piazza where a banner advertises the Istituto degli Innocenti. Although far more discreet than his dome, yet no less important, Brunelleschi's modest

Istituto is considered to be the first Renaissance building. Once the city's orphanage and now home to a small museum, the tall columns and unabashed arches of the building's exterior inimitably display his innovation.

At the top of the stairs I enter the museum only to look up and see a familiar face watching me. Ghirlandaio's eyes are bold as he irreverently stares out from a crowd of pious adorers and heralding angels in a painting at the end of the corridor. His look of confidence is unmistakable, but now staring back I understand his conviction. At times audacious, and always boldly recognizable, the city of Florence is, after all, the very signature of its artists.

Born and raised in Northern California, Chelsea Bauch now lives in New York City where she is a student at NYU and continues her writing. She is interested in studying human migration, from pilgrims to immigrants, to better understand her own itchy feet.

CAROL KAUFMANN

* * *

An Uneasy Peace

In 2000, a holiday became something else.

STAND IN THE HEART OF SARAJEVO, TILT UPWARD AND turn slowly in a 360-degree circle. Craggy mountains rise sharply above a cozy valley, its meandering roads dotted with homes. I salivate over the possibilities of countless hikes on my unusual vacation—a combination of an overdue visit with a friend who's been away from home too long and a firsthand look at a war-torn city under siege for three years, a natural curiosity for a journalist. Later in the evening, I casually mention my hike to Lydia and her colleagues, Americans and Europeans transplanted there to reconstruct the city.

"You will not, under any circumstances get off the paved road!" they warn. "The hills are mined, like the rest of the mountains in Bosnia. There's no way to detect where they are and the Serbs didn't exactly leave a map. Last week, a child was killed when he stepped in the wrong spot."

Mines? I wince, certain my crinkled brow portrays disbelief. Sure, headlines attempt to depict the horror, but without actually setting foot in a tarnished landscape, how can one fully comprehend what such restrictions mean? Mines are for battlefields, not cities, but still, my friends warn, about a million remain. The alluring mountains began to look like a prison, my cell for the next ten days of my vacation. But residents of this once elegant European town, a former Olympics host, face a much longer sentence. "You should have seen Sarajevo before the war. It was a completely different city," says Adina, an energetic and bright-eyed college student who lived through the three-year ethnic conflict of Serbs, Croats, and Muslim Bosniaks vying for dominance. "Now, it's like a psychiatric ward, where everyone walks around shell-shocked." She says all this as a matter of fact, as if she has told the story many times.

How has war changed Adina's life? How can a foreigner begin to understand what war does to a place and its citizens? What questions do you ask? Immediately, tiny glimpses of what Adina meant become apparent. Stress on the street is palpable. From a distance, these physically hearty, Slavic people look like they could endure multiple harsh winters and take on hurricanes, but up close on the street they appear dazed, locked in a permanent state of confusion. I watch them walk into oncoming traffic, oblivious to the accident waiting to happen. Is this from sheer distress, or do they simply no longer care? Pedestrians collide into me, their bumps force me to regain balance but the offenders keep walking as if nothing has happened. Maybe it's because of their superior height and frame, but there's likely a deeper reason. For a country that has lost a third of its population, a little jolt in the street probably has no effect.

The very hills that help make the town charming quickly begin to feel suffocating. To compensate, I run. Every day I hit the asphalt, careful to stay on the sidewalks. Running provides a street-level way to cover vast territory in a new city and I've learned a great deal by huffing and puffing through various cities and countrysides, but Sarajevo is my toughest exercise yet. Decimated gray-block office buildings still open for business despite conditions that would make OSHA officials shiver. The National Library burned by the Serbs stands on the river's edge. Many of Sarajevo's literary treasures went up in flames—and so did property deeds, contracts, and other records that give citizens confidence they possess a piece of the town. Nearby, the famous crumbling stone bridge that marks the assassinations of Archduke Ferninand and his wife still crosses the river. Elegant curving mosques built by the Ottomans stand next to faded yellow architecture of the Austro-Hungarian Empire. Families and conversations fill apartment buildings riddled with scars from bullets and grenades, laundry hangs from windows with jagged glass. Dilapidated cars fill the parking lots. Men in their twenties or thirties missing limbs amble awkwardly by. Others wear patches to cover empty eye sockets. Bosnians, Croats, and Serbs blend together on the sidewalks. Most of them, even the women, tower over me. On the surface, they appear indistinguishable to me. Only during the call to prayer are Muslims identifiable as they trod toward one of the city's many mosques.

No one else jogs here, save the United Nation's troops. The camouflage-covered peacekeepers breeze by, heads erect and cocky. I nod in appreciation for their part in maintaining the outward calm of the city and take note of the different insignias of their countries on their sleeves. Sarajevans have mixed feelings about troops on their turf. But without them, would the palpable tensions erupt?

My morning jog hurts, even on the path by the Miljacka River that separates the town. The cars lack catalytic converters and spew grimy black emissions from their tail pipes, tea kettles blowing their tops. Metallurgic plants pump bigger plumes that lie stagnant in the valley's wall of mountains. The residents seem oblivious to the heavy pollution—probably the last thing on their minds—and the international community must have adjusted, but I never breathe freely. The dirty air lingers, infecting the mood. Walkers shoot confused and often hostile looks as if they've never seen a jogger and don't want to now. On my second run, I decide to ditch the baseball cap and white t-shirt for something a little more gray and inconspicuous. The daily ritual becomes a guilty pleasure; exercising here seems luxurious and trivial. I feel ashamed after one block and long to retreat to Lydia's apartment, safe from the looks. The very act of exercise gives me away. Clearly, I'm not suffering.

The flowing Miljacka does provide a tiny respite. Residents seem less guarded on this tree-lined path. Old men don nice suits for an afternoon stroll, young teenagers push and shove each other, and small children in bright clothes scamper around their mothers, laughing. Normal. But I knew there was a difference between my normalcy and theirs. The best and brightest of the city found a way to leave during the war, most fled to Europe. Remaining residents live with loss of jobs and family members. Their homes provide temporary apartments for affluent aid workers trying to rebuild the city and mitigate further disaster. And my only concern for health and welfare is to breathe fresh air and soothe the rumbling of my hungry stomach.

A marketplace called the Bascarsija in the cobbled streets of the old Ottoman part of the city, offers options for lunch. On the streets of inviting craft stalls grouped according to trade it's not difficult to find what I'm looking for. Pizza is a common dish in the Balkans—and a staple in my diet. Some restaurants use ketchup for tomato sauce, so I make attempts to look at the pies before placing an order. At the third restaurant, an affable young guy no more than eighteen doesn't seem to understand I want plain pizza, despite many gestures and attempts to communicate. The waiter looks about Adina's age and I wonder if he's going to college or what his future holds. I recall the stories of Adina's family smuggling food during the war; their dinner would often come from the same market, if it came at all. I stop my plea for real tomatoes. The teenager, doing his best to please, looks confused. This large international community living in his hometown can't say "pizza" in his native tongue, yet he's really trying to help. I smile, put my hands up in a whatever-you-have-is-fine gesture and take what I'm served. I eat it all and tip the waiter 100 percent, a total of six dollars. Enough of my demands.

A quaint haven of a shop, owned and operated by women who lost their husbands and homes in the war, lies just around the corner. It's a bright, clean, and airy place about the size of a mid-level manager's office with shelves of lovely hand-knitted sweaters, shawls, gloves, and hats. The October chill isn't severe enough for the thick cable-gauge knit, but I buy some goods anyway. My repeat appearances leave no impression, and I'm quite positive I don't look like the usual clientele. Each time I hand her my money, no traditional verbal token of appreciation follows—only vacant eyes and a half smile.

I have never known such wide-scale loss. I have never seen scorched earth. I can't communicate with the residents of Sarajevo. My small monetary contributions and the smile I offer don't amount to a hill of beans because I don't know what it means to suffer. I probably don't convey real empathy, only confusion.

Every few blocks in the hilly, patternless neighborhood streets lie graveyards, but not ones with centuries of history. The tombstones are all new with tall, white pillars on which, despite the year of birth, the year of death reads either 1992 or 1993. Cemeteries usually mean an array of tombstone types and ages, mostly moss-covered and forgotten—not ones marked by gleaming white marble. But here they're part of Sarajevo's daily rhythm. A trip to the corner store includes walking past pillars, an obvious reminder of the chasm in the city's history.

It's here I'm drawn to an old Muslim man and his slow, deliberate stride, and forget to consider the "rules" in a Muslim cemetery—if non-Muslims are allowed. I follow him down the gray stone path stopping about twelve feet behind him. He stands by the grave of a young boy, who according to the dates on the tombstone died at age twenty-two. He holds out his hands, palms facing the sky and mumbles something, his eyes closed. I think it must be a prayer, but maybe he is simply asking, "Why?"

Why indeed. I have used my vacation days to try to understand how people cope with a tragic conflict by coming to witness what remained. But I can only stand outside at a distance, looking in like a child witnessing a terrible crime. Despite the pervasiveness of evidence here, I'll never fully understand.

Carol Kaufmann is a staff writer at National Geographic *magazine. Her work has also appeared in* The Washington Post, George, Big World *travel, and* AOL's Talk City *website. She is also currently working on her first book. Since she can remember, she has measured all she buys against the cost of a plane ticket—and usually opts for travel. She lives in Alexandria, Virginia.*

* * *

Souvenirs

*Years after youthful sojourns in the City of Light, a mother
and daughter return, sharing memories of a place
that came to symbolize life, love, and loss.*

M. DE MÉNEVAL IS NOT THE TYPE I'D EXPECT TO SEE ON
all fours: a small, graying man, crisp of carriage, with an astonishing aquiline nose. And this is not a place that promises
such informality—a bourgeois salon with its large oil portrait
of an austere ancestor, its ancient bandoliers marking the walls
with Xs, and its glass cabinet filled with such Empire relics as
pieces of royal china and a fan from Empress Eugénie.

"*Et voilà*," he calls out ebulliently, lifting a lithograph from
the bottom of an ornate chest so that my mother and I can
see. There, on horseback, is Napoleon III, reviewing his
troops. And there, just behind him, is M. de Méneval's "*arrière-
arrière grandpère*," Napoleon's private secretary and the guy
who earned the impressive "de" in the family name.

I had never imagined, when I impulsively invited my
mother to Paris for her sixty-fifth birthday, that we would
end up *here*, in Versailles, sipping tea and chatting in French
with Claude and Monique de Méneval. Sure, I knew that my
mother's junior year abroad had been one of the formative

experiences of her life. But hadn't she moved on, settling for a humble life in rural Hawaii, never returning to France, letting her ties loosen?

She had, in my view, not so much abandoned her taste for all things French as chosen to pass it on, to me. She pulled me off the beach to read *Madeline and the Bad Hat* and *Eloise in Paris*. She bought me a small spiral notebook, inscribing its brown cover with MON PETIT CAHIER DE FRANÇAIS and listing words for me to memorize. Although our everyday diet consisted of things like tuna-noodle casserole and Hamburger Helper, she occasionally gave my brother and sister and me a taste of her Continental past by serving a cheese soufflé or chocolate mousse. Once or twice she treated us to stories of the French gypsy who'd taught her to read palms—and then she proceeded to predict our futures.

Tales of gypsies were eventually supplanted by tales of le Baron-Louis de Méneval, scion of the *petite noblesse*, and la Baronne, head of their formidable household in the 17th *arrondissement*. Long on pride and short on funds, the enchanting de Ménevals had chosen the socially acceptable way to improve the family cash flow—by taking in a college student. My mother must have fit the bill perfectly: she had studied French all her life (even winning a statewide award in Ohio), but she wasn't just a French nerd. Raised by a socialite from Massachusetts, and named "Madeleine" after her, she had followed her mother's footsteps by attending Smith College. By then my mother had lost her mother, and she always spoke of the de Ménevals with a fondness usually reserved for family.

Now here I am in Versailles, connecting the dots: Before me are all the possessions—inherited by the eldest son of le Baron-Louis and la Baronne—that filled my mother's descriptions of her "home" in France. And here are the intersections between a family and a country, whose history Claude is proudly enumerating. Here, too, is the relationship between Claude and my mother: the once stiff rapport between a competitive twenty-three-year-old law student and a smug twenty-one-year-old American girl is now reinventing itself as a warm friendship between a retired businessman turned Napoleon expert and a photo-toting granny from Hawaii. But, more than anything, here are my mother's deep ties to Paris—which, because they preceded me, have remained largely a mystery.

The longing for such connections had sparked the idea of our trip. Then, midway through the planning stages, my father was given less than a year to live. Though he and my mother had been divorced for thirty years, the news devastated us both. We considered postponing, until a new urgency swept aside our misgivings. *Go. Now. While there's time.* In the face of losing Dad, I yearned to draw closer to Mom. Planning the trip got me through some hard months.

There was lots of planning. With the help of the Internet and two Paris services, we finally selected two *pieds-à-terre*: a large studio on the Ile de la Cité, and a one-bedroom on rue du Fer à Moulin, in the 5th *arrondissement*. Apartments would afford us corners of privacy and our own washing machine, and their kitchens would give us an excuse to load up on fresh bread from Poilâne, cheeses from Androuët, and mustards from Hédiard.

But apartments also let us experience Paris not as tourists coming and going from a hotel, but as residents. Being on Ile de la Cité means waking to the eight o'clock bells of Notre Dame, lunching in the lovely Place Dauphine, taking in an evening violin concert at St. Chapelle, and snagging ringside seats for the Saturday-night street theater kicked off by nine guys in surgical scrubs and a gay man in a bunny costume with a few strategically placed fresh carrots, green foliage flopping. In the 5th *arrondissement*, we visit with the *boulangère* down the block, blaze through the rue Mouffetard market every day, and take mint tea in the Arab Café de La Mosquée, with its blue-and-white-tiled fountain, fig trees, and round brass tables.

Mom and I easily agree on how to spend our days. We don't go to a single museum. We skip the Eiffel Tower. We tune in to the surprises of the quotidian rather than the pre-dictability of tourist destinations. We decode billboards and shop signs. We enjoy the bump and bustle of Paris buses, where schoolchildren rub elbows with immigrant workers, and adolescents prattle on into cell phones. And we visit churches daily: in the eloquent quiet of St. Paul and St. Germain-des-Près, we light candles for Dad.

Mom spends one morning on the Ile de la Cité scouring the map. Soon she is leading me across the Seine on a foot-bridge, around the tiny chapel of St.-Julien-le-Pauvre, and then straight to rue de la Huchette, a narrow medieval alley. She stops in front of a crude stone façade.

"My dear friend David brought me to the Caveau de la Huchette on my birthday in 1953," Mom muses, casting her glance to the Greek restaurants now lining the street. "This was just an old alley then, with centuries of grime." Pointing to pictures of dancers on a subterranean parquet, under stone arches, she continues: "Steep, turning steps descended to a cave-like room. Sidney Bechet and his Blue Notes played! A gang of men all dressed in black turtlenecks—they were called '*apachés*' then—arrived. One of them—very handsome— asked me to dance. At first I demurred, but David insisted I dance with him. By chance I was wearing a black cashmere turtleneck and a flared red skirt. He was very polite with me. And he was the most wonderful dancer—the smoothest…" I sense in Mom's voice the hint of something dark, forbidden, thrilling; later I learn about the underworld of the *apachés*, and the rough tango they practiced.

"Afterward, in the foggy mist from the river, David and I circled around a small Greco-Roman church. We walked back across the city to the seventeenth, past bakers in basements—one blew flour at us from a bellows. We crossed the Place de la Concorde, completely empty. I was carried part of the way because my feet hurt."

And so I start to learn the secrets of my mother's time in Paris, to become familiar with the subterranean corners of her history. And she, in turn, learns mine. My Paris is a place of unfamiliar longings suddenly made all too familiar. A place of romance witnessed from a distance (those kids kissing on the bridge), and loves unrequited. A place you can desire but never possess.

Mom knows little about my falling in love in my early twenties with a French photographer. Jacky and I shared poetry, love letters, and, briefly, a room in a sprawling house on the St. Cloud train tracks. We met in San Francisco, but it was in Paris, after a ten-month separation, that Jacky took me up in his bear-like arms, burrowed through my jumble of curls, searched for "*le creux de ton cou*," inhaled deeply, and whispered, "*Je retrouve l'odeur de Connie*" (I am rediscovering the scent of Connie).

But it is also here that Jacky and I made our own Odyssean journey by foot, starting at 1:00 A.M.. from Châtelet and ending at 4:00 A.M. near the Bois de Boulogne, when Jacky gently let me know that he intended to live alone, needed to *be* alone. An artist needs *la solitude*, he said, without a trace of grandiosity.

And now, fifteen years later, Jacky invites us to an exhibition of still photographs at the Canadian Cultural Center that he has taken for a film, *The Red Violin*. There, he adds, we can meet Nam, the French-Vietnamese woman for whom he has abandoned *la solitude,* and their son, Ulys. Never am I so happy to have my mother's company. I am struck by uncharacteristic shyness; she holds my hand while I gaze at photos, she makes small talk with Nam, and she praises Jacky on the handsomeness of his son.

Jacky's first words to my mother—*Je la connaissais quand elle était toute petite* ("I knew her when she was a little girl")—call Bob Dylan to mind (not just "she breaks just like a little girl," but also "I was hungry, and it was your world"). And they also remind me of that peculiarly French kind of intimacy—witty, affectionate, and brutally detached. He looks better than ever, his auburn hair now brushing his shoulders, and I find that I am still susceptible, still able to be pulled in by his tender words and then spit out into the dark Paris night.

My mother does not directly address the whorl of confusing emotions within me as we leave the cultural center and wander along Les Invalides. "Would you like to stop by that wine bar you've been curious about?" she asks instead, with exquisite delicacy, placing her hand softly on my shoulder. And so we submit together to the attentions of Au Sauvignon's proprietor, who determines that we shall leave his establishment tasting the very best France has to offer.

As Mom and I continue to explore the mysteries of Paris together, we continue to refine our mother-daughter act. It starts with the language we both love. Mom's French is formal, correct. Mine is informal, current. With the artists and boutique owners in Village St. Paul, I chat away as Mom intently listens. I can see their wheels turning, their scenarios spinning. *The mother must be French—trim figure, strong nose, elegant sweep of white hair. The daughter's French is good, yes, but the unkempt curls, the running shoes, the earnest manner! Not French, no.* Then I mash a few pronouns, Mom answers a question, and their stories shatter around us like dropped Limoges.

Not that I do all the talking. In an antique store in the Marais, an eccentric, leather-skinned patron points me downstairs to his collection of '40s French soap wrappers. (Flat, light, and cheap, *etiquettes de savon* are the perfect souvenir.) Having dispensed with me, he extravagantly sets two director's chairs in the doorway, facing out, and flirtatiously invites "*Madame*" to join him "*sur la plage.*"

To track down the de Ménevals, Mom had taken the lead. She pored through an old white pages directory, thinking that at least the children—Claude, Françoise, Christian, and "Bébé"—would still be in Paris. She found a Claude de Méneval listed, but it was up to me to translate our urgent desires into graceful French. I dialed the number, identified myself, and asked after Claude. The man who answered—he was much too young to be a contemporary of my mother's—explained that Claude, once a roommate, now lives in Poland. "Perhaps you are looking for the father," he added. "I believe he lives in Versailles."

And so we ended up at the train station in Versailles. The moment Claude steps out of his blue Renault, my mother gasps. "He hasn't changed at all," she whispers. He and my mother approach each other without a trace of doubt, clasping hands and kissing both cheeks. Then we get into the car, me joining two towheaded and very curious little boys in the back seat. Unlike Claude, who has retained the formalities of the 17th *arrondissement*, Monique is a down-to-earth Bretonne equally at ease welcoming us into their modern townhouse on the edge of Napoleon's woods, passing delicate porcelain teacups and crisp cookies laced with chocolate, and firmly insisting that the grandchildren, Luc and Daniel, sit still.

After an exchange of gifts and the finding of the magnificent lithograph, Claude suggests a tour. Mom visited the palace years ago, so she picks the gardens. All six of us pile into the Renault as our private guide, who has filled his retirement by learning about this place, reveals the intrigue behind the endless canals, the Grand Trianon, and Marie-Antoinette's faux peasant village. When we part, the Paris my mother and I now share acquires another facet.

On our last night in France, Mom and I treat ourselves to *Turandot* at the Opéra de Bastille. We arrive early and banter with two young, idle ushers. Hearing that Mom has come back to Paris after forty-five years, they ask excitedly, "What was Paris like in 1954?" "How do you find it different?" She answers in French, basking in our interest, telling us how *belle* it is now, the trees ever more majestic, the façades scrubbed of coal dust, the shadows of World War II banished, and the men in green keeping the Boulevard St. Germain spotless.

In Act III, we both weep quietly in our front-row balcony seats as the slave-girl Liù expresses her "deep, secret, unconfessed love" and anticipates her untimely death. We weep for the loss of Liù, for the pending loss of my father, for the loss of youthful romance, for the loss of rekindled friendship, for our last moments together in Paris. To console ourselves, we stop at the Café le St. Médard for a *crème brûlée*, a last look at the crowd, a last listen to the fountain. There I realize I have lost an earring. It is half of a pair of lovely mabe pearls, traced in gold, given me by my father on my recent birthday, the last I will spend with him. I am momentarily heartsick, and then decide that an earring is the only thing I've really lost on this trip, and I can live with that.

A few weeks later, back home in California, a small package arrives from my mother. It is a pair of pearls.

Constance Hale's lifelong fascination with French is rivaled only by her lifelong fascination with English. She is the author of Wired Style *and* Sin and Syntax, *and as a journalist has written about Latin plurals and internet clichés. She has also covered national politics, the digital culture, and the spread of hula on the U.S. mainland. She lives in Oakland, California, and Hale'iwa, Hawaii.*

JO BROYLES YOHAY

The Power of a Good Book

A 1930s story comes to life
in the twenty-first century.

"IT'S THAT BLOODY BOY—HE'LL KILL THE LOT OF US—
Look at the table—knee-deep in scorpions—every matchbox
in the house is a death-trap…"

So goes the dialogue in well-known naturalist Gerald
Durrell's exuberant minor classic, *My Family and Other Animals*.
The book gives his account of the London-based Durrells'
five-year sojourn in the 1930s on the Greek island of Corfu.

The words exploded from Gerald's brother Lawrence, then
twenty-three, who would later gain fame as writer of four
novels in the *Alexandria Quartet*. "He had finished lunch,
leaned back in his chair, and opened a matchbox to light a cigarette." (It was 1935; smoking was still *de rigueur*.) "Agitated
scorpions, fleeing captivity, hoisted themselves out of the box
and scuttled across the luncheon table. Bedlam ensued. Margo,
fifteen, screamed, Leslie, seventeen, overturned chairs, and
their large, boisterous dog Roger barked wildly. At the other
end of the table sat their diminutive mother—a widow, looking like a tiny, harassed missionary in an uprising. All that the

283

bloody boy (ten-year-old Gerald, a budding animal enthusiast) had intended was to move the scorpion family from its home in the garden wall into the house for scientific scrutiny. An empty matchbox had offered perfect transport."

The summer I read *My Family and Other Animals* aloud to my son Jacob, I fell in love not only with the marvelously crazy household of Durrell characters, but with the land of Corfu itself. With Gerald, we prowled the olive-clad countryside and searched marshlands for animal life. We picnicked with the family on deserted beaches and overheard zany conversations with local peasants. As we belly-laughed our way through the chapters, I put Corfu on my list of places to visit someday.

Such is the power of a good book that last January, ten years after the thigh-slapping summer, I commandeered my friend Susan to join me for a week on the island as a kind of Durrell pilgrimage. By then I had also read several more of Gerald's three dozen books on his life as an animal preservationist. All of them, full of lively wit, were runaway successes. Since the mid-'50s when they began to appear, millions of copies have been sold to enthusiastic fans. I had also savored Lawrence's gorgeous descriptions of Corfu in *Prospero's Cell*, which fortified my resolve. I knew, of course, that today's Corfu would be wildly different from the pre-World War II era of the '30s (a time long before poured-concrete condos threatened to cover the earth's surface). But I was determined to see if I could find any remnants of the Durrells' 1930s Corfu.

Since summer's snarled traffic and sun-seekers would intrude on our search for the past, we opted for winter instead. January temperatures promised to be in the high 50s, a blessed relief from Manhattan's deep-freeze. For flavor, we decided on period transportation. Instead of flying to Corfu, we wanted to arrive a la the Durrells, by rail and boat—methods

I often pick anyway as a means of eavesdropping on a culture. Since a train from London takes more time than we could spare, we settled for a flight from New York to Rome, a five-hour train overland from Rome to Bari, on the Adriatic coast, and an overnight ferry to Corfu, which dangles between the southern tip of Italy and the western shore of mainland Greece.

Approaching by sea was a perfect choice. I slipped from my cabin at daybreak and hurried on deck, eager for my first glimpse of the island. The moon still hung in the growing light as sickle-shaped Corfu appeared. Craggy mountains swooped down, yielding to hills stained with the green of olive groves. As we drew closer, curved beaches glinted white along the shore. Across the Adriatic, a scant two kilometers away, stood the stark, snow-clad mountains of Albania, and beyond them, mainland Greece. We chugged through a large bay and docked at Corfu Town, the capital, perched on a promontory by the sea.

We spent our first day ambling around the elegant little city. Laid out by fourteenth-century Venetians, the town bears the imprint of other occupiers, too—French, British, Turkish—but the architecture clearly recalls La Serenissima. Graceful three- or four-story houses loom over narrow alleyways. The sea is visible from almost everywhere.

A huge green Esplanade fronts the water; directly behind is The Liston, an arcaded street designed by the French to resemble Paris' Rue de Rivoli. Together they form the local point of town life. An arched roof shelters numerous outdoor cafés (even in January!) and an entry to a small hotel where the Durrells' stayed for two weeks while they searched for a villa to rent. I could easily picture them shambling up from the port in a magnificently dilapidated horse-drawn cabî though today's curbs are lined with Smart cars and Fiats.

We wandered through the narrow, cobbled streets of the old town and visited two forts that jut up above the rooftops. One has origins in the sixth century when the ancient city was destroyed by the Goths; the other dates from the twelfth century. A morning market, specializing in farm produce and fresh fish, occupies the dry moat of the so-called "new" fort. The colors of stacked vegetables and fruits were a feast for the eyes, the local shoppers a feast for the lay-anthropologist heart. Fishermen, bronzed and muscular, offered their catch; elderly women in their best black clothes bargained for red mullet and octopus; young mothers with babies poked at just-picked oranges for juiciness; old men, as twisted as olive trees, gathered in clumps to talk.

When we spied the red onion dome of the sixteenth century Church of Agios Spiridon, I had a flash of recognition and rushed inside. The small interior glowed with the light of candles and, just as Gerald had reported, the mummified body of Saint Spiridion, the island's miracle-working patron saint, was enshrined in a silver coffin in a tiny room to the side. Several days a year, the coffin is opened to allow the faithful to kiss the slipper-clad feet of the mummy. I laughed out loud when I remembered a scene in which Mrs. Durrell (known to the reader as Mother), hopelessly entangled in a crowd, got separated from the children as the mob surged forward to bend, kiss the feet, and murmur a prayer. Thinking that public slobbering presented a health risk, Mother gestured frantically to Margo who was ahead of her. Finally she hissed at Gerald over the wedge of humanity, "Tell Margo—not to kiss—kiss the air.... Too late. Fifteeen-year-old Margo crouched over the slippered feet, kissing them with an enthusiasm that enchanted and surprised the crowd. She thought the saint might cure her acne, she explained afterward."

Ours was not an open-coffin day. We joined a line of assorted locals who filed by to kiss the foot of the closed coffin. Mother would be glad to know that I kissed the air. Sifting through a bookstore for a road map, we stumbled on an English-language section, a surprise because we had heard no English spoken among the mere smattering of tourists. I was even more startled to find a small guidebook, locally published, called *In the Footsteps of Lawrence Durrell and Gerald Durrell*. So we weren't the only pilgrims. The woman at the counter explained that quite a few people, especially British, visit Corfu because they loved reading the two brothers. "Some even stay," she added. I bought the book with mixed feelings. Specific directions for finding such things as "the strawberry pink villa" were definitely a boon. But my sense of originality was sorely shaken. When you fall in love with a book, a kind of possessiveness develops.

The next morning we headed our rental car for the countryside. Taking a well-maintained two-lane macadamed road, we hurried past the tourism-marred stretch of beach north of Corfu Town, cringing at signs, in English, announcing family fun at a water slide or souvenir shop. The brash strip seemed thoroughly de-Greeked. Mercifully, after fifteen miles, the scenery changed, giving way to the heart and soul of Corfu: the olive trees. They seemed to be everywhere, interspersed with spires of black cypress and flanked by the strong color of ripe oranges and lemons. Enormous trunks were pitted with hundreds of holes and gnarled into hunched, arthritic shapes. Some, we learned, are 600 years old.

Over the next week, we explored by car and on foot. The island is small enough to reach any point within a couple of hours, so we moved at a leisurely pace, starting out each day with a Durrell "destination" in mind, then radiating out from there. Following directions from the local guidebook, we walked up a hill off the coastal road, through a small stand of olives, and stood outside the gate of the once-pink villa where the scorpions had wreaked havoc. Another day, we walked through the marshlands where Gerald had gathered specimens of marine life while a jet screeched over our heads on its approach to the local airport. We stood on a beach and gazed across the water to the tiny island where Margo had fled to nurse a broken heart. We ignored a truck barreling along the busy road behind us.

We followed impossibly steep, winding roads to hilltowns with spectacular sea views, sat in tavernas and sampled regional specialties such as *bourdetto*, a spicy fish stew, and the town's local wine. We stopped in a roadside shop for picnic supplies and saw shelves lined with canned Christmas pudding and a rack of greeting cards made in England—evidence of transplanted residents.

Evenings we returned to Corfu Town; hotels elsewhere on the island remain closed during off-season. Though it would have been nice to stay in small villages, we couldn't complain. Our large corner room in a 300-year-old hotel had huge windows facing the sea with Albanian mountains as a backdrop.

On our last day in Corfu, we went in search of Lawrence's favorite swimming spot, which he called "our private bathing-pool—four puffs of cypress, deep clean-cut diving ledges above two fathoms of blue water, and a floor of clean pebbles." We drove to Kalami, twenty miles north of Corfu Town. The tiny village squats beside the water; steep hills jump out of the sea behind it. In the quiet morning, we parked and continued on foot, following directions from our local guidebook. We followed an uphill road out of town, then turned onto a footpath that dipped and wound through the half-light of ancient olive groves. No car, no house, no person spoiled the depth of the forest. At last we had found the period atmosphere we had come for.

At last, the path opened onto a cove surrounded by rocky ledges and cypress trees. We climbed on the rocks, then sat on the deserted beach to listen to the crashing surf. True, it was January. True, last night's cool rain had us wearing jackets on a cloudy beach famed for the prismatic clarity of Greek light. But we shivered happily because, for the moment, our sense of time had shifted. The cove with its four puffs of cypress must have looked precisely like this in the 1930s. The ancient olive trees we had passed under must be the exact ones that shaded the Durrells on their way to picnic.

A family we had met in a book had led us to a place we never would have found on our own. We lifted our water bottles in tribute to the lovable, spirited Durrells.

Jo Broyles Yohay lives in Manhattan and writes frequently about travel for The New York Times *and other publications.*

MICHELE ANNA JORDAN

✦ ✶ ✦

The Provençal Sky

The colors of imagination become the colors of reality.

UPON MY RETURN FROM TEN DAYS IN PROVENCE THE
questions, of course, have been inevitable: Did you have a
good time? (Yes.) What did you do? (Everything.) How was
the food? (Wonderful.)

I try to speak but the answers, if they come at all, come
more slowly than the questions, or else they come in a flood-
tide of words, of whirling verbal images, too many words to
be spoken at one time by one person. I open my mouth and
colors escape: the dazzling blues and mauves and fuchsias of
the Aix sky at sunset; the emerald greens and delicate blues of
the Mediterranean; the astonishing liquid yellow of the sun.

I don't really want to talk at all; I want to find another way
to transfer my experience, to take this tangled web inside of
me, this inner stew of feelings, scents, tastes, images, sensations
all bundled together, this fierce convergence of desire and re-
lease, a great tumbling ball of human yarn, and hand it to you,
let you hold it up and turn it in the light so that you, too, may
know the astonishing beauty, pleasure, satisfaction, relief, and

longing that is my Provence. But alas, I am left with only the word, with inadequate human language and a tale the telling of which is beyond me. How to say something so simple and profound as that I arrived home at last, without sounding romantic and hyperbolic, a silly dreamer? Maybe I am specifically that; maybe that's how I arrived at my destination at long last, after twenty-one years of failed attempts. Perseverance furthers, I recall from my old days with the *I Ching*.

I am a talker, that much is certain. If you know me, you know this. I speak easily and often, and probably too much, imposing a constant narrative overlay onto everything I do, think, and feel. But this time it hasn't happened and what might someday be the story I tell myself and others about my time in Provence, the narrative of it all, as it were, for now still flutters in the soft sea breezes, out of my reach. I have only images to offer you.

I am standing in a parking lot on the outskirts of Toulon. A tall, thin man is shoving what looks like old, broken fence boards under a three-legged iron tripod, feeding a raging fire. On top of the tripod is a huge, battered pot into which the man, who has a cigarette hanging from his lips, dumps a couple of buckets of water, then a platter of different shapes, sizes, and colors of fish and shellfish, live, kicking crab, big round chunks of peeled potatoes all go plunging in. The water quickly turns orange with saffron; the air is filled with the scent of garlic; the temperature of the water slowly rises and finally, after an interminable amount of time, the crabs' kicking slows and stops. I watch this for a while, the man feeding the fire and pulling on his cigarette, and then I walk to the courtyard behind the house, where I am handed a glass of white wine.

Time passes. If I look far into the distance I can just barely see the Mediterranean. The sun is warmer than I've felt it in months but with the pleasant breeze I don't notice the burn, the dangerous rosy glow I will discover that night and that is only now beginning to fade. From the house, a woman brings out bowls of a thick yellow sauce that I recognize immediately: aioli. Aioli in Provence. I stare, captivated, then raise my head and look around. Someone is carrying the fish, piled high on huge platters made of cork, to the table. Someone else fills my glass with wine and yet another person asks me a question. In French. I understand and respond, in spite of the fact that it has been years since I could hold my own in a conversation in the language I so love. I look across the courtyard and see my friend Louise. "Michele, are you happy?" she asks wisely.

Another image: I am walking through narrow streets towards the center of a tiny medieval town. A woman in a black sweater, long skirt, and golden beads is sweeping her doorstep. She is very old, older than I can ever imagine myself being. She must feel me watching her; she looks up, our eyes meet and linger. We smile.

Another day—near the end, at least for now. Overhead, the sky is the color of a peacock's breast, shimmery, nearly metallic blue. Towards the east, the drape of night is beginning to close over us, highlighting the day's lingering colors. The blue overhead fades westward into a dramatic periwinkle, which in turn gives way to an intense lavender dissolving into a brilliant fuchsia horizon. A few hundred yards in the distance, the great fountain, already lit by yellow lights, glows. The enormous ancient plane trees that line the Cours Mirabeau, in their stark winter nakedness just two days ago, are covered now with tiny buds, like stars in the fading light. Listening carefully, I swear I can hear the music of the fountains above the chatter of the clientele that lounge in café after café along the famous promenade of Aix-en-Provence. Briefly, I let myself lean against a nearby friend, needing the palpable sensation of another's presence as I feel as if I will float away into the very ether of this land I've longed to see for an eternity. If ever I have been at home, it is at this precise moment.

Another image lingers. A late dinner—the best kind, to my thinking—with a friend has left me drowsy with contentment. The next day the group will depart for the States and I will go by train from Marseilles to Nice for my flight to Paris. Closeness dissolves into ever widening distances, both personal and geographic, and I snuggle deep into the large hotel bed, my nightgown as silky and black as the Marseilles night. The arms of Europe that opened so wide in welcome are closing around me, gently lifting me if not exactly home, then certainly back to the world where, inevitably it seems, I must live, at least for now.

Michele Anna Jordan is the author of fifteen books about food and wine, including The BLT Cookbook, The New Cook's Tour of Sonoma, Salt & Pepper, *and* California Home Cooking. *She writes for a variety of national publications and hosts two radio shows on KRCB-FM. She has won numerous awards for both cooking and writing, including a 1997 James Beard Award, and makes her home in Sonoma County, California.*

Acknowledgments

This book wouldn't have been possible without the inspiration and talent of two friends, Travelers' Tales publisher James O'Reilly and executive editor Larry Habegger. Thank you for sharing your editing and writing expertise, insights and patience with me. Sincere thanks to Susan Brady who is always cheerful and keeps us on task from start to finish. Thank you also to Sean O'Reilly, Krista Holmstrom, Judy Johnson, Jhana Bach, Christy Harrington, and Jennica Peterson.

And to my parents, Ruth and Bill Bond who gave me roots and wings and never told me I couldn't "do it." Special thanks goes to my daughters and husband, who believe in me, and make my life so very rich and meaningful.

"The Working Class" by Judy Wade published with permission from the author. Copyright © 1998 by Judy Wade.

"Smoke, No Fire" by Ferne Arfin published with permission from the author. Copyright © 2004 by Ferne Arfin.

"Yearning for the Sun" by France Mayes originally published as "Under the Etruscan Wall" in *House Beautiful Magazine*, December 1993. Copyright © 1993 by Frances Mayes. Reprinted by permission of Curtis Brown, Ltd.

"Restoration" by Lollie Ragana published with permission from the author. Copyright © 2004 by Lollie Ragana.

"In a Soldier's Care" by Nancy Hill published with permission from the author. Copyright © 1998 by Nancy Hill.

"Pilgrim's Progress" by Catherine Watson published with permission from the author. Copyright © 2003 by Catherine Watson.

"Naturally Baked" by Claire Berlinski published with permission from the author. Copyright © 2003 by Claire Berlinski.

About the Editor

Marybeth Bond is a well-known name in the world of travel. She is the award-winning author/editor of five women's travel books in the Travelers' Tales series. She was the travel expert for CBS *Evening Magazine* and was also a featured guest on the *Oprah Winfrey Show*.

She has appeared on over 250 television and radio shows and her Travelers' Tales book, *Gutsy Women*, translated into three languages, was featured on the *Today Show* and *Oprah*.

Her travel articles have been published worldwide in magazines such as *Islands*, and *Shape*, and newspapers such as the *San Francisco Examiner* and *Kuala Lumpur Star*. Marybeth is also the travel columnist for a Northern California newspaper and adventure editor for *travelgirl* Magazine.

Her resume includes a marketing career for Xerox and Honeywell, consultant for Fortune 500 companies, travel editor/expert for ivillage.com and Outside Radio, and a frequent guest on CNN, Oxygen, NPR, and "Ask the Experts" (*Reader's Digest*).

She has been a spokesperson for numerous companies, including British Airways.

As a professional speaker, Marybeth has entertained audiences across the USA and internationally, speaking to groups as diverse as The Explorer's Club in New York, to Merrill Lynch and Business and Professional Women.

Marybeth has hiked, cycled, climbed, dived and kayaked her way through six continents and more than seventy countries around the world, from the depths of the Flores Sea to the summit of Mt. Kilimanjaro. She has trekked across the Himalayas and ridden camels across the Thar and Sahara Deserts. At age thirty, she left her corporate job in the computer industry, put all her possessions in storage, bought a one-way ticket to Bangkok and took off. She continued to travel for two years around the world solo. This is when she met her future husband in Kathmandu. In the past two decades she has traveled with her daughters and husband from Lombok to Luxor, Zanzibar to Kilarny.

Marybeth is a member of the American Society of Journalists and Authors, the Society of American Travel Writers, and was an advisor for Northwestern University's Medill School of Journalism.

Marybeth lives in Northern California with her husband, two children and a yellow lab named "Tuscany." Visit her Web site at www.marybethbond.com.

TRAVELERS' TALES

THE POWER OF A GOOD STORY

New Releases

THE BEST TRAVELERS' TALES 2004
$16.95

True Stories from Around the World
Edited by James O'Reilly, Larry Habegger & Sean O'Reilly
The launch of a new annual collection presenting fresh, lively storytelling and compelling narrative to make the reader laugh, weep, and buy a plane ticket.

INDIA
$18.95

True Stories
Edited by James O'Reilly & Larry Habegger
"Travelers' Tales India is ravishing in the texture and variety of tales."
—*Foreign Service Journal*

A WOMAN'S EUROPE
$17.95

True Stories
Edited by Marybeth Bond
An exhilarating collection of inspirational, adventurous, and entertaining stories by women exploring the romantic continent of Europe. From the bestselling author Marybeth Bond.

WOMEN IN THE WILD
$17.95

True Stories of Adventure and Connection
Edited by Lucy McCauley
"A spiritual, moving, and totally female book to take you around the world and back."
—*Mademoiselle*

CHINA
$18.95

True Stories
Edited by James O'Reilly, Larry Habegger & Sean O'Reilly
A must for any traveler to China, for anyone wanting to learn more about the Middle Kingdom, offering a breadth and depth of experience from both new and well-known authors; helps make the China experience unforgettable and transforming.

BRAZIL
$17.95

True Stories
Edited by Annette Haddad & Scott Doggett
Introduction by Alex Shoumatoff
"Only the lowest wattage dim bulb would visit Brazil without reading this book."
—Tim Cahill, author of *Pass the Butterworms*

THE PENNY PINCHER'S PASSPORT TO LUXURY TRAVEL (2ND EDITION)
$14.95

The Art of Cultivating Preferred Customer Status
By Joel L. Widzer
Completely updated and revised, this 2nd edition of the popular guide to traveling like the rich and famous without being either describes, both philosophically and in practical terms, how to obtain luxurious travel benefits by building relationships with airlines and other travel companies.

Women's Travel

A WOMAN'S EUROPE $17.95
True Stories
Edited by Marybeth Bond
An exhilarating collection of inspirational, adventurous, and entertaining stories by women exploring the romantic continent of Europe. From the bestselling author Marybeth Bond.

WOMEN IN THE WILD $17.95
True Stories of Adventure and Connection
Edited by Lucy McCauley
"A spiritual, moving, and totally female book to take you around the world and back."
— *Mademoiselle*

A WOMAN'S WORLD $18.95
True Stories of Life on the Road
Edited by Marybeth Bond
Introduction by Dervla Murphy

— ★ ★ ★ —
Lowell Thomas Award
—Best Travel Book

A MOTHER'S WORLD $14.95
Journeys of the Heart
Edited by Marybeth Bond & Pamela Michael
"These stories remind us that motherhood is one of the great unifying forces in the world"
— *San Francisco Examiner*

A WOMAN'S PASSION FOR TRAVEL $17.95
More True Stories from A Woman's World
Edited by Marybeth Bond & Pamela Michael
"A diverse and gripping series of stories!"
—Arlene Blum, author of
Annapurna: A Woman's Place

Food

ADVENTURES IN WINE $17.95
True Stories of Vineyards and Vintages around the World
Edited by Thom Elkjer
Humanity, community, and brotherhood comprise the marvelous virtues of the wine world. This collection toasts the warmth and wonders of this large extended family in stories by travelers who are wine novices and experts alike.

FOOD $18.95
A Taste of the Road
Edited by Richard Sterling
Introduction by Margo True

— ★ ★ ★ —
Silver Medal Winner of the Lowell Thomas Award
—Best Travel Book

HER FORK IN THE ROAD $16.95
Women Celebrate Food and Travel
Edited by Lisa Bach
A savory sampling of stories by the best writers in and out of the food and travel fields.

THE ADVENTURE OF FOOD $17.95
True Stories of Eating Everything
Edited by Richard Sterling
"Bound to whet appetites for more than food."
— *Publishers Weekly*

THE FEARLESS DINER $7.95
Travel Tips and Wisdom for Eating around the World
By Richard Sterling
Combines practical advice on foodstuffs, habits, and etiquette, with hilarious accounts of others' eating adventures.

Travel Humor

SAND IN MY BRA AND OTHER MISADVENTURES $14.95
Funny Women Write from the Road
Edited by Jennifer L. Leo
"A collection of ridiculous and sublime travel experiences."
— *San Francisco Chronicle*

LAST TROUT IN VENICE $14.95
The Far-Flung Escapades of an Accidental Adventurer
By Doug Lansky
"Traveling with Doug Lansky might result in a considerably shortened life expectancy...but what a way to go."
— Tony Wheeler, Lonely Planet Publications

HYENAS LAUGHED AT ME $14.95 AND NOW I KNOW WHY
The Best of Travel Humor and Misadventure
Edited by Sean O'Reilly, Larry Habegger, and James O'Reilly
Hilarious, outrageous and reluctant voyagers indulge us with the best misadventures around the world.

NOT SO FUNNY WHEN $12.95 IT HAPPENED
The Best of Travel Humor and Misadventure
Edited by Tim Cahill
Laugh with Bill Bryson, Dave Barry, Anne Lamott, Adair Lara, and many more.

THERE'S NO TOILET PAPER...ON THE ROAD LESS TRAVELED $12.95
The Best of Travel Humor and Misadventure
Edited by Doug Lansky

——— ★ ★ ★ ———
*Humor Book of the Year
— Independent Publisher's Book Award*

——— ★ ★ ★ ———
ForeWord Gold Medal Winner — Humor Book of the Year

Travelers' Tales Classics

COAST TO COAST $16.95
A Journey Across 1950s America
By Jan Morris
After reporting on the first Everest ascent in 1953, Morris spent a year journeying across the United States. In brilliant prose, Morris records with exuberance and curiosity a time of innocence in the U.S.

THE ROYAL ROAD $14.95 TO ROMANCE
By Richard Halliburton
"Laughing at hardships, dreaming of beauty, ardent for adventure, Halliburton has managed to sing into the pages of this glorious book his own exultant spirit of youth and freedom."
— *Chicago Post*

TRADER HORN $16.95
A Young Man's Astounding Adventures in 19th Century Equatorial Africa
By Alfred Aloysius Horn
Here is the stuff of legends—thrills and danger, wild beasts, serpents, and savages. An unforgettable and vivid portrait of a vanished Africa.

UNBEATEN TRACKS $14.95 IN JAPAN
By Isabella L. Bird
Isabella Bird was one of the most adventurous women travelers of the 19th century with journeys to Tibet, Canada, Korea, Turkey, Hawaii, and Japan. A fascinating read.

THE RIVERS RAN EAST $16.95
By Leonard Clark
Clark is the original Indiana Jones, telling the breathtaking story of his search for the legendary El Dorado gold in the Amazon.

Destination Titles

ALASKA $18.95
Edited by Bill Sherwonit, Andromeda Romano-Lax, & Ellen Bielawski

AMERICA $19.95
Edited by Fred Setterberg

AMERICAN SOUTHWEST $17.95
Edited by Sean O'Reilly & James O'Reilly

AUSTRALIA $17.95
Edited by Larry Habegger

BRAZIL $17.95
Edited by Annette Haddad & Scott Doggett
Introduction by Alex Shoumatoff

CENTRAL AMERICA $17.95
Edited by Larry Habegger & Natanya Pearlman

CHINA $18.95
Edited by James O'Reilly, Larry Habegger & Sean O'Reilly

CUBA $17.95
Edited by Tom Miller

FRANCE $18.95
Edited by James O'Reilly, Larry Habegger & Sean O'Reilly

GRAND CANYON $17.95
Edited by Sean O'Reilly, James O'Reilly & Larry Habegger

GREECE $18.95
Edited by Larry Habegger, Sean O'Reilly & Brian Alexander

HAWAI'I $17.95
Edited by Rick & Marcie Carroll

HONG KONG $17.95
Edited by James O'Reilly, Larry Habegger & Sean O'Reilly

INDIA $18.95
Edited by James O'Reilly & Larry Habegger

IRELAND $18.95
Edited by James O'Reilly, Larry Habegger & Sean O'Reilly

ITALY $18.95
Edited by Anne Calcagno
Introduction by Jan Morris

JAPAN $17.95
Edited by Donald W. George & Amy G. Carlson

MEXICO $17.95
Edited by James O'Reilly & Larry Habegger

NEPAL $17.95
Edited by Rajendra S. Khadka

PARIS $18.95
Edited by James O'Reilly, Larry Habegger & Sean O'Reilly

PROVENCE $16.95
Edited by James O'Reilly & Tara Austen Weaver

SAN FRANCISCO $18.95
Edited by James O'Reilly, Larry Habegger & Sean O'Reilly

SPAIN $19.95
Edited by Lucy McCauley

THAILAND $18.95
Edited by James O'Reilly & Larry Habegger

TIBET $18.95
Edited by James O'Reilly & Larry Habegger

TURKEY $18.95
Edited by James Villers Jr.

TUSCANY $16.95
Edited by James O'Reilly & Tara Austen Weaver
Introduction by Anne Calcagno

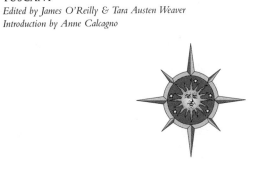

Footsteps Series

THE FIRE NEVER DIES
One Man's Raucous Romp Down the Road of Food, Passion, and Adventure
By Richard Sterling
"Sterling's writing is like spitfire, foursquare and jazzy with crackle...."　　　　　*—Kirkus Reviews*

$14.95

ONE YEAR OFF
Leaving It All Behind for a Round-the-World Journey with Our Children
By David Elliot Cohen
A once-in-a-lifetime adventure generously shared, from the author/editor of *America 24/7* and *A Day in the Life of Africa*

$14.95

THE WAY OF THE WANDERER
Discover Your True Self Through Travel
By David Yeadon
Experience transformation through travel with this delightful, illustrated collection by award-winning author David Yeadon.

$14.95

TAKE ME WITH YOU
A Round-the-World Journey to Invite a Stranger Home
By Brad Newsham
"Newsham is an ideal guide. His journey, at heart, is into humanity."　　　　　*—Pico Iyer, author of The Global Soul*

$24.00

KITE STRINGS OF THE SOUTHERN CROSS
A Woman's Travel Odyssey
By Laurie Gough
Short-listed for the prestigious Thomas Cook Award, this is an exquisite rendering of a young woman's search for meaning.

$14.95

ForeWord Silver Medal Winner
— Travel Book of the Year

—— ★ ★ ★ ——

THE SWORD OF HEAVEN
A Five Continent Odyssey to Save the World
By Mikkel Aaland
"Few books capture the soul of the road like The *Sword of Heaven*, a sharp-edged, beautifully rendered memoir that will inspire anyone."
　　　　　—Phil Cousineau, author of The Art of Pilgrimage

$24.00

STORM
A Motorcycle Journey of Love, Endurance, and Transformation
By Allen Noren
"Beautiful, tumultuous, deeply engaging and very satisfying. Anyone who looks for truth in travel will find it here."
　　　　　—Ted Simon, author of Jupiter's Travels

$24.00

ForeWord Gold Medal Winner
— Travel Book of the Year

—— ★ ★ ★ ——